Understanding Publi
Administration

CW00558604

Previous books in English by Michiel S. de Vries

(2015) *The application of NPM in transition countries.* Brussels: Bruylant. (With J. Nemec)

(2015) *Quo Vadis? Local governance and development in South Africa since 1994.* Brussels: Bruylant. (With P. S. Reddy)

(2013) *Training for leadership.* Brussels: Bruylant. (With G. Bouckaert)

(2012) *Public sector dynamics in Central and Eastern Europe.* Bratislava: NISPAcee press. (With J. Nemec)

(2012) *Global trends in public sector reform.* Brussels: Bruylant. (With J. Nemec)

(2011) *Was Ella Fitzgerald right? Good enough governance and the effectiveness of government.* Inaugural speech, University of Aruba, Oranjestad.

(2011) *Value and virtue in public administration.* London and New York: Palgrave Macmillan. Reprinted in 2014. (With Pan Suk Kim)

(2010) *The importance of neglect in policy making.* London and New York: Palgrave Macmillan.

(2009) *The story behind Western advice to Central Europe during its transition.* Bratislava: NISPAcee press. (With I. Sobis)

(2008) *Improving local government.* London and New York: Palgrave Macmillan. (With P. S. Reddy and S. Haque)

(2000) *Calculated choices in policy making: The theory and practice of impact assessments.* London: Palgrave Macmillan, New York: St Martin's Press.

Understanding Public Administration

Michiel S. de Vries

Radboud University Nijmegen

Institute for Management Research

First published 2016 by
PALGRAVE

Palgrave in the UK is an imprint of Macmillan Publishers Limited, registered in England, company number 785998, of 4 Crinan Street, London, N1 9XW.

Palgrave Macmillan in the US is a division of St Martin's Press LLC, 175 Fifth Avenue, New York, NY 10010.

Palgrave is a global imprint of the above companies and is represented throughout the world.

Palgrave® and Macmillan® are registered trademarks in the United States, the United Kingdom, Europe and other countries.

ISBN 978–1–137–57545–6 hardback
ISBN 978–1–137–57544–9 paperback

This book is printed on paper suitable for recycling and made from fully managed and sustained forest sources. Logging, pulping and manufacturing processes are expected to conform to the environmental regulations of the country of origin.

A catalogue record for this book is available from the British Library.

A catalog record for this book is available from the Library of Congress.

Printed in China

Contents

List of Figures, Tables and Maps

Figures

Tables

Map

Foreword

In 2009, I was approached by a South African professor who was preparing an introductory course in Public Administration. He asked if I knew of a book that would be suitable to use in his classes. When I became responsible for the publications of the International Association of Schools and Institutes in Administration (IASIA), many more professors approached me with the same question. This was the start of a project which resulted in this book. I presented an initial proposal at the IASIA conference in Bali. I was advised and encouraged by many colleagues and friends from all over the world. I sent preliminary versions to Christina Andrews at the University of São Paulo, Brazil, Lisheng Dong from China, Luiz Estevam Lopez Goncalves of the Fundação Getulio Vargas in Brazil, Juraj Nemec of the Masaryk University in Brno, P. S. Reddy of the University of KwaZulu Natal, South Africa, Sofiane Ben Mohamed Sahraoui from the Bahrain Institute of Public Administration, Iwona Sobis from the University of Gothenburg in Sweden and many others, to comment and provide illustrations from their regions. I may be the sole author, but I could not have completed this book without the help of friends.

Is this just another introductory Public Administration book? I don't think so. This book is different because existing introductory books often introduce students to the specific public sector arrangements as they exist in their own country. This book provides an introductory perspective on eight themes which are thought to be crucial for understanding the public administration in every country around the world. It focuses on issues that affect every country, and it presents the various ways these countries approach and deal with them in practice. This book does not contain comparative analyses or normative judgements about such actual practices, but it does include practices from a range of countries as examples and illustrations, in order to make this book interesting for students in Asia, Africa, Latin America, the Middle East, Central and Eastern Europe, and Organisation for Economic Co-operation and Development (OECD) countries.

The subjects discussed in Chapters 2 to 8 are key themes because they form the foundation for much Public Administration research still conducted at present. There are no conclusive answers to the dilemmas and issues involved, and thus the debate about the themes continues. The key themes provide an ideal organizational structure for the book since these themes continue to be interesting to scholars and students in Public Administration who are eager to know what this discipline is all about and how the public sector works.

What are the key themes? This book addresses the provision of collective goods and the pros and cons of alternative service delivery arrangements, the merits of centralization and decentralization, the dilemmas surrounding bureaucratic organizations, the necessary traits of management and leadership in the public sector, the motivation and integrity of public officials, the dilemmas involved in public decision making and the problem-solving capacity of public policy making. It highlights a number of theories to address these themes. These include Herbert Finer's theory on the history of government, theories on the legacy of colonialism and path dependencies, Max Weber's theory on bureaucracies, Geert Hofstede's theory on cultural dimensions, the theory on Public Service Motivation, Irving Janis's theory on groupthink, Herbert Simon's theory on bounded rationality and Thaler and Sunstein's approach to nudging, as well as the wisdom from antiquity contained in holy scriptures, and in teachings from such famous thinkers as Confucius, Hammurabi, and Plato.

Determining what to include and what to exclude is a necessary task in writing an introductory book, but is, nonetheless, an unpleasant process. So much more could be said about each of the themes and so many other themes and theories could have been incorporated. Some readers will miss separate chapters on public finances, on human resource management in the public sector, on policy analysis and on the emerging use of ICT and the consequences thereof. These topics are touched upon in different chapters, but given limitations of space and the complex nature of these matters, these subjects had to be excluded as separate themes.

Also, the book may for some readers still be too much focused on theories from scholars in Public Administration from developed countries. Unfortunately this has proven to be inevitable given the purpose of this book. There are limits in what needs to be discussed in such an introductory book. More advanced and in-depth theories on particular and specialized topics from scholars outside the West could not always be included, no matter how interesting they are.

Luckily, two Palgrave editors, Steven Kennedy and Lloyd Langman, as well as two anonymous reviewers, assisted me in this process. Finally, I am grateful to Julie Bivin Raadschelders, who corrected grammar and style issues and highlighted a few unintelligible sentences contained in preliminary versions.

MICHIEL S. DE VRIES
NIJMEGEN, NETHERLANDS
JUNE 2015

Chapter 1

Introduction: Understanding Public Administration

This book's intent is for you to think, consider and reconsider, and reflect on the business of government from a Public Administration (PA) perspective. It focuses on key questions related to working inside government as a public administrator or civil servant, on behalf of citizens. While you might not (yet) be convinced that Public Administration is an interesting subject, it is important to realize and appreciate that the actions of government affect us all.

In some countries, the government is omnipresent. The alarm clock that wakes you in the morning is powered by the public utility that is subject to public regulations. The water and toothpaste that you use to brush your teeth is tested and monitored for safety and quality by similar public agencies. The food that you eat was bought from someone who was required to have a permit from the government in order to sell it. The money you use to buy the food is printed by government and obtains its value, in part, through the government policies. In some countries, you might be expected to dress in a specific way, and government might impose this by law, particularly if you are a woman.

Public traffic laws regulate how we walk, ride or drive to work, and the houses you pass on your way to work are most likely built the way they are because some government agency allowed them to be built in that manner. Perhaps you use public transport that is enabled and regulated by government. Perhaps you have children who attend school because education is obligatory for certain ages, as determined by law. Even what your children learn and how they learn it can be determined or influenced by government. The teachers themselves have an education and credentials established and necessitated by public regulations. At your office, there might be working conditions that are more or less enforced by public law regarding working hours, minimum wages, safety measures and accessibility for disabled people. Perhaps the first thing you do is start up your computer and check your email. In many a country, email is under surveillance of security agencies.

1

You have only been awake for two hours, yet the influence of government on your life and in your activities has been substantial. In some countries, governmental influence on an individual's life continues throughout the entire day even though he or she is utterly unaware of it. That is, until something goes wrong. Then, the individual becomes explicitly aware of rules and regulations, and possibly the police, the justice system, a fire department, a hospital and eventually an undertaker, all of whose activities are equally subject to publicly maintained regulations.

When you leave the country – carrying your passport issued by your government, of course – you might experience things differently. Not only is there another language, but rules and city structures can be different; not to mention that when you cross the street, you have to be extra careful if the cars drive on the other side of the road than in your home country. Roads might be better maintained than in your own country or they might be neglected, the streets might be cleaner or dirtier and people dress and behave differently. The military might be visible in the streets, there might be cameras watching you all day, and you need to adapt to this new reality. The differences become even more noteworthy when you travel to another continent. Perhaps the teachers just don't show up, the tap water might make you ill, the electricity might be intermittent, and after heavy rainfall the whole place may be flooded. You might even see street names that use a different alphabet or characters, and you may need a map or guidebook to understand where you are, how you got there and which way you should go.

This book is not about streets but about governments. The questions are nonetheless similar. How do they function, how did they come about and where are they going? The related questions are the key themes of the study of Public Administration on the *internal workings* of government: Why do we accept government authority? Where is power concentrated? What is bureaucracy good for? Who wants to work for government? What motivates those individuals? And does the public sector need to change? Similar questions arise concerning the *external workings* of government: What are the main societal problems that governments face? Why do public policies often fail to resolve these problems? Why does public decision making produce less than optimal outcomes? Why are policies rarely implemented as designed, and how can we evaluate such policy making?

This book is for students seeking to understand why government is highly visible in some countries and much less visible in others; why the role of government is much more restricted in some countries than in others; why there are fewer regulations in some countries and nobody even adheres to them in other countries. In the last case, government may have a minor impact on citizens' daily lives. It may maintain a police force and an army, but other public involvement and oversight may be absent. At the most basic level, public expenditures reflect these differences. In some countries, public expenditures account for over 40% of gross domestic product (GDP) (for instance, Belgium, Cyprus, Hungary, Italy and New Zealand), while in other countries, they account for less than 15% (for instance, Ethiopia, Guatemala, Cambodia and Indonesia). Such general figures do not reveal many details about how governments actually operate, where they spend their money, how they are organized, what policies are in place and whether their citizens tend to comply with such rules. They only provide a general idea about variations in public involvement in the daily lives of citizens, and they also suggest that even in countries where the government is less visible, its role within the state is still significant.

This book goes one step further and provides a more detailed view of the workings of government. It is an introduction to Public Administration for students enrolled in an introductory PA course, and it will acquaint students with the theory and practice of the internal and external workings of governments. It is about the internal organization and the management of the public sector and how governments steer societies through policy making.

What is Public Administration?

This book takes a broad perspective on public administration including its political, economic, legal and social dimensions. Every regime, whether it is a religious state, a monarchy, a democracy or a military regime, is in need of an organization – administrative, advisory and executing – that provides (semi-)public goods through policies and programmes and ensures that people contribute to that provision through taxes and/or participative contributions.

In ancient times, the family, courtiers, military commanders, guards, tax collectors and personal staff assisted kings (Finer, 1997, p. 42). In those days, the staff was relatively small. The staff provided the king with information and advice and executed his commands. In the religious state of the Aztec regime, a well-respected class of warriors, priests and nobility, as well as artisans, physicians, teachers and long-distance traders who served the regime as ambassadors and spies supported the high-level priests in taking care of public affairs. In military regimes, the military and administrative staff execute the commands from the military leaders. In modern forum-type regimes, elected politicians find their staff in departments and ministries at different levels of the state, and also in the army, the police, welfare agencies, public schools and what are called street-level bureaucrats.

This is no small business. The growth of governmental outlays and revenues related to GDP is enormous, and the twentieth century saw extremely dramatic growth. The average public revenues across the whole world are well over 30% of GDP and public expenditures are even higher (see Table 1.1).

Table 1.1   *The role of government in different parts of the world in 2015*

Public expenditures and revenues as a percentage (%) of gross domestic product (GDP)		
Country group name	*General government expenditures*	*General government revenues*
Advanced economies	39.58	36.33
Euro area	48.74	46.48
Major advanced economies (G7)	40.18	36.36
Other advanced economies (advanced economies excluding G7 and Euro area)	32.46	31.95
European Union	46.77	44.21
Emerging market and developing economies	31.13	27.41
Commonwealth of Independent States	36.39	32.91
Emerging and developing Asia	28.75	25.91
Emerging and developing Europe	39.67	37.40
ASEAN-5	21.36	18.76
Latin America and the Caribbean	33.26	28.51
Middle East, North Africa, Afghanistan and Pakistan	36.32	28.97
Middle East and North Africa	37.97	30.31
Sub-Saharan Africa	22.39	18.72

Source: International Monetary Fund Economic Outlook (2015) World Economic Outlook Database, October 2015

While there is a huge variance in the role of government in different regions, there is no doubt that the public sector is the major employer and largest sector in all states, and in many regions it is also the largest debtor.

This administrative apparatus, including the people who work in it and the work it does, constitutes the public administration and is the central topic of this book. Public Administration as an academic discipline is 'centrally concerned with the organization of government policies and programs as well as the behavior of officials (usually non-elected) formally responsible for their conduct' (cf. Dwight Waldo, in Mosher, 1975, p. 181). Because the discipline and the object of the discipline are both termed public administration, the discipline is typically written in capital letters, i.e. Public Administration, and the object of the discipline in lower-case letters, i.e. public administration. Hence, Public Administration is the study of public administration.

Notwithstanding this description, defining Public Administration remains a tricky business. In the USA the discipline is often said to have originated in an 1887 article entitled 'The Study of Public Administration' by Woodrow Wilson. However, in that article Wilson himself repeatedly referred to earlier studies on Public Administration. He mentioned, for instance, eighteenth-century Prussia under Frederick the Great, who appointed the first university professorates in what was called Cameralism to study the government apparatus and to train a new class of public administrators. He also refers to France under the reign of Napoleon, who tried to optimize the administration in France and the territories he occupied, and to England, where the main question according to Wilson was how to curb the executive power of government. He could have gone back much further in time, to writers and philosophers such as Confucius, Kautilya, Plato and Cicero, because government and its administrative apparatus have been studied since ancient times.

Wilson's article became famous because he distinguished Public Administration from the disciplines of politics and of law, emphasizing that it is a means of putting politics into practice, implementing laws, and organizing and managing the public sector. In his view the main questions underlying Public Administration were:

[H]ow shall our series of governments within governments be so administered that it shall always be to the interest of the public officer to serve, not his superior alone but the community also, with the best efforts of his talents and the soberest service of his

conscience? How shall such service be made to his commonest interest by contributing abundantly to his sustenance, to his dearest
interest by furthering his ambition, and to his highest interest by
advancing his honor and establishing his character? And how shall
this be done alike for the local part and for the national whole?
(Wilson, 1887, p. 221)

This is congruent with the classic meaning of administration. The word
'administration' is derived from the Latin word *'ministrare'* meaning
'being of service' or 'being helpful'. Together with the word 'public'
the translation for public administration would be 'serving the public
good'. In this view, Public Administration is the discipline that studies
how the public sector does serve the public good through developing
and implementing public policies and what is needed to conduct this
business in an efficient, effective, legitimate and rational way, in order
to optimize serving the public good.

Not everyone views Public Administration as a separate discipline
from political science. Indeed, a key theme in Public Administration
is the self-reflection on whether it is a distinct academic discipline, an
element of study in political science, economics, social science, management sciences or law, or an interdisciplinary study drawing from those
areas. In many countries political science and Public Administration
are combined in one department, while in others Public Administration
is taught in an economics department or one of the other disciplinary
departments.

Partly dependent on the location of Public Administration within
specific institutional settings within universities – that is, within a law
department, a department of political science, management sciences or
social sciences respectively – specific aspects of public administration
dominate among its scholars. Some emphasize the organization and
management aspects of administration, thus underscoring the connection between public and business administration. Others see Public
Administration as a sub-discipline within political science, focusing
mainly on political–administrative relations and the inherent political
nature of the public sector. Still others see the discipline to be embedded
within economics, within the study of the implementation of laws, or
stress the public side of Public Administration thus relating it mainly
to social sciences. In some countries Public Administration has been
disconnected from Public Policy, resulting in separate schools in Public
Administration and schools in Public Policy, while in other countries
Public Policy is seen as a crucial part of Public Administration.

In different countries different models dominate and sometimes multiple models are seen within one and the same country. This is one of the reasons why discussions on the nature of the discipline and its definition are ongoing. Varying views exist on the question whether Public Administration is an academic discipline in itself or whether it is a sub-discipline of law, political science, the social sciences, or economics or whether it is an interdisciplinary endeavour between those disciplines. This also results in disputes about what PA should study, how it should study its object and what its boundaries are – if there are any.

A basic issue in these discussions is what constitutes a scholarly discipline. Does it need to have its own object of investigation, its own explanatory theories, its own descriptive terminology, and its own body of knowledge and paradigm(s)? To what extent is it dependent on theories and research conducted in the other disciplines mentioned above? In spite of varying opinions with regard to these questions, there is something distinctive in Public Administration.

In relation to *political science*, Public Administration is not primarily concerned with explaining political conflicts and the struggle for power. Rather, it investigates the effectiveness and efficiency of the provision of (semi-)public goods, the rationality and legitimacy of policies and programmes, the organization and management of the public sector, and the organizational behaviour of the people working in the public sector. Clearly, political conflicts and the struggle for power may influence the effectiveness and efficiency of public service provision and affect its legitimacy and rationality. If scholars in Public Administration include these factors in their analysis, it is to consider them as explanatory variables that affect the conduct of the public administration and public administrators.

Economics theories are also important for the study of public administration. Notions of scarcity, efficiency, macroeconomic development, microeconomic behaviour, and the consequences of the *homo economicus* and self-interest, are not only relevant for the private sector but also apply to the conduct of public administration and public administrators, and then not only in relation to issues of public finance. Public Administration scholars need to understand budgeting processes and the limitations posed by economic constraints. As with political science, economic factors and theories are important in the study of Public Administration for their explanatory power regarding the conduct of policies and programmes, but they are not the primary object of study within the discipline.

Sociology and its theories on public order and violence, stability and change, organization and management, organizational behaviour and the creation and functioning of societal groups are also relevant for Public Administration. Sociology addresses key themes of Public Administration, especially when applied to policy-making processes, building and maintaining institutions, and understanding the evolution of norms and values in social groups.

Theories and the rule of *law* form a core element of good governance. Legitimate behaviour, legal procedures, diligence and precision are also indispensable for work in public administration. If the public sector's actions are not legitimate and legal procedures are routinely ignored by those working in the public sector, why would one expect ordinary citizens to abide by the law?

It is undeniable that public administration as a practice and Public Administration as a study require knowledge from the four disciplines mentioned above and preferably others, such as social psychology, for understanding decision making, and history, for understanding long-term trends and dynamics. This is something entirely different than asking whether Public Administration is just an element of those studies. Those disciplines provide indispensable elements for understanding public administration, but they do not provide a comprehensive framework for the study.

The questions posed in Public Administration differ from those asked in other disciplines. The dependent variable, i.e. the phenomenon one wants to explain and understand, also differs from the dependent variables in other disciplines. At times, the knowledge from another discipline is relevant for answering questions posed in Public Administration. In this sense, basic knowledge of all of these disciplines is useful and even elementary for understanding the workings of public administration.

In some cases, the integration and application of theories developed in other disciplines result in the development of new theories within Public Administration. Nobel Prize winner *Herbert Simon* developed the theory on bounded rationality. Simon challenged the basic economic assumption that self-interested actors will always try to make optimal choices in terms of the costs and benefits for themselves. Simon presented an alternative: most people, including public officials, will settle for decisions that are 'satisficing'; decisions where the benefits outweigh the costs even though other choices are more profitable. (For more information on this theory see Chapter 7.)

More recently, *Elinor Ostrom* won the Nobel Prize for work on collective action in the management of common pool resources. These resources are primarily natural resources such as fish, water, grasslands, and they are like public goods, but difficult to manage, as they face overuse, depletion and congestion. Ostrom called this 'the tragedy of the commons' (see Chapter 3 p. 65).

Simon and Ostrom are two examples of the contribution of Public Administration to the understanding of human and organizational behaviour.

Public Administration is also different from other disciplines in that it seeks to understand problems occurring in the public sector in order to improve public administration. It does not gather knowledge for the sake of knowledge, but in order to apply it in practice. In this sense, Public Administration is an applied science.

This section argued that Public Administration takes a distinctive position between political science, economics, law and sociology, and that it uses elements and theories created in those disciplines in research on its own object of study, i.e. public administration. It also pointed out that in integrating theories from different disciplines, Public Administration scholars develop theories and research unique to PA.

Furthermore, Public Administration is distinct in that it not only attempts to understand, but also uses this knowledge to improve public administration. As such, it is also an applied discipline.

The character of this book

The main difference from other introductions to PA is that this book is based on an international perspective. It is not so much about the government in your country, but about government in general. This book includes developed, developmental as well as developing countries and countries in the north and south and in the east and west. The differences in context and in governing are substantial, but the dilemmas – the key themes – that governments struggle with are similar. Moreover, their varying responses to similar dilemmas are edifying. So, this book invites you to look beyond the borders of your country, to see the differences, to understand them and to make judgements about alternative courses and developments in the governing of nation-states.

Many assume that how public affairs are arranged and which rules are followed – and the existence of public policies in general – is predetermined. This book argues otherwise. From one country to another, and from one region to another, one can observe significant differences in the internal organization of government and how it develops policies for society. For instance, in some countries all of the power and authority is in the hands of central government, while in others it is decentralized to local or regional governments. In most countries government is composed of a national branch, a local sector and a mid-level/regional structure, but some countries have a fourth or even a fifth level while still others have only one level. In some countries the opinions of the population may be decisive in determining what policies are developed, while in other countries the only opinion that counts is that of the central-level authority. In some countries there is a strict divide between state and religion, while in others the two are closely related, and in still others religious leaders solely determine the workings of the state. Some countries are democracies, while others are kingdoms, military-ruled polities, one-party states or theocracies.

This book treats the internal and external workings of government as variable instead of fixed. It provides a basic insight into the pros and cons of the alternatives, without prescribing what would be optimal. This is for the reader and student to decide based on sound critical analysis, theoretical knowledge, and insight into the complexities of such choices and the merits of the alternatives.

This perspective of public arrangements as a choice among alternatives could easily result in 'value-relativism', i.e. that anything goes and all options are equally good. That is not our intention here. The United Nations Universal Declaration of Human Rights is a foundational tenet, and it plays an inescapable role in evaluating the public sector. It recognizes the inherent dignity of all human beings and establishes equal and inalienable rights for all people. It also translates this into the actions required of governments and limits public interference when it violates human rights. The universality of the declaration is set out in the second article:

> Everyone is entitled to all the rights and freedoms set forth in this Declaration, without distinction of any kind, such as race, color, sex, language, religion, political or other opinion, national or social origin, property, birth or other status. Furthermore, no distinction shall be made on the basis of the political, jurisdictional or international status of the country or territory to which a person belongs, whether it be independent, trust, non-self-governing or under any other limitation of sovereignty. (United Nations, n.d.)

It also urges governments to address and ameliorate many societal problems relating to education, housing and medical care. And it limits the actions of governments by stating that no one shall be subjected to torture or cruel, inhuman or degrading treatment or punishment.

The variation in public arrangements from country to country should not suggest that such arrangements are easily changed or modified; it is only evidence of differences concerning the essential elements of the public sector. These elements comprise the key themes of public administration, and each chapter in this book addresses a key theme in Public Administration. The chapters are written to invite the reader to participate in that discussion based on substantive arguments. They are not about an absolute truth or the final word on governments. Rather, the chapters introduce those themes and elements and present some of the theories developed over the years, varying arguments and varying outcomes of research.

After reading this book, you will not be an expert in Public Administration as a discipline or as a practice. This is an introductory book, intended to provide a basic understanding of classic questions in Public Administration as well as some of the answers that have been advanced throughout the years. In order to gain a more in-depth understanding of Public Administration, further reading and study on each topic introduced in this book is necessary.

The structure of this book

Chapter 2 begins with a discussion of the *raison d'être* of the public sector, why people transfer their authority to make binding decisions to governments, what types of regimes exist and how government penetrates the states in different parts of the world. It argues that the provision of collective goods is one of the main reasons for governments to exist, but also that because of the specific features of collective goods, there is an ongoing discussion about the way these are provided for and about alternative service delivery arrangements.

In Chapter 3, the focus is on intergovernmental relations and the importance of centralization and decentralization. What is best for the resolution of societal problems? Should central government take care of most of the problems or is local government better equipped in such matters? These questions provide an entrée into organizational theory and, more specifically, bureaucracy, which Chapter 4 then turns to. This chapter argues that organizational theory cannot provide answers as to whether one type of organization is superior as such. It all depends on characteristics of the context, the tasks of the organization and the people working in the organization. Therefore, Chapter 4 concludes that the organization and management of government needs to be examined in context and in light of the recent research into this topic.

The structure of this book

2. Why do governments exist and why study them?	Origins of government Regime types The provision of collective goods
3. What does a typical government structure look like?	Central, regional and local government Path dependency Decentralization
4. What is the role of a bureaucracy?	Organizational theory Political–administrative relations Bureaucracy
5. Who works in government?	Human resource management Recruitment and careers Capacity building, socialization and training Management and leadership
6. What motivates government officials?	Job motivation Morality
7. When do public decisions result in optimal outcomes?	Why decisions do not always produce optimal outcomes
8. How can public policies solve social problems?	Why public policies often fail to resolve public problems and even lose their connection to the underlying problems
9. The need for appreciation of the public sector	The need to reformulate and balance Public Administration theory in order to defend against the criticism of government

Chapter 5 explores the individuals who work in government. It introduces issues in human resource management and addresses problems of capacity building, recruitment, socialization and careers. This chapter concludes with recent research on necessary traits for leadership and management.

Chapter 6 addresses the mindset of public officials, their public service motivation and their ethics in terms of values, norms and virtue. This chapter concludes with measures taken to reduce corruption inside the public sector and the use of performance measurement and management as tools to enhance the performance of public officials.

These internal features of the public sector are important because they influence public decision making and the policies that are developed. Chapter 7 examines the content of decision making in general and public policy decision making in particular. It discusses different theories about why decisions do not always result in optimal outcomes and how to improve decision-making processes.

Chapter 8 focuses on policy-making processes and further explores why public policies do not always provide a solution to the problems they address. It addresses major problems in the world, including differences between simple and complex problems and their impact on public policy making. It introduces the impact that context can have on public policies.

The book concludes with a call for appreciation of public administration. This final chapter evaluates the difficult, sometimes adversarial, circumstances in which public administrations have to perform and the dilemmas, unhelpful reforms and constant criticism that they face.

The themes in this book

The structure of this book suggests contextualizing the workings of government in order to acquire an adequate understanding of them, and that is the first common theme of the book. This is especially true for those nation-states that were once colonies since they often still bear the burdens of those eras. Chapter 3 explores this in detail. Government systems of former colonies often resemble or still contain remnants of the structure imposed on them by the European colonial powers during occupation, whether it fits the culture of their society or not. The same goes for the artificial borders of those nations that are often inhabited by diverse tribes and seldom form a unified state. Such features of nation-states in terms of territory, population, government and sovereignty define many of the problems they face even today. This book provides building blocks to better understand the extent to which context – from macro level to micro level as well as the other way around – determines outcomes.

This has implications for public organizations internally and for public policies externally because public management principles and public policies cannot be seamlessly transferred from one context to another. The success of these internal and external operations must always be considered in the context of time and place (cf. Painter & Peters, 2010; Pollitt, 2013). As Brazilian Guerreiro Ramos pointed out, valid foreign theories and practices might, and perhaps must, be applied outside the context in which they were developed, but only if they are adjusted to the local, regional and national context (Ramos, 1965).

A second common theme of all chapters is that they present theoretical perspectives related to the topic of the chapter. These perspectives are not the only ones possible, nor are they necessarily the best in terms of empirical corroboration. They are, however, perspectives that are still frequently used in Public Administration research. Theories are important because they structure our thinking about what is actually taking place in practice. Without theories, one can easily get lost in the myriad of factors and complexities involved. Theories also direct our observations to what those theories suggest are crucial. Chapter 2 highlights theories on the provision of collective goods. Chapter 3 examines path dependency theory as it applies to colonization patterns and their aftermath. Chapter 4 takes a closer look at theories of bureaucracy. Chapter 5 discusses organizational culture theories and their impact on management and leadership. Chapter 6 looks at theories on organizational behaviour, values and ethics. Chapter 7 examines framing, irrationality and groupthink as factors that disturb decision-making processes. And Chapter 8 discusses the uncertainty and dynamics of social problems, the tools available to resolve them through policies and how to ensure a connection between public policies and the problems they need to address.

All of these theories point to tendencies that are not necessarily optimal for the functioning of public organizations. The chapters address centralization, bureaucracy, top-down management and selfishness, as well as the dominance of irrationality in decision-making processes, the bias in framing problems and symbolism in policy development. Public Administration proposes alternatives and solutions for these natural tendencies – conceived as a prevailing disposition to move, proceed or act in some direction or towards some point, end or result, if barriers, counterforces, institutions or other mechanisms to prevent them are absent – and the dilemmas they create.

This is the third common theme in all chapters, which reflects Public Administration scholars' opinion on the nature of the study of government from a Public Administration perspective. Government is not only about power, as political philosophers such as Machiavelli have argued. Rather, government is based on a duality of power struggles and ambitions of individual rulers: on the one hand their attempts to stay in power and their willingness to initiate political conflicts over that power; and on the other the justified necessity for government of a population that accepts that power – more specifically, power transferred into government authority – because it receives something in return, namely public goods. Public Administration is especially concerned with the second part of the equation. Instead of emphasizing conflicts and power struggles, it stresses the importance of rationality and legitimacy in the internal and external workings of government in order to optimize the benefits for the state. It does not naïvely judge such politics as insignificant, but it attempts to offer an understanding of the workings of government and formulates recommendations to make them more efficient, effective, rational and legitimate within the context of such politics. So when Chapter 2 discusses the merits of collective goods, Chapter 3 decentralization, Chapter 4 the merits of bureaucracy as a form of public organization, Chapter 5 the distinction between management and leadership, Chapter 6 administrative integrity, Chapter 7 the problems in decision making and Chapter 8 the problem of developing public policies, the contents are not only countering the one-sided focus on politics in government and arbitrary decision making by politicians, they are discussing key themes of Public Administration.

Finally, studying the working of government involves more than just a consideration of economic costs and benefits. The study of Public Administration seeks to examine economic value in the framework of the ethics, norms and values involved, i.e. using normative value to understand and evaluate the workings of government. As a result, each chapter includes a discussion of ethics. Values and norms are partly reflected in laws, but they are more implicit in varying cultures and traditions, and this brings us back to the first common theme: the need for contextualization.

This book concludes by summarizing the essentials of the previous chapters and extending a plea for more appreciation for what governments – under difficult circumstances and impossible boundary conditions – are still able to accomplish.

Further reading

Haque, M. Shamsul (1999). *Restructuring Development Theories and Policies: A Critical Study*. New York: SUNY Press.

Painter, Martin & Peters, B. Guy (eds.) (2010). *Tradition and Public Administration*. Basingstoke: Palgrave Macmillan.

Pierre, Jon (2013). *Globalization and Governance*. Cheltenham, UK and Northampton, MA: Edward Elgar.

Pollitt, Christopher (2013). *Context in Public Policy and Management: The Missing Link?* Cheltenham, UK and Northampton, MA: Edward Elgar.

Chapter 2

Why do governments exist and why study them?

This chapter addresses the main reasons for the existence of governments. The role of the public sector in society is a common subject of discussion and criticism, inspiring debates on topics including taxation, inefficient public service delivery, ineffective public policies and irrational decision making. This leads to the question of why governments exist in the first place. Why are people willing to pay taxes, comply with the rules as determined by their government, and even work for the government? What is it that allows a group of people to have the authority to govern a country or nation and to exercise political direction and control over the actions of the members, citizens or inhabitants of communities and societies? (cf. definition of 'government', Merriam-Webster dictionary).

This chapter contains varying answers to these questions, which generate references to the nature of humankind, religious convictions, the evolution of civilization, coercion and the provision of public goods that resolve collective problems. The chapter continues with a discussion of public goods. What makes public goods different from private goods, and what problems exist in the provision of public goods?

Which public goods are provided as well as how they are provided depends in part on the type of political regime. Four types of political regimes are distinguished: the palace type (kingdoms), the temple type (religious states), the club type (interest group dominance) and the forum type (democracies). It will quickly become evident that while such pure types previously existed, nowadays regimes are more commonly mixed, combining, for instance, a kingdom with a democracy, or even a religious state with democratic elections or a king and certain dominant interest groups.

Notwithstanding the differences between regime types, one common feature is that they all need some organizational capacity or an administrative apparatus, i.e. a public administration. I described in Chapter 1 how the study of public administration is Public

Administration, a discipline distinct from political science, law, economics and sociology. In this chapter I will start to explore Public Administration's key themes.

Terminology

State and government

Although the terms 'state' and 'government' are sometimes used interchangeably, they do refer to different phenomena. A state is broader in that it consists of a population, a territory, a government and sovereignty. Government is part of a state. A state is also typically a nation, and both terms are used here. In practice, a state can refer to the regional level of government in some nations, i.e. the United States, and the states in Germany and Australia. In order to distinguish such regional states from our definition the term 'nation-state' is used.

The state (or nation)

A nation-state comprises all of its inhabitants, but not all inhabitants are part of its government. People rarely protest against their nation-state, but they do against their government. One speaks of the nation-state of India, or the nation-state of Brazil, referring to a territory that exists of an Indian or Brazilian population, a well-defined territory, a government and sovereignty.

Territory

Defining nation-states by their territory is not always as easy as its definition suggests. Although most territories are delineated within nations, in South East Asia the ownership of some islands is still disputed between sometimes powerful nations. Between Greece and Turkey in the Aegean Sea, there are some rocky, uninhabited islands that flood twice a day. Does a territory include these, and if so whose territory? It is not a trifling question, because the ownership of fishing areas surrounding these areas depends on it. In Latin America, the Falkland Islands still cause tension in UK–Argentinian relations; China and the Philippines continue to dispute ownership over certain islands in the South China Sea as do Japan and Russia over the Kuril Islands.

Population

Similar problems arise concerning the population. The population can be defined as a group of persons who live on a commonly shared territory, but also more specifically as a group of people who share complementary communication habits, at least part of a common culture and language, have a common understanding of many things and attach shared meanings to words (Deutsch, 1974, p. 120). Who belongs to a population? The answers vary around the world. Sometimes belonging to the population depends on where one is born; at other times the nationality in the passport is the determining factor. There are also nations which allow political rights to certain groups, such as the right of active and passive participation in elections to migrant workers, and thus look upon them as part of the population of the nation.

Sovereignty

The sovereignty of nation-states can also be the subject of dispute. Most nations are recognized by other nations. This constitutes external sovereignty; that is, independence and the right to self-government. Internal sovereignty refers to the authority over a territory to rule and make and enforce laws. Authority refers to a claim of legitimacy by which one's power or right to give orders, make decisions and/or enforce obedience is supported. Sometimes the claim of legitimacy can be found in an individual's or organization's ability to do what is advantageous for the state, be it on the basis of one's wisdom, strength, skills, knowledge, past behaviour or even height or body type. This is charismatic authority.

In other cases the claim of legitimacy is based on tradition, for instance kings, caliphs, emperors, popes, pontiffs, or chief-imams are legitimate rulers in religious states. In such traditional authority the person with authority is the anointed leader by virtue of being the heir of a dynasty or by divine command. The world has many different traditions in this respect. Finally, authority does not necessarily have to be assigned to an individual per se. Authority can also lie in rules and laws, and it can be based on a position that allows anyone occupying that position to exercise authority based on that law, i.e. rational–legal authority.

Government

A government, as a constituting element of a nation-state, is defined as the totality of political and administrative organizations and institutions within that nation, authorized to allocate collectively binding values and services, i.e. public values and services. The government system plays a crucial role in developing, deciding upon, executing and enforcing public policies and thus steering a nation's socio-economic development. Often a nation-state's government monopolizes certain functions, such as the right to use violence through its police and army, the maintenance of public order and safety, the right to print money, the right of legislation, the right to levy taxes and the right to discipline individuals.

Why people transfer authority to government

Nowadays, nearly every territory belongs to some kind of nation-state. Although not all constituting elements are always present, there is always a government. This has not always been the case throughout history, so why would people transfer the power to settle their problems and conflicts to an external authority like government?

One of the answers can be found in the *nature of humankind*. Human beings are social animals. As twentieth-century Italian political scientist Mosca wrote, 'Men have an instinct for herding together and fighting with other herds' (Mosca, 1939, p. 165) and Aristotle wrote that 'man is by nature a political animal'. If Aristotle lived in the twenty-first century, he might have said that it is in our DNA to organize ourselves and to establish hierarchical relations in the best interests of all the people involved. Some seek power while others seek the protection that this power provides. Therefore, it is in humanity's best interest to form primitive or more extensive kinds of government. These can range from informal leadership within a family to the more formal organization required to rule larger communities. This idea suggests that rulers will be considered legitimate as long as they take care of the interests of the ruled.

These general notions have been reformulated into psychological theories such as social identity theory, in which people need to identify with a group for their self-esteem, and hierarchy and power within these groups are accepted as long as this contributes to their identity vis-à-vis other groups. Social dominance theory views humans as having a biological drive for social inequality and an evolutionary past that predisposes them towards hierarchy and competition between groups. According to this theory, every individual has a degree of attraction to authoritarian social relations, and a tendency to buy into the 'legitimating myths' deployed to defend them. Social justification theory assumes that individuals need social structures in order to legitimize them. Individuals want to support the status quo and to see it as being there for good reasons (cf. Blaug, 2010, pp. 41–43).

A second answer is that *not all problems are individual problems.* Many problems are shared by groups of individuals. In ancient times, people feared for the loss of their own and their families' lives and property at the hands of violent neighbours, roaming tribes and natural disasters. This resulted in collective fear and necessitated group action, including organization and management, to counter the problems. This collective action often resulted in some form of government because organization requires leadership. According to seventeenth-century philosopher Thomas Hobbes' warning in *Leviathan* (1651), if people did not organize, there would be a continuous struggle of all against all, which would be detrimental for all.

Originally, people lived in tribes of one's kinship. The eldest, or the strongest or the wisest within these families solved problems and mediated conflicts. When serious troubles emerged because of potential conflicts with other tribes, for instance over women, one of the conflicting parties was bound to lose the conflict and lose power. Tribes disappeared or were subdued or taken over by larger entities. In other cases flooding, drought, earthquakes, et cetera, posed serious threats that necessitated collective action. Individuals alone were unable to deal with the consequences of these natural disasters, so cooperation and organization became a necessity. For instance, in countries such as Mesopotamia, China and Mexico, irrigation required substantial investments that could not be made individually. Collective action was required, and a managing organization (government) was needed. Of course, in different parts of the world different problems dominated, resulting in different types of organizations. In some regions, especially mountainous or isolated areas and among nomadic people without permanent residence (territory), and in the absence of threats, tribes could survive for a long time. Even nowadays, some communities, for instance in Africa, India or Afghanistan, are better characterized as tribes than as (parts of) nations.

The need for collective action is the most basic reason for an organization; organizations exist to fulfil purposes that a group of individuals have in common (Laski, 1939). Hence, it is a kind of trade-off. People join in taking responsibility for an army, a city wall or other protection, this in turn requires organization and leadership, i.e. government, and the new entity diminishes the original problem.

A third answer is *the evolution of civilization*. The evolution from nomadic life dominated by hunter-gatherers to settlers who developed agriculture, and later on the emergence of trade and the division of labour, resulted in the emergence of cities, which were sometimes political centres, trade centres or religious centres. Living together in cities is more complex than living together in tribes or small villages. Increasing population density – more people living together in a small space – gave rise to more collective problems and conflicts, and the need of an authority to solve those problems and conflicts. Because of cities' increasing size, functions previously handled within the family were transferred to non-kinship structures, i.e. 'structural differentiation'. In ancient times, cities were under the recurring threats of nomadic tribes, attacks by competing cities and civil unrest. This necessitated some form of organization and government overarching the family structure. Initially, governments built and maintained armies, built city walls to defend the cities from outside threats, built facilities to maintain order and safety within the cities and built infrastructure, such as harbours, to facilitate trade. The first known cities (3500 BC) in the region of Sumer, between the Euphrates and the Tigris rivers, were composed of a palace, a temple with a ziggurat, a court, a harbour, schools, irrigation canals and dykes, and fields, farms and cattle folds in the suburbs (Finer, 1997, p. 109). Hence, city states emerged with some form of city government. Later conquests of one city by another resulted in the emergence of city states with kings and emperors ruling over a number of cities and the surrounding land. The first records of such development are found in Sumer.

A fourth reason for the emergence of government is *religious convictions*. The belief in natural laws and divine order, substantiated by holy manuscripts, supported the idea that leadership was the instrument of divine order to enforce divine laws. Many believed that states and nations emerged and leaders were chosen based on divine power. This resulted in the religious state where religious leaders, such as priests, shamans, imams or prophets, held authority. Their authority was based on divine command, and the actions of the worldly leader as well as of the population were subject to their judgement. In medieval Islam, the sultan was the representative (*khalifa*) of Allah. Originally in Islam, the main requirement for being imam was to be *muftahid*, possessing the ability to organize an army and defend the frontiers and handle the affairs of Muslims. Of course, the imam also had to be an excellent individual in the eyes of Allah. In Abrahamic religions, a king is the sword of God on earth. In a religious state, the religious leader protects his people in the name of the divine power. He has to create conditions in which the people can live the good life and he must be exemplary in accordance with the laws as outlined in the first five books of the Bible or in the Quran.

A fifth reason for the emergence of government is that it was *forced on people* by other people through violent actions or the threat of such violence. Individuals and groups differ in strength and the strongest impose their will on the weaker. In conquests, one nation or tribe defeats the other and imposes its rule on the vanquished. In this case, transferring one's authority to a government is not a choice, but a fait accompli because the losers lack the means to oppose government. In this situation, the rulers have a minimal amount of legitimacy; they are accepted because they enforce their acceptance through might. This government also enforces taxes, beliefs, preferences and collective goods on the people, without the latter asking for or needing it. From a historical perspective – and with the benefit of hindsight – this reason is perhaps the most realistic explanation for the emergence of nations, states and governments.

In ancient history, rulers became rulers by conquering one city after another. The earliest great conquerors in ancient times were the Qin Dynasty in China and Sargon the Great from Sumer, which is nowadays Iraq, Alexander the Great from Macedonia, Cyrus the Great from Persia and his grandson Darius I. In medieval times, Gothic King Theodoric the Great, Attila the Hun, Genghis Khan from Mongolia, Timur Tamerlane, from what is nowadays Uzbekistan, and Mahmud of Ghazni from Afghanistan were the great conquerors. More recent conquests linked less to an individual and more to states or nations include the Spanish Empire that colonized Central America and parts of what is now the USA and Latin America. The British Empire, under various rulers, conquered almost half the world. It did this in competition with the Portuguese and the Dutch merchants who colonized territories over a thousand times the size of their own nations in the seventeenth and eighteenth centuries. More recent individual conquerors include Napoleon of France and Adolf Hitler of Germany. With a merciless show of strength, they were able to subdue up to five million square miles of territory. The main authority of such governments and individuals was found in their use of brute force.

Whatever the reason, the establishment of governments resulted in organized states. In some of them, governments made it possible to build infrastructure that individuals or small kinship groups could never have built alone. These included temples to honour the divine power, irrigation systems, fountains for drinking water, marketplaces to facilitate trade, an army and city walls to protect the citizens against roaming tribes – even the building of the Great Wall of China. These were public goods because they required a more formal organization, a collective effort to produce something that benefited everyone and excluded no one.

European powers exploited their nationals or colonies. The colonial powers were not interested in providing collective goods on behalf of their colonial territories to resolve certain collective problems, but rather to benefit themselves by depriving the colonies of their wealth and natural resources. The mining, agriculture and plantation systems were not for local use and benefit, but they were developed to benefit the colonial power. Forced labour resulted in the massive movement of people from one area to another, rural to rural, rural to urban and even as slaves to the Americas. It also resulted in poor working conditions in the colonies, family break-up and changing values and beliefs. For instance, during colonialism, the number of Christians in Africa increased enormously and the dominant feeling there of belonging to an extended family transformed into the dominant feeling of belonging to a nuclear family.

History shows that building legitimacy solely on brute force is not only unreliable, but it is ultimately detrimental for the oppressed as well as for those in power. From the late eighteenth century through the end of the nineteenth century, the Americas warred themselves into independence. Between the end of the nineteenth century and the Second World War, Central European, Middle Eastern and some Asian and Pacific and Oceanic countries gained independence. After 1945, the African countries and many more countries in South and South East Asia became independent.

Today, governments still find legitimacy on primarily the same five grounds. In many nations, government is still believed to be legitimized by divine power (religious states) or by its promotion of the common interests and the self-interest of the population (democracies). There are also still nations where the rule of force dominates the rule of law (military states). Some scholars view such nations as lacking authority. These scholars differentiate authority from power; in the former, there is an inherent inclination to accept decisions while in the latter, the threat of force is always present and people only accept decisions out of fear. In most states, governments have established a system of law and order and use force to uphold the law. And in most states, the use of force is monopolized in the police and military under the control of government as a means to maintain political stability and non-violence and to protect the state against internal and external threats. The consequences of the state monopolization of force can differ from country to country given the wide range of choices for balancing the interests of those in power and managing the collective problems of the population as a whole.

In spite of these differences, the provision of collective goods to resolve collective problems forms the basic legitimacy of any modern-day governments. Nowadays, complex problems in many countries require more than simple collective action for the protection of life and property against violent tribes and natural disasters. These problems include education, infrastructure, socio-economic welfare, economic development, health care, housing, environmental sustainability and working conditions to mention just a few. There is variation across states – and groups within states – in how these issues are viewed. Some view them as collective problems that require collective action that results in public goods, and some see them as individual problems that are primarily the responsibility of the person involved. Some of these issues related to public goods will be discussed in the next section.

The logic of collective action

Government comes into existence through the organization of individuals or groups with common interests who try to further those interests by creating a government. This government produces public goods, through collectively binding decisions for the benefit of all, to which all citizens are expected to contribute and from which all citizens benefit. This public good might be a dam to prevent flooding, an army to fight off attacks by roaming tribes, or a police force to uphold the law.

This would be self-evident if public goods had the same features as private goods, but this is not the case. In fact, the production of public goods is highly controversial simply by virtue of the fact that they are public. The people who contribute to the provision of a public good complain about others who contribute less or nothing. They complain that it takes too long, that it is inefficient or that it could be done better. By their very nature, public goods are contested and discussed. Some even doubt whether there truly are goods that are public or private in nature. Roads, temples, palaces, fountains and marketplaces were originally public goods, but they might also be built by the private sector in which users pay for their service and use. For instance, in eighteenth-century Europe, offices belonging to the public sector, such as a tax office, could be bought and owned by individuals. Today, a similar phenomenon takes place in privatization, the transfer of the provision of goods and services from the public to the private sector – although collective, i.e. governmental, action is required in areas such as environmental pollution or combating terrorism. The principle remains the same: when a problem cannot be or is not handled by individuals or groups of individuals themselves, when many individuals have an interest in the resolution of the problem and when government is expected to find an efficient and effective solution, the pressure for collective goods provided by the government increases.

Private goods can be purchased and consumed or used in exchange for money. Just because one person can acquire a private good does not imply that everyone can acquire it. Consider a Happy Meal at McDonald's; you pay for what you get, and if you do not pay, you do not get it. Such goods are *excludable*, meaning that only the people who pay for them are able to enjoy their benefits. Unlike private goods, *public goods are non-excludable*. Public goods are goods that cannot feasibly be withheld from individuals in a group if there are others in the group who are able to consume/use them. Everyone benefits from the existence of a police force, an army, a lighthouse, street lights or a public park.

In addition, whereas private goods are mostly *rivalrous*, meaning that one person's use of them decreases the quantity available for someone else, *public goods are non-rivalrous*. Many people can consume them or use them without diminishing their value or exhausting their supply. One might even argue that the more people profit from a public good, the more efficient and effective the good is.

Furthermore, public goods require a collective contribution. Everyone is supposed to contribute to the creation and maintenance of that public good, even if they do not profit from it individually. As a result, the economic value of public goods is determined in a different way than the economic value of private goods. Whereas the economic value of a private good is the maximum amount that a person is willing to pay for it, the value of a public good is the maximum amount that all the people are willing to pay for it. In the case of public goods, payments can be obligatory in the form of taxes, but they can also be voluntary, as in voluntary actions to maintain and beautify a public park.

Public goods are also judged based on criteria other than their economic value. Even if the provision of the public good is costly from an economic point of view, other criteria may deem it necessary. Such public goods include environmental quality, access to education, labour laws, poverty alleviation, public health care, et cetera. Although some scholars have tried to frame the existence of such policies primarily in terms of economic cost and benefits, ethical standards in terms of norms and values pose the primary reasons for developing policies and public goods in these areas.

For instance, the Universal Declaration of Human Rights, which many national governments signed, outlines the basic public goods that every government should provide. It also defines those policies every government should abstain from.

According to this universal declaration, everyone has the right to life, liberty and security of person. No one shall be held in slavery or servitude; slavery and the slave trade shall be prohibited in all their forms. All people are equal before the law and are entitled without any discrimination to equal protection of the law and no one shall be subjected to arbitrary arrest, detention or exile. No one shall be subjected to arbitrary interference with his or her privacy, family, home or correspondence, or to attacks upon his or her honour and reputation. Everyone has the right to the protection of the law against such interference or attacks. Everyone has the right to a nationality and no one shall be arbitrarily deprived of his or her nationality nor denied the right to change his or her nationality. Everyone has the right to a standard of living adequate for the health and well-being of him- or herself and of his or her family, including food, clothing, housing, medical care and necessary social services, and the right to security in the event of unemployment, sickness, disability, widowhood, old age or other lack of livelihood in circumstances beyond his or her control. Motherhood and childhood are entitled to special care and assistance. All children, whether born in or out of wedlock, shall enjoy the same social protection. Furthermore, according to this declaration, everyone has the right to rest and leisure, including reasonable limitation of working hours and periodic holidays with pay. Everyone has also the right to education and parents have a prior right to choose the kind of education that shall be given to their children.

The Universal Declaration of Human Rights sets a common standard of achievement for every state, in that its governments shall strive to promote respect for these rights and freedoms and by progressive measures, national and international, to secure their universal and effective recognition and observance.

In theory, this all makes perfect sense and one might even expect that because such goods and services are in everyone's interests, that everyone would attempt to further these interests and there would be a corresponding growth of public goods. This idea, is nonetheless, disputed.

In his famous theory on the Logic of Collective Action published in 1965, Mancur Olson was one of the first to dispute the idea that groups of individuals with common interests usually attempt to further those interests. On the first page of his classic book, Olson writes that:

> The idea that groups tend to act in support of their group interests is supposed to follow logically from this widely accepted premise of rational, self-interested behavior ... If the members of some group have a common interest or objective, and if they would all be better off if that objective were achieved, it has been thought to follow logically that the individuals in that group would, if they were rational and self-interested, act to achieve that objective. (Olson, 1965, p. 1)

Notwithstanding this idea, according to Olson this is not the case in practice 'even if all of the individuals in a large group are rational and self-interested, and would gain if, as a group, they acted to achieve their common interest or objective, they will still not voluntarily act to achieve that common or group interest' (p. 2).

Why would individuals not contribute to such common goods? Olson responds that in sizeable states, individual efforts will not have a noticeable effect on the establishment of such goods, and given the definition of public goods, individuals can enjoy public goods anyway if they are produced or initiated by others, irrespective of their own individual contribution. In other words, people will act as *free riders*, enjoying the outcomes – which cannot be denied to them because that is the essence of a public good – while minimizing their own contribution to such goods.

According to Olson, this problem increases with the size of an organization or the size of a state. With increased size, the noticeable effect of individual contributions decreases, while the benefits for each individual do not increase. Hence, the probability that individuals will voluntarily contribute to common goods decreases with the size of the group.

This is not the only problem with public goods. Another problem is that the linkage between supply and demand is not as direct as in private goods. Since contributions to public goods are shared, it is easy to assert the need for one; a public road might be paid for by everyone in the municipality even when only a small number of individuals actually use it. In theory, this implies that *public goods have a tendency to be overproduced*.

Other problems related to public goods are that their benefits are not always limited to the boundaries of the state, such as in the case of scientific knowledge. According to Olson, a government cannot be expected to provide collective goods when its benefits fall in significant proportion outside the nation's boundaries.

A further problem is that public goods might not be produced efficiently (cost inefficiency) or provided efficiently (allocative inefficiency), because they are paid for by others. As Olson writes, 'The types of collective goods and externalities with which governments have to deal are not only diverse in their scope and locale, but are presumably also becoming more numerous and important over time' (p. 172).

Furthermore, Olson believes that collective goods have a tendency to increase societal conflict because there will tend to be disproportionality in the burdens of providing the good. The disproportionality is called the 'exploitation of the great by the small' (p. 3). Because the wealthy often pay higher amounts of taxes than the poor do, they thus contribute disproportionally to public goods. Conflicts can also arise out of diverse needs, wants or values with respect to the provision of collective goods and services.

If public goods cause such problems and conflicts, why do they exist at all? Indeed, some scholars favour the privatization of all public goods; they assume that if the free-market mechanism is applied, production will be more efficient and the resulting competition will enhance the quality of such goods. Other options have also been proposed to deal with the problems while retaining (part of) the features of public goods.

One suggestion is to provide *semi-public goods*, in which the collective builds a public facility and individual users are required to pay in accordance with the use thereof. Entrance fees for entering a public place, school fees, parking fees, public transport fees and personal contributions for health care are examples of the creation of semi-public goods. The user does not have to pay all the costs, because these are provided for by the collective, but is required to contribute individually dependent on the personal benefits and use of the public service. In the case of a dam to prevent recurring flooding, residents below the dam will obviously benefit more from the dam than those above it. This difference in benefit could be reflected in variable contributions to the construction of the dam. Unlike pure public goods, semi-public goods are expected to reduce overconsumption and overproduction.

One solution to reduce free riding is by requiring contribution to public goods, for instance through obligatory taxes and regulations enforced by law, administrative control and the justice system. In this case, individuals have no choice but to contribute to the production of public goods. Regulations can also compel conscription into the army or voting in elections.

Laws and regulations are not the only means to enforce contributions to public goods. Compliance can also be brought about through social norms and moral obligations. In this way, the self-interest that might lead one to try to escape from contributing to a public good is countered by moral obligations, feelings of solidarity, faith, beliefs, the fear of disapproval of others, et cetera. Whether such social norms and moral obligations are effective in reducing the free-rider problem depends partly on the legitimacy of the provider of such goods, as the previous section describes.

In conclusion, varying opinions about the pros and cons of the provision of public goods and services by government exist and the dominance of either point of view varies over time and place. In some nations, health care is a public good; in others, it is a private good; and in still others, it is a semi-public good. The same goes for education, military service and many less important goods; for instance, parking.

Regime types

Not only does the provision of goods and services vary over countries, the forms of government (regimes) that provide public goods vary. *Regimes* refer to the basic mechanisms, rules and cultural and social norms that determine who is in charge of government operations. In democracies, individuals transfer the right to decision making to politicians through elections. The political leaders, being elected by the polity, are thus legitimized to make decisions on behalf of and for the people, but this is not the only type of regime nor the only way decisions can be made.

Figure 2.1   *Four main regime types*

S.E. Finer (1997) described the different forms of government that have existed throughout history starting with the Sumerians and ending with the modern state. He identified four main types (see Figure 2.1): the palace, the forum, the temple (in Finer's classification 'church') and the club (in Finer's classification 'nobility'). These are ideal types, i.e. types of government in their purest form. These ideal types are not likely to be found in their purest form, but they are constructed to distinguish and analyse different forms of government. Hybrids such as a church–palace combination or a palace–forum combination are much more common.

The palace type

According to Finer, the palace is a metonym for the people who inhabit it and where those people work (Finer, 1997, p. 38). It is the seat of the monarch and his or her servants. In its purest form, power is concentrated in the hands of one man or woman only and this person is not accountable to anyone, neither to divine power nor to his or her people or the law. Rituals and symbols, like the orb and the crown, are important for legitimacy.

The monarch stands above the law, because it is in his name that laws are made. King Louis XIV of France said in his address to the Parliament of Paris in 1655, '*The state, that is me*' (cited in Dulaure, 1834, p. 298). Such a remark points to the issue that in palace-type regimes, there does not have to be a distinction between public and private goods. Someone like Louis XIV was known for his amalgamation of the private and the public.

Royalty are not necessary for a palace-type government. In some states, there is a kind of super-presidential government in which all power is concentrated in the hands of that one president. In such states, there is no real separation of powers, elections are a farce and the president acts like the sun-king. The palace type is also rather closed in terms of succession and decision making. This relative closure results in political intrigues and conspiracies. Another disadvantage is the small distance – or even absence of distance – between private and public affairs, of which greedy presidents and kings sometimes take advantage.

The forum type

At the opposite end of the palace type is the forum type. Decisions are openly discussed in front of the population through the forum, the parliament or nowadays indirectly through the media. Plurality exists and decision makers are accountable to the population, either directly to that part of the population that has political rights or indirectly through a parliament or a senate. Modern democracy in its purest form is characteristic of this type of government, and present-day Switzerland comes nearest to this pure type because it is the only country where important decisions are decided upon directly by the population through referenda. Public goods are provided according to the earthly desires of the populace and the legitimacy of their provision is based on the trust and support of the ruled. This would also be defined as legitimacy based on rationality because a greater variety of interests are considered in decision making, and compared to the palace type more knowledge is shared before reaching a decision. This type is not without problems, however. These include the possibility of the oppression of the minority by the majority, the time it takes to make decisions – a process which is of course more complex than in the palace type where one man makes the decision – the overproduction of public goods and the costs involved in the provision of public goods. Like the pure form of the three other government types, no states conform totally to the forum type. It is more typically combined with some kind of club-type government, a religious state or even a monarchy such as in the United Kingdom.

The temple type

In this type of regime, political power is based on divine rules and regulations as prescribed in ancient texts. Its main characteristic is that rulers – often the religious leaders – are accountable to the divine power and restricted in their actions by the contents of holy books and their regulations. This results in very strong legitimacy. The rule of law is established in the holy book(s) and interpreted by the religious leaders to provide solutions for modern-day problems. There is no separation of religion and government or church and state, and religious leaders dominate over political leaders. These are religious states. In ancient times, the Aztec Empire approached this pure temple type. In its purest form, the priests, who are learned people, make decisions, regulate societal conflicts and solve problems through rituals and actual ruling. Many religious states still exist today, although often in combination with one of the other types. Rites and rituals play an important role in these states, and religious leaders are recognized by their clothing. Their ascetic behaviour that exudes the legitimacy of selfless caring and worshipping makes it clear that the leader is indeed a religious person and has reached spiritual excellence. Only religious officials can occupy positions of power in this type of government or regime, and a relatively large part of public goods are allocated to places of worship and institution building is religion based.

Unlike the forum-type regime where overproduction of public goods is expected, in the pure temple-type regime one expects fewer public goods based on state-wide public contributions. Most religions emphasize the importance of charity by individuals and societal groups instead of the government. The latter is seen as a last resort. In order to maximize legitimacy, religious institutions instead of the state will provide most of the public goods. Problems arise in such systems when the spiritual leaders fail to protect the country and when religious morality conflicts with the interests of the state, for instance if perceived needs of stability and innovation clash. Another source of conflict is the appearance of hypocrisy when spiritual leaders act differently to the way in which they require the population to act.

The club type

The club type consists of people who have similar interests such as nobility, merchants, party-members or military. Belonging to and having an important position in that grouping can provide a sufficient power base to rule the country. In the club-type regime, government is composed of one group representing a dominant, one-sided interest. Access to power is limited to those individuals who are seen as members of the club. You are of noble birth by a hereditary principle or not. You have had a successful military career or not. You are the owner of a multi-billion company or not. The particular interest such leaders represent is the dominant interest in the state. This is primarily defined in terms of possession. In medieval times, it could be agriculture. In seventeenth-century Holland, the main source of income was trade and those who controlled trade had power. Nowadays, we think of large industries and banks, whose influence is sometimes greater than that of government and military regimes. Although there are not that many examples of states in which such one-sided interests formally constitute this kind of government, there are many nations that are dominated by the military, with presidents who have been bankers and where nobility is still highly influential. There are also states, such as the former Soviet Union, in which party membership is the only way to obtain an influential position in government. The source of legitimacy in these regimes is that the individuals who govern the country received extensive training in the party or the military, gained position from birth as in nobility or otherwise achieved their station through their career in trade or business. Hence, the predictability of how such leaders will act is high; their legitimacy is based on the assumption that if they have been successful in a specific business or service, they will be equally successful in government.

There are three main problems in such regimes. First, the interests that the minority or club represents within the state are not necessarily beneficial for the state as a whole. Second, it is equally questionable whether the people who have proven to be skilled in their own business can translate that skill into the successful provision of public goods. Third, if the provision of goods benefits only that group or part of the state, i.e. members of the club, while exploiting or seeming to exploit the remaining groups, the legitimacy of this regime type becomes problematic. In the end, and in extreme cases, the only route for such governments might lie in the use of brute force, which often means the end of the regime.

Mixed regimes are more common than pure types

Most often, regimes occur as a combination of the ideal types. For instance, the palace type is often combined with the temple type. In this case, the monarch's legitimacy is also based on the extraordinary powers and characteristics attributed to the monarch as given to him or her by some divinity, or in the ancient Chinese Empire, as mandated by heaven in which the emperor is seen as the link between humanity and the cosmos. In Japan, the emperor is viewed as a descendant of the Sun-Goddess.

The forum type is often combined with either or both the club type and the temple type. Even in ancient Rome, the source of the term 'forum', political power was combined with devotion to the Gods and a strong role for spiritual leaders. Now, many countries try to combine traditional regime types with the forum type, creating a democracy in which the political leaders are elected, but in which there is still more or less influence of the religious leaders, the special interest groups or the monarchy.

Also, through time, government types within nations or states can change. Although regime changes are never easy and often painful, they do occur. Many reasons account for regime change throughout the world including foreign conquest, internal uprisings, revolutions and wars of independence. Regime change can be gradual, as in some decolonization processes, but it is typically accompanied by violence and political instability. Change is sometimes caused by conflicts of interest between different factions inside the state – the monarch, the spiritual leaders, the people and the dominant interest groups. At other times, the leadership has blundered or is unable to provide the public goods needed. In some cases, regime changes result from an altered national environment – wars or changing external threats. Important underlying causes for regime changes can also be found in demographic and cultural changes, such as secularization and urbanization, and in technological change. Actual regime change is based on the perceived need for such change and involves the shifting balance of legitimacy as seen in the following trade-offs, which are only some of the possible dilemmas in this regard:

- The (perception of the) success and failure of the existing regime internally in providing the necessary public goods.
- The (perceived) threat posed by the regime to other states.
- The (actual and perceived) incongruence between specific (dominant) interests and the general interest or between conflicting interests.
- Changes in the dominance of religion vis-à-vis secularization.
- The changing emphasis on tradition in relation to the need for innovation.
- Dominance of conservatism in relation to the (perceived or actual) lack of progress.
- The (perceived) exploitation of the minority by the majority or of the majority by a minority.

Clearly, the existence of conflicts is inherent to governments. Conflicts are not the exception but more or less the essence of politics in government. They arise out of the struggle for power and authority by different actors involved and the fight over *who* will control the government. The conflicts can be about the preferred regime type and the nature of government, about the need for government in general, about the success and failure of government in protecting the interests of the polity, about the efficiency and effectiveness of the provision of public goods, about whether something is or should be a public good, et cetera. This is the political side of government.

Recent research on the provision of collective goods

Recent theoretical developments on governmental provision of collective goods as a response to collective problems provide a useful illustration of the applied nature of the discipline. As explained earlier, the provision of collective goods is, in a classic sense, the *raison d'être* of government and it is one of the key themes in Public Administration. Through collectively binding decisions, governments produce public goods to which all citizens are expected to contribute and from which all citizens benefit without exclusion.

Because of their collective nature, the provision of such goods and services is frequently criticized. Regardless of the validity of the criticism, the inherent dilemmas involved in their provision results in a varying support for public sector provision of these goods and services over time. Until the 1970s there was a strong belief, especially in economically developed countries, that an expansion of the welfare state was essentially a government guarantee of the good life from the cradle to the grave. The provision of governmental public services would especially enable those individuals with few opportunities otherwise to advance. During the 1980s, it was believed that collective goods had to be transformed into semi-collective goods that required individual contributions, or even more preferably, into private goods that removed them from the public sector altogether. Privatization emerged in health care, public transport, education, pension systems and even prisons and traditional police tasks such as traffic control.

The conservative, anti-government political agendas of Prime Minister Margaret Thatcher and President Ronald Reagan during the 1980s and the budget deficits that many governments faced, as well as the publication of *Reinventing Government* by David Osborne and Ted Gaebler in 1992, and journal articles by Christopher Hood in 1991 and 1995, served as catalysts in the worldwide acceptance of the principles of what became known as New Public Management (NPM), a novel paradigm for the functioning of the public sector everywhere.

Denhardt and Denhardt (2003, p. 136) summarized the American version of NPM in ten principles: government should be catalytic (steering rather than rowing); community owned (empowering rather than serving); competitive by injecting competition into service delivery; mission driven instead of rule driven; results oriented; customer driven; enterprising; anticipatory; decentralized; and market oriented. Action by any actor other than the central government was preferred over the provision of public services by central government. Other actors included customers, civilians, businesses or local governments. The American version of NPM especially attacked the idea that such a thing as public services needed to exist and that they needed to be provided by the public sector.

The European version of NPM was less radical. Christopher Hood argued for an improvement of public service delivery by introducing hands-on management, performance measures, an emphasis on output and controls, the introduction and disaggregation of competition in the public sector, and copying private sector management styles and input discipline (Hood, 1991, 1995). According to this European view, public service delivery needed to improve its management and act more like a business. The European version of NPM was especially intended to solve inefficiencies in the provision of public goods.

While the success of these reforms varied, both in terms of improving governmental service delivery and in involving private partners in service delivery, NPM ideas continued to dominate public sector reforms over the late 1990s and early twenty-first century. NPM was especially lauded for its ideas of including private sector practices in the delivery of public sector services and for its ideas of substituting the public sector with the private sector.

However, this thinking was criticized from the outset. NPM practices were criticized for viewing individuals only as customers and not as citizens or partners, for suggesting solutions that did not create efficiency or that took care of individual interests but neglected the public interest, and for ignoring the moral, public norms and values that resulted in scandals in privatized services and agencies.

The question of how to avoid the problems that NPM sought to remedy without returning to a monopoly on the provision of public goods by the public sector became the new research question for scholars reflecting on alternative service delivery mechanisms. Their point of departure was that while some services were better off in the private sector and some in the public sector, the more important issue was the number and type of actors involved, i.e. citizens, non-profit organizations, international organizations, charities, et cetera. There are multiple combinations of actors and these combinations depend on the context and the policy area, as well as the phase, goals, financing, implementation and functions of service delivery. The research turned towards the relationship of service providers, service producers and consumers, and how the various contractual and organizational forms developed by these entities depended on legal, political, economic and social reasoning.

The search for effective and efficient alternative modes of service delivery has continued to be one of the key themes in Public Administration, ranging from full privatization to public–private partnerships, contracting out, concessions, co-production, transforming collective goods into semi-collective goods, et cetera. Furthermore, the role of government in these arrangements has become a crucial question. Should it be dominant, facilitating, regulating, steering, rowing or serving?

Recently the discussion was broadened by bringing the question to the fore of whether efficiency and effectiveness of service delivery are the most important criteria to judge the quality of service delivery or whether there are even more important criteria such as inclusion, citizenship, collaboration, engagement and equity. In such 'value-governance' the public sector, together with empowered and responsible citizens, is expected not only to create public value but also to ensure public values in which normative and unifying elements are crucial. The crucial question is how to accomplish this.

Conclusions

This chapter addressed the first key theme in Public Administration: why it exists. After distinguishing governments from states and nations, it turned to the following question: Given that the work of the public sector is constantly discussed, disputed and despised, why do we have government, and why is it relevant to study its administrative apparatus? It listed five reasons for the existence of governments: the nature of humankind, the existence of collective problems, the evolution of civilization, religious convictions and the forced imposition of government on people.

Subsequently, it explained that the main function of government is the provision of public goods, and compared public goods to private goods and explored whether public goods really exist.

One of the key themes in Public Administration is managing the inherent disadvantages and negative side effects of collective goods while providing a solution for collective problems. How do we handle the issues of free riders, overproduction and overconsumption of collective goods, the inefficiency in the production and provision of collective goods, the generalized resistance to collective goods, and the conflicts and problems that are inherent in such goods? Do we need to rephrase these questions in order to understand and resolve them?

The chapter continued by describing different types of governmental regimes: the palace type, the temple type, the club type and the forum type. It explained that as ideal types they are rarely, if ever, visible in their pure form. Instead, most regimes exhibit some combination of these types. Besides the obvious differences, for instance in how they handle the provision of collective goods, all regimes require some organization – administrative, advisory and executing – to handle the provision of (semi-)public goods through policies and programmes, and to ensure that citizens contribute to that provision through taxes and/or participative contributions.

Further reading

Fukuyama, Francis (2011). *The origins of political order*. London: Profile Books.

Heady, Ferrel (1996). *Public administration. A comparative perspective.* (5th edn.) New York: Marcel Dekker.

Lindert, Peter H. (2004). *Growing public. Social spending and economic growth since the eighteenth century*. Vols 1 & 2. Cambridge: Cambridge University Press.

Osborne, David & Gaebler, Ted (1992). *Reinventing government*. Reading, MA: Addison Wesley.

van Creveld, Martin (1999). *The rise and decline of the state*. Cambridge: Cambridge University Press.

Chapter 3

What does a typical government structure look like?

The varying regimes described in the previous chapter, as well as varying levels of socio-economic development, the different periods of time in which states emerged and their varying histories, culture and geo-political location suggest that there might be huge variance in the structure of governments. While differences are evident, remarkably, in most states around the globe – at least superficially – governmental structures are rather similar.

Although there are some exceptions in small nations, most governments typically consist of at least three levels: central (or national) government, regional government and local government. Further variations exist when there are additional layers between regional and local government and when there are subdivisions within a governmental layer. The latter is especially the case in large metropolitan cities.

The national level usually includes a head of state, a president, king, emperor, et cetera. Next to the head of state, there is sometimes a separate head of government along with either appointed or elected ministers, and a legislative institution, parliament, senate or assembly. At the regional level, the governor is the appointed or elected head, and at the local level there is the mayor, the aldermen and the municipal council.

Governments do not differ much in this way of structuring, but there are substantial differences in the hierarchical relations among the central government institutions and those between the three levels of government, especially in how authority is divided and powers are separated. In unitary states, the central government has most of the power and authority. In federal states, much of the power and authority lie in the hands of regional government, and in decentralized states, power and authority rest with the local governments.

Notwithstanding such differences, the argument is that within the central government as well as between central, regional and local governments, there is a natural tendency towards centralization. In developing countries, this tendency is enhanced by path dependencies from the legacy of previous colonization. After independence, four laws apply. First, the division of authority is copied from the colonizing power's constitution at the time of independence. This is followed by Michels' Iron Law of Oligarchy predicting the emergence of centralization. Third, nineteenth-century moralist Lord Acton's observation that power corrupts and absolute power corrupts absolutely becomes evident. Fourth, the drawbacks of the first three laws result in civil war and a limiting of the separation of powers until a new balance is attained. In many of these countries, a tendency towards centralization is visible not only in intergovernmental relations, with subnational governments being subordinate to central government, but also within central government, with either the head of state or the head of government concentrating power. Centralization seems to be the most obvious and dominant solution for solving the pressing problems that exist in those states.

A key theme for Public Administration is finding a rational counterpart for the detrimental effects of such power concentration. Solutions include, for instance, decentralization and bottom-up instead of top-down decision making. This chapter focuses on decentralization, that is, the transfer of power and authority from central government to the subnational level. The merits of bottom-up versus top-down decision making are addressed in chapter 8, p. 202. Researching and theorizing about the merits of decentralization focuses on intergovernmental relations and examines the optimal division of authority and power between the three levels of government. This chapter addresses the purposes of each level and the path dependencies that determine the varying division of tasks and responsibilities among them in different countries. It concludes with a discussion on the merits of decentralization.

Terminology

Central, *regional* and *local government* are each a set of legislative and executive institutions and organizations responsible for authoritative decision making over a certain territory. For central government, that territory is the nation. For regional government, the territory refers to a region within that nation, a territory with a single, continuous and non-intersecting boundary between local and national governments (cf. Marks et al., 2008, p. 113). For local government, the territory is the municipality.

The head of state

The *head of state* is – formally – the highest ranked person. This is usually a single individual such as a prince, king, queen or emperor in a monarchy or a president in a republic. The functions of the head of state vary. Some have a ceremonial and symbolic role in the external representation of the nation, and internally as the symbol of national unity and of the legitimacy of the government and the state. This is the case in many European monarchies as well as in Japan, where the emperor is devoid of any independent discretionary executive powers. At the other extreme, there is super-presidentialism, in which all executive, legislative and even judicial powers are concentrated in this one person, with only symbolic control of a parliament. This model is evident in Central Asia.

In between are many different arrangements, with the head of state sometimes being formally a ceremonial function but in practice an all-powerful position, for instance because it is combined with other functions. An example is China where the presidency itself is ceremonial, but the president (chairman) is nonetheless all-powerful because of his simultaneous position as General Secretary of the Communist Party of China and as Chairman of the Central Military Commission.

The head of government

In addition to the head of state, there is or can be a *head of government*, i.e. the prime minister, chief minister, state-minister, chairman of the executive council, *Bundeskanzler*, *primer ministro*, Secretary of State, *başbakan*, mayor of the palace or sultan. To a varying degree, this individual is in charge of the executive and the administration of all affairs of state, and thus responsible for executing and upholding the laws. He is also dependent on the authority relations vis-à-vis the head of state. In many states, the head of government is the *primus inter pares* – the first among equals – in a cabinet of ministers.

Not every state has a separate head of government in addition to the head of state. In those cases, both functions are combined in one person. This is the case in the USA where the president is head of state as well as head of government. In this country, it is the president who has to 'take care that the laws be faithfully executed', and 'preserve, protect and defend the Constitution' and it is the president who leads the executive branch of government as well.

Ministers

Most national governments have one or more *ministers* responsible for the administration and execution of policies in specific areas: a minister for defence for military affairs; a minister for finance, for collecting taxes, budgeting and the tax offices; a minister for foreign affairs, for international relations and the embassies; a minister of the interior, for domestic affairs in the government system as such, including the administrative apparatus and intergovernmental relations; a minister for education, for schooling and education; and a minister for justice, for the policies of the public prosecutor, maintaining and enforcing the legal system and preserving public order, including the policies regarding the police. The number of ministers as well as their domains can vary greatly. For instance, in Aruba, an unusual combination of policy areas is combined within the different ministries. In that microstate in the Caribbean, the prime minister oversees the ministry of general affairs, science, innovation and sustainable development; other ministries include a ministry of economic affairs, communication, energy and environment, and a ministry of tourism, transport, primary sector and culture.

The legislative

The next institution is the *legislative council*, with the power to enact, amend and repeal laws, to approve, amend or reject budgets, and to oversee and control the workings of the executive. Again, the real power of this institution depends on the separation of powers and the division of authority among the head of state, the head of government and this assembly. It is known in different countries under varying names such as parliament, congress, *Diet*, (National or People's) Council, (National or People's) Assembly, Senate or House of Representatives. The exact functions of the legislative vary over countries, as does its organization. Sometimes there are two chambers, such as the upper and lower house, the Senate and the House of Representatives or the first and second chamber, between which the powers and authority can greatly vary.

The judiciary

The third institution is the *judiciary*, which applies and interprets the law in specific cases through the court system in the name of the state.

It has the authority to adjudicate legal disputes between parties and carry out the administration of justice in civil, criminal and administrative matters in accordance with the rule of law (cf. Walker, 1980, p. 301).

The constitution

The institutions mentioned above have different names and varying degrees of power across countries. The *constitution* of a country often reflects the actual powers and authority of each of the mentioned institutions, their mutual relations and the separation of the executive, legislative and judiciary powers. It establishes basic and fundamental principles about how a state is governed at each level. It may delineate who is in charge and who can appoint and dismiss others. For example, is the head of state dependent upon the head of government or on support from the legislative council, or is it the other way round and can the head of state dismiss the head of government and parliament? The constitution also provides information about the term of office for the three branches, how officeholders are recruited, i.e. appointed or elected, whether reappointment or re-election is possible, who is responsible to whom, et cetera. Furthermore, the constitution can provide the principles of intergovernmental relations – between central, regional and local government – prescribing whether regional and local governments also have legislative powers, or whether these are reserved to central government.

In fact, constitutions are a reflection of the centralization, i.e. separation of powers and authority, within each governmental level and the centralization, i.e. separation of powers and authority, among different governmental levels. The constitution can also define the rights and obligations of citizens and their entitlement to protection by government and from government through articles similar to those found in the *Universal Declaration of Human Rights*, and specific provisions such as referenda, appeal to an ombudsman or further control of government's policies by a national auditor's office.

The constitution does not always reflect the actual separation of powers or levels of authority. In Russia, for instance, the constitution stipulates that the head of state – the president of the Russian Federation – and the head of government – the prime minister, officially called the Chairman of the Government of the Russian Federation – are two separate functions, the latter being appointed and subordinate to the former. The president has most extensive powers in being granted an important role in the appointments of top officials such as the prime minister as head of government, in the drafting, signing and vetoing of legislation, and in the implementation of domestic and foreign policy. According to the constitution, the president is elected for a period of four years and can be re-elected once. However, when the Russian president Putin had served twice in 2008 and couldn't be re-elected again, he simply switched position with his head of government, Medvedev, for four years, apparently without losing any of his previous powers, and returned as president in 2012.

The stability of government structures

Terminology can help us know what we are talking about, but it does not provide insight or understanding as to why governments differ in the distribution of powers among their institutions. In order to understand present-day government structures in many states in Africa, Asia, Latin America and the Caribbean, one needs to go back to the Europe of England, France, the Netherlands, Portugal and Spain of the nineteenth and twentieth centuries, and to the USA and the Soviet Union after the Second World War.

The colonial powers left an administrative legacy of which the remnants are still visible today. England significantly impacted institutional development with its Westminster model of government. France had a presidential model, and Spain and Portugal ruled Latin America through a system of viceroyalties, military rule and patronage until the nineteenth century.

Although there are crucial political differences between these regimes, they also have some common characteristics resulting from the fact that they were all highly centralized systems, with overseas central government making, executing and applying the laws. In addition to the humiliation of the native people in the colonies through imposed migration and exploitation, and the violent manner in which these powers colonized the countries, a crucial feature in Public Administration terms was how small communities in the colonies were governed.

Spanish colonization started with building cities and mission posts. French colonization was characterized by the absence of local rule, euphemistically called indirect rule, resulting in the continuation of traditional leadership and very little institutionalization at that level, especially in rural areas. The ruling of localities during English colonization varied depending on whether the colony was a settler colony, a trading post or an exploitation territory. In the latter two cases, it was considered efficient to maintain the traditional structures, as long as orders from the central level were obeyed, since this decreased the number of officials required in the colonies. Local-level governance only emerged in settler colonies.

A third characteristic was limited access to the public sector in the colonies, except for the happy few who received a proper education at one of the few governmental or mission schools and/or those who had a personal family background that ensured loyalty to the colonial power. During the Spanish colonization in the Americas, individuals aspiring to a job in government were required to prove their families had been loyal to the Spanish regime and were Christians for more than ten generations. The Spanish laws, known as *limpieza de sangre*, or Purity of Blood, restricted access to the powerful offices in the colonies to those individuals born in Spain (*peninsulares*) or to those who were born out of Spanish parents (*criollos*). Finally, yet importantly, a system of patronage dominated and was retained with a mutual exchange of (financial) support, encouragement and privileges within a selective group. Although many colonies ultimately revolted against the oppressive colonial powers, many of the administrative systems established during the colonial period were retained.

Path dependency theory

The stability of institutional structures and their dependence on their historical development is the focus of path dependency theory. The essence of this theory is that the best way to understand the situation in a nation is by investigating its past and that remnants of this past will always be visible. In examining a nation's history, one will see the origins of historically grown habits and customs that regulate ordinary life in terms of traditions, culture, values and norms, laws, and regulations. This explains the stability of structures and institutions in a state. Changes occur because of – often – minor institutional alterations which may have unexpectedly large positive or negative effects on the development of the state.

This theory is part of institutional analysis which suggests that institutions have their own dynamic. The two scholars in political science and economics most famous for developing this theory are Paul Pierson and the Nobel Prize winner Douglas North. According to North, 'Institutions are the rules of the game in a society or, more formally, are the humanly devised constraints that shape human interaction' (North, 1990, p. 3). In this theory, institutions are of utmost importance. North illustrates this by pointing to the Dutch trading market in the seventeenth century. Amsterdam became the centre of trade in wood, grain and spices from all over the world. The institutions set up for this market can explain why Amsterdam became the centre of international trade. For example, the commodities the merchants traded varied in quality, and samples did not always provide ample information about the quality of the total bulk of goods. Some traders cheated by putting the finest quality of the merchandise on top thus giving a biased image of the average quality of the total goods. Because of the complaints by traders who felt cheated, the Dutch government guaranteed the quality of goods and banned cheating traders from the market. This small change in an institution had a huge effect. Knowing that a sample was representative for the whole bulk of goods reduced the transaction costs enormously, and resulted in easier and more profitable trade. The Dutch government also guaranteed compliance to contracts, which reduced the transaction costs of trade even further.

By setting up such institutions and rules of the game, the behaviour of the traders was constrained, and because the outcomes were positive, such institutions became self-reinforcing. At first, they applied only to that part of the market in which there were most complaints. Later on, the rules applied to all goods traded and not just in Amsterdam. Still later, the regulation of different policy areas evolved. This is the *self-reinforcement of institutions*.

The example illustrates the central concepts of path dependency theory. Institutions are set up in order to solve an existing problem and, in this case, to provide a public good, namely the guarantee that government ensures honest – or at least less deceitful – trade. When institutions create positive outcomes, they tend to self-reinforce. When these outcomes result in learning, especially in a reduction of uncertainty, by providing information on what you can expect from the institution and what the institution expects from you, and when the start-up costs of building alternative institutions are high, the acceptance of coordination through these institutions increases. The institution has started a life of its own in that it becomes difficult, if not impossible, to initiate radical changes in the institution or to eliminate it. When more and complementary institutions are set up, it becomes even more costly to radically change them or to abandon them, because changing one institution can have serious implications for other institutions. Often, there are 'configurations of complementary institutions in which the performance of each is affected by the existence of others' (Pierson, 2000, p. 78).

This does not mean that institutions are immutable, but it does mean that institutional change will be incremental instead of radical. Institutions are expected to proceed according to a certain 'developmental pathway', and are simultaneously subject to gradual or incremental change (Thelen, 2004).

Such changes occur at so-called critical junctures in which crucial events happen and choices are made. Examples of such critical junctures are found, for instance, in those wars of independence that were fierce and bloody as seen, for instance, in the process towards the creation of the USA in their revolutionary war against the British Empire in the eighteenth century, and the fight in Indonesia against the Dutch colonizers in the aftermath of the Second World War. The resulting enmities made the leaders of the newly established states hardly inclined to copy the government system of the previous colonizers to their newly independent states.

In the newly established USA of 1776, the Declaration of Independence testified against all the wrongdoings of its previous colonial power and this made it no surprise that the US constitution was modelled consistent with ideas critical of the centralized ruling of the English colonizers. The first part of the constitution was based on the ideas of the eighteenth-century French political philosopher Montesquieu, emphasizing the need for the separation of legislative, judicial and executive powers. Origins can also be traced to the Bill of Rights, drafted in England in 1689 after the Glorious Revolution. This is reflected in the idea that individuals are allowed to have arms for their defence, the trial in court by jurors and the freedom of speech. Furthermore, the ideas of the English philosopher John Locke on liberty and the curbing of governmental power were reflected, as well as the theory of the French philosopher Voltaire that the relation between government and the people is a two-sided relation based on a 'social contract' and not a one-sided hierarchical relation in which the people are at the mercy of the arbitrary decisions of their rulers.

A second example of such a critical juncture resulting, however, in quite a different outcome is found in Indonesia in 1945 when it fought its way to independence after 350 years of Dutch colonialization and five years of Japanese occupation during the Second World War. The Indonesian leader in the revolution, Sukarno, formulated what is called in Indonesian *Pancasila,* five principles that would constitute the political philosophy of the independent Indonesian State. Central were the primacy of the belief in the one and almighty God, taking care of human rights, national unity, Indonesian-style democracy and social justice. The five points were a reaction against the characteristics of the exploitative Dutch colonial system and the inhumane Japanese occupation. They were an attempt to define a unified independent Indonesia, completely different from its colonial power in its structure of government which emphasized unity instead of freedom, denied the separation of church and state and opted for an indirect form of democracy.

More recent critical junctures occurred in Central Europe after the fall of the Berlin Wall in 1989, in South Africa with the abolition of the apartheid regime in the early 1990s and in the Middle East in the so-called Arab Spring that started in 2011.

Such choices, especially such major ones, but also minor ones, can have dramatic consequences for the future development of the institutions, and they can be self-reinforcing. This is the principle of 'locked in' choices. Choices made today affect possible and likely choices in the future. The system evolves along a particular path that is 'locked in'.

Institutional change can occur because of its contribution to the general interest, but also because of the actions of political actors driven by selfish or organizational interests who wish to change the rules of the game to serve their own positions. As such, a *conversion* may occur in which the goal of the institution changes to serve a different goal. This would be the case when a head of state eliminates the position of head of government and concentrates those powers and duties in his or her own hands. Another well-known illustration is the phenomenon of *layering*, in which one avoids the difficulty of changing or eliminating an institution by adding new institutions on top of the existing ones. This happens when additional layers are established between local and regional government or between regional and central government in order to avoid the difficulty of amalgamating local and regional governments.

Although creating the independence of states is a critical juncture in their development, existing institutional arrangements continue and are often only changed incrementally in conformity to path dependency theory. Shamsul Haque mentions three historical stages that contain the mechanisms through which path dependencies worked in the transition from colonial to postcolonial government, where the postcolonial structure resembles the colonial system despite the radical societal changes. The first is education in the colonial era and the preparation of postcolonial leadership during colonialism. The second is the postcolonial training of the administration under the label of technical assistance and through exchange programmes. And the third is the continuing export of reform programmes from one country to another and the mimesis that occurs as a result.

With regard to the education of postcolonial elites, it is illustrative to note that in Africa many future leaders received their early education at the same school, the Achimoto School in Accra, Ghana. Notable students included future Ghanaian presidents Nkrumah, Akufo-Addo, Atta Mills and its future head of state John Rawlings as well as Robert Mugabe, the future president of Zimbabwe, Dawda Jawara, the future head of state of Gambia and Adamu Atta, the future governor in Nigeria. Most of the postcolonial leaders attended university in either the USA or England where they were taught the merits of the governmental system of these countries.

As to the second point, while formal occupation ended in many African countries in the 1960s, the influence of the colonial powers on the development of these states continued – although not always with positive outcomes. Colonial European officers in Africa and Asia either retained their positions in the independent governments or attained 'new' positions in the United Nations (UN) development administration and advised the newly independent countries on government structure and provided technical assistance. And with regard to the third point, reforms, the UN together with the World Bank and the International Monetary Fund (IMF) continued to give advice and guidance and exert pressure on African and Asian governments, especially, to modernize their apparatus in conformity with changes taking place in some OECD countries.

Given the path dependence of the governmental institutional structure, the dominant colonial structures imposed by the European powers left their legacy on the colonies even after they became independent. The Ghanaian scholar in developmental Public Administration and policy, Joseph R. A. Ayee, argues about Africa that, irrespective of the colonial power, postcolonial developments are mainly due to the characteristics of the colonial era that 'left a legacy that created conditions to foster the development of highly personalized and leadership-dependent political systems' (Ayee, 2008, p. 10). His argument is that colonialism resulted in social fragmentation, economic backwardness and international vulnerability. This posed enormous challenges for African leaders in terms of state building, nation building and economic development. At the time that most African countries became independent, these problems were seen as only to be resolved through strong central government which was consistent with the structure and habits the independent states experienced as colonies in the colonial state and which was furthered by the dominance of the idea at that time that only central planning could result in development (Ayee, 2008, pp. 10–12).

The next section will discuss this impact of colonialism on current governmental structures of the French 'presidential' system, the English 'parliamentary' system and the Spanish 'patronage' system.

Three colonial powers, three types of government

This section describes the legacy of the Spanish, British and the French Empires. These powers controlled many countries and left a legacy in the administration of those countries which is still visible today in the division of power among head of state, head of government and the legislative branch. Their colonial realms are shown in Map 3.1.

The background of European expansion

In order to better understand the different types of government and European expansion, we have to return to the classical era of Rome. The Roman Empire started with a regime based on a separation of powers, with a forum, a senate, a judiciary and executive. With the expansion of the empire, this gradually evolved into a palace-type regime with highly concentrated and centralized power in the hands of successive emperors. The ideal of these increasingly palace-type regimes was empire building. This was subsequently seen among kings and emperors in medieval Europe. If we advance through history to the late eighteenth and early nineteenth centuries, the concentration of power in the hands of the head of state reached its apotheosis in the emergence of absolute kings who were accountable to no one but themselves, such as Louis XIV in France, George IV in England, Peter the Great in Russia, Frederick II of Prussia, the House of Habsburg in Austria and Spain, and the House of Osman during the Ottoman Empire in Turkey. During this period, the heads of state were all-powerful, competing in extravagance with their colleagues by building enormous palaces and often bringing their nation-states to near bankruptcy by waging expensive wars, which in France caused revolutions at the end of the eighteenth century.

The Age of Enlightenment – also known as the Age of Reason – provided the philosophical background for the reaction to such

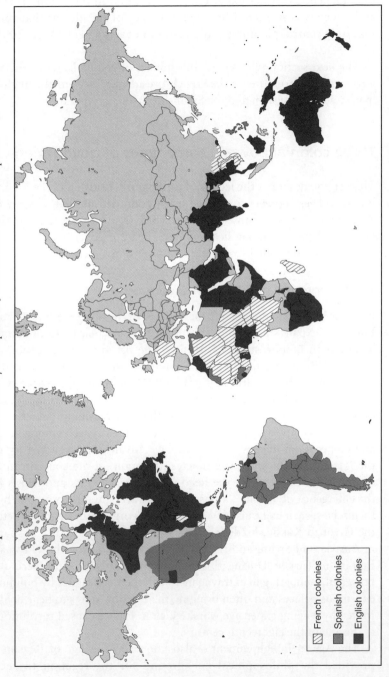

Map 3.1   The colonial realms of the Spanish, British and French Empires

French colonies

Spanish colonies

English colonies

absolute concentration of powers and its negative effects. Rousseau, Voltaire and Montesquieu in France and John Locke in England challenged the idea of the divine right of kings to govern, the prevailing idea of traditional authority. Rousseau substituted it with the idea of the social contract, in which government is based on and requires the consent of the people. According to these thinkers, the people are sovereign and government needs to protect the people, especially their freedom and their property. Locke's ideas also allow citizens to withdraw from the contract and to dispose of a government that does not live up to the social contract. Montesquieu rediscovered the early Greek and Roman traditions in which a separation of powers – the executive, legislative and judiciary – existed in order to prevent one of these powers becoming as dominant as the absolute kings had been.

These ideas of the Enlightenment were received in various ways by governments of the time. It took nearly a century before Locke's seventeenth-century ideas became accepted and widespread.

In the late eighteenth and early nineteenth centuries, the ideas influenced the actual construction of the constitutions on which governments were to act. The US Declaration of Independence (1776) and the Constitution (1789) were based on these ideas. The French Declaration of the Rights of Man and of the Citizen (1789) and the constitutions of other European countries such as Poland (1791), the Netherlands (1798) and Spain (1810), also borrowed from the ideas of the Enlightenment. Since that time, most European and North American countries have divided governmental power among the head of state, the head of government and legislative bodies. This has resulted in a continuous struggle over power among the three branches, and varying arrangements regarding the dominance of each of these bodies in the different countries have developed. These arrangements have also had consequences for the resulting arrangements in their colonies, even after decolonization.

Below the focus in depth is on Spanish, British and French colonization and the legacy of their presence after decolonization, in order to illustrate the determinative impact of path dependences on such arrangements. Other colonial powers also influenced government formation around the world.

The very first imperial dynasty may well have been China, which ruled in Korea, Vietnam, Mongolia, Tibet and countries in Central Asia. In the Middle East, the Parthian Empire covered the areas surrounding the eastern part of the Mediterranean and the Black Sea, all the way to what is now called Afghanistan. At the height of its reign, the Turkish Ottoman Empire possessed the European Balkans and almost the entire Middle East and North Africa, and it left a legacy of bureaucracy and rule of law. The Portuguese had colonies in the Americas (Brazil), Asia (East Timor, Macau) and Africa (Cape Verde, Angola, São Tomé and Principe, Guinea-Bissau and Mozambique), and the Dutch in the Caribbean, Africa (South Africa) and Asia (New Guinea, Indonesia). The Russians colonized Central Asia and Siberia.

Although it is not referred to as colonialism, in the period after the First World War, the USA and the Soviet Union agreed to divide power over Europe between them, with Central and Eastern Europe and Central Asia falling under the (one-party) club-type regime of the Soviet Union and Western Europe under the democratic and free-market (forum-type) regime of the USA. However, given the introductory character of this book, it will only describe in detail three main colonial powers and their legacies for developing countries.

The French presidential system

Around 1960, most of the French colonies gained their independence. Just two years before, in France itself, the Fifth Republic had replaced the previous Fourth Republic. The main alteration was the increased power of the head of state, i.e. the president. Starting with the next term, 1962, the president would be elected by direct and general elections. The president received a seven-year term and the power to name and dismiss the prime minister (in French 'premier' as head of government) and dissolve the parliament. The president, and not the head of government, now had new powers and authority to determine policies, and the president would be the one to guide the premier in terms of which policies to pursue (Safran, 1998, p. 18). Under this new constitution, the president is the one who ensures the functioning of governmental authorities, and is the arbiter of political and institutional conflicts, the principal appointing officer and the commander-in-chief of the armed forces (Safran, 1998, p. 178). The Fifth Republican Constitution limited the powers of the parliament by limiting the length of parliamentary sessions, reducing the number and power of legislative committees and limiting parliamentary influence on the budget-making process. Furthermore, it gave the prime minister a dual responsibility to the president as well as the parliament. As for judicial, executive and legislative powers, these would be shared, but the president would have the initiative and the right of arbitrage to observe and interpret the constitution (Safran, 1998, pp. 13–14). Some have interpreted the

Fifth Republic as a quasi-monarchical executive because most of its decision-making power is concentrated in the function of the president. Hence, in this presidential system, central government itself is centralized. The power and authority for legislative and executive matters are concentrated within the function of head of state.

In terms of intergovernmental relations, the French system is also centralized. In France, there are three layers in addition to the central government: the regional governments, departments and local governments (communes). These subnational layers have very little legislative or independent decision-making powers. The departments are subdivisions of national government and function merely as the constituency for the general assembly elections. The communes can be seen as the basic administrative unit, implementing national policies and having responsibilities only for 'technical policies' such as traffic control, fire protection, urban transport, sanitation, sports facilities, and maintenance of nurseries and schools (Safran, 1998, p. 279).

This centralized system functioned similarly in the African colonies, but not in French Indochina. The main reason for the difference is that Vietnam, Laos and Cambodia became independent in 1954 as a consequence of the Geneva Convention when France was still in the Fourth Republic and when the head of government was still dependent on parliamentary approval. Despite the long-lasting war in Indochina, which started immediately after Vietnam's independence, all three countries adopted a semi-communist system and, notable here, with a more or less symbolic head of state and a more powerful parliament/general assembly and head of government. Furthermore, unlike the situation in West Africa, there was no widespread emigration of French people to Indochina. Indochina was mainly an economic interest, with Saigon a major port for the transport of profitable goods such as rubber, tea, rice, coffee, pepper, coal, zinc and tin.

All the French colonies in West Africa had the same general governor, stationed in Dakar, and each one had its own lieutenant governor, who together with a representative from the colony was seated in the Grand Council of West Africa. Below the lieutenant governor there were the *cercle* commanders. *Cercles* were the smallest administrative units although they still comprised huge areas. These *cercle* commanders appointed and, when deemed necessary, dismissed the African 'chefs de canton' and 'chefs du village' whom they controlled from a distance. If such chiefs became too powerful, the cantons were simply broken down into smaller ones. The chiefs were appointed mainly based on their proven loyalty to the French and were responsible for collecting taxes, recruiting forced labour and applying French law. As to forced labour, every indigenous person was obliged to work part of the year on behalf of the colonial power. This included working on all infrastructure such as roads, mines, plantations and forests.

It was a centralized system because all orders from France went through the general governor who commanded the lieutenant governors who in turn commanded the *cercle* commanders who in turn commanded the chiefs. The grand council only had consultative status. Although universal suffrage had been granted to all people in the French colonies in 1956 under the Fourth Republic of France, they could only vote for parties from which the winning party could appoint the vice-president. The real power 'presidency' stayed in the hands of the French governor. This only changed after complete independence. From then on, the presidents of these newly independent states were directly elected, and the French enforced this in part. At the end of September 1958, French Premier Charles de Gaulle forced the territories to support the Fifth Republic Constitution and gave them the choice to remain an overseas territory, to become an autonomous member state within the French community or to become a French department. Most countries in West Africa opted for the autonomous member state status, while many small French islands in the Caribbean opted for the continuation of being an overseas territory.

Hence, despite decolonization, the governmental systems in these newly independent states remained centralized, as they promised to in their adoption of the French Fifth Republic Constitution. The continued dominance of the power of the president in relation to the council/parliament and the prime minister is evident as are the neglect of governance in the villages and the absence of capacity building at the local government level. The only capacity built was on the 'national' and '*cercle*' levels, and positions at those levels were reserved for French nationals, many of whom left after independence, thus leaving the new states virtually empty-handed.

With a public administration-lacking capacity, only few states, such as Ivory Coast and Madagascar, remained stable (for some decades). The reason in the former case was the continued rule by popular President Houphouët-Boigny, who was repeatedly re-elected as a result of one-party rule and remained in power for 24 years. Adding to the stability were his continued close relations with France and the subsequent influx of French teachers and advisors, Ivory Coast's natural resources in coffee, pineapples, palm oil and cocoa, and the country's relative prosperity at the time of independence.

Many other newly independent states were not as lucky. They suffered under the classic adage that 'power corrupts and absolute power corrupts absolutely'. Their presidents were more interested in retaining power and increasing their own wealth than in providing collective goods to their population – especially to those parts of their population that belonged to a different ethnic group. Subsequently, many of these countries experienced ethnic civil war. Their presidents banned opposition or minimized the influence of it, imposed one-party rule and imprisoned or even publicly executed political rivals and overly ambitious allies. The presidents could eliminate the position of head of government and concentrate all executive and legislative power in their own hands. In the Central African Republic, President Bokassa even crowned himself emperor. Although such excesses are no longer visible, the government systems in West Africa remain highly centralized.

These are some characteristics of governments in the former French colonies:

1. A tendency towards centralization in all its aspects, within central government as well as in intergovernmental relations, with a dominance of the head of state over the head of government and the parliament at the central government level, and minimal or no power and authority at the subnational and especially the local level.
2. A severe lack of capacity building at the subnational and especially the local level.
3. An inclination within government to emphasize the utility of government for the rulers instead of the ruled.

The British 'Westminster' system of government

The English were as harsh in their colonies as the French, but in the twentieth century when many of its colonies became independent states, their government system differed from the French system. In what is called the Westminster system, the head of state (queen) is a ceremonial position, while the executive powers are in the hands of the head of government (prime minister) based on support from the parliament (lower house). Although, formally, all laws must have royal assent, in practice the parliament has the legislative powers and the head of state cannot deny assent when a law is based on a parliamentary majority. Also, although the monarch names the head of government, this is always based on parliamentary consent and support from the majority in the lower house and the advice of the previous prime minister. Furthermore, if the head of government, the prime minister, loses support from parliament he or she must resign and call for new elections. Hence, the main feature of this system is that the executive is accountable to the legislative and that the two are separated.

Within central government, the Westminster system is less centralized and top-down than the French presidential system, and it has more checks and balances and a separation of powers. Centralization in intergovernmental relations in the colonies – between central and subnational governments – is similar to the French system.

Centralized government was even more visible in those British colonies that were not settler areas for English emigrants, but served mainly as areas for economic exploitation. The latter – especially the African colonies and India – were governed by indirect rule, in which military force and maintaining order were all that mattered, and local issues were left to the indigenous leaders. In the colonies that were seen as settler areas – because of climate – more effort was put into direct governance, even at the subnational level (North America, Australia, the southern part of Africa and New Zealand).

After their independence, countries with large numbers of English immigrants were more inclined to imitate (parts of) the English government system and to adopt the Westminster system. Hence, this system is still operational in South Africa, Australia, New Zealand and Canada, where the powers of the head of state are limited and the head of government retains most of the executive powers and is dependent on the support of a parliament/assembly/general council. This came at a cost, though, namely the repression of the indigenous population by English emigrants and their descendants: in South Africa, through the apartheid regime, in Australia, through the oppression of the Aboriginals, in New Zealand, where the Maori suffered, and in Canada, where Native Americans and Inuit were denied rights for a long period of time.

There was limited emigration from England to India, and many Indian villages not inhabited by English immigrants were governed by indirect rule. They lacked local government structures and the governance of these areas was left to local traditional leaders. Nevertheless, India retained the Westminster government system after independence, with the president elected indirectly by an electoral college and the prime minister retaining executive powers, based on support from the majority of seats in the lower house of parliament.

In many African countries, postcolonial times were more turbulent because of ethnic conflicts between indigenous tribes. In many countries, this resulted in the abolition of one of the pillars of the

Westminster model, that is, the free and direct election of parliament based on a multi-party system. Because of the turmoil and civil wars, most states changed, through the seizure of power by one of the conflicting parties, into a one-party state (e.g. Tanzania, Sierra Leone, Kenya) or through *coups d'état* into a military regime (e.g. Nigeria, Uganda).

These are some characteristics of former colonies in the Westminster system:

1. A tendency towards checks and balances within central government with the legislative, the parliament, being dominant, the head of state having very limited powers and the head of government being the executive based on support from a majority in the parliament.
2. Centralized and hierarchical intergovernmental relations, as in the French presidential system, but with variations in governance structure at the local level depending on the number of English immigrants in such localities. The greater the number of immigrants, the more direct the rule. The lower the number of immigrants, the more indirect the rule. In the latter cases, governance was left to traditional leaders resulting in an absence of subnational capacity building.
3. After independence, the system was retained in all those countries in which sufficient institution building had taken place during the colonial era and into which massive emigration from England had taken place. It proved unsustainable in those countries where such institution building had been absent. In the latter case, such countries deteriorated into civil war and transformed into club-type regimes.

The Spanish colonization of the Americas

The Spanish began colonization before the French and English, and their colonization efforts ended earlier as well. There are additional important differences. After Columbus discovered what was later named the Americas at the end of the 1400s, the Spanish Crown conquered a large part of this continent. Spain was a combination of an absolute monarchy and a religious (Catholic) state since the Pope officially granted its king and queen the title of '*Reyes Catholicos*'; the Moorish as well as Jewish inhabitants were forced into the Catholic faith by being offered the choice between conversion, expulsion or elimination; and the influence of the clergy was substantial. This served to establish unity through a common faith and laid the basis for a unitary state. This was necessary because Spain had had its internal conflicts. In addition to the king, Spanish rule consisted of independent and mutually conflicting nobility owning large pieces of land (*latifunda*) with rebellious serfs working their land and towns with varying interests, especially the merchants. Notwithstanding religious unification, the problems remained. Because of the wars Spain fought with England, France, Holland and Turkey, it needed increasing amounts of money and the country could barely bear these costs alone – hence, the colonization of the Americas. The Americas were conquered with a twofold mission, namely to extract as much money as possible to finance Spain's wars and to bring the Catholic faith to the natives. It started in what is now Mexico and extended north and south. The one country in Latin America that Spain did not possess, Brazil, was a colony of Spain's close neighbour Portugal, which was accepted by the two because of papal interference and decree.

Spanish colonization differed in a number of points from the English settler colonization. The conquest was just as violent and painful for the indigenous population; it is estimated that of the 30 million original Mexican inhabitants, only three million survived the Spanish occupation. The difference between the colonization of the Americas by the English and Spanish is that many of the former emigrated to escape religious prosecution, while the Spanish emigrated mainly to bring the Catholic faith to the indigenous people. The mission of the English in the north was agriculture, while the mission of the Spanish was to extract the gold and silver from their colonies and bring it to the king of Spain. If there were no gold or silver mines, e.g. in Chile, there were cattle, and the Spanish nobility were transformed into big landowners which was a symbol of power in their tradition.

Whereas the English emigrants were peasants, the Spanish conquerors were of noble birth, not willing to work the land but only to own it and to have servile and converted labourers forced to work it. The English came in families, while the Spanish inflow consisted mainly of men. During the entire period of Spanish colonization, approximately two-thirds of the Spanish were male. While the English did not consider marrying Native Americans, this was not a problem for the Spanish in Central and Latin America. They were even encouraged by the Crown to do so, but their children would have a lower status than children of pure Spanish ancestry would have. The highest status was reserved for those born in Spain of Spanish nobility (*peninsulare*). Next came those born in the Americas but still of Spanish ancestry (*criolos*). Below the *criolos* were those of mixed blood (*mestizos*), and lowest in the societal hierarchy were the indigenous population and the slaves. The Spanish and European hierarchy was directly translated onto the colonies. As Finer observes, of the 170 viceroyals between 1535 and 1813, only four were born in the Spanish Americas (Finer, 1997, p. 1389). This hierarchy and inequality was reflected in the recruitment for public offices. The nature of inequality in the Spanish colonies was somewhat different from the hierarchy and inequality in English and French colonies. By law, the indigenous people were free instead of being slaves, with the freedom to move, to have possessions and with relatively easy access to courts. They were converted by persuasion instead of force, they were paid (minimally) for their work and their working hours were restricted by labour laws. No matter how low the wages were and how severely the Spanish exploited the indigenous population, the latter had more rights than the indigenous populations in French and English colonies and were sometimes protected by the Catholic clergy.

The main feature of colonization by the Spanish was that they started by building and governing towns. This was similar to the situation in Spain itself. An official councillor also acting as judge on behalf of the crown (*corregidor*) and a mayor (*alcalde*) governed these towns. Later on, a *corregidor de indios* appeared to govern the rural areas. Unlike the colonization of the French and English described above, the basic unit for Spanish colonial government was the town. Still, beautiful specimens of such colonial towns exist, for example in Mexico City, Antigua, Santo Domingo, Cartagena and San Juan. All towns were built according to Spanish law with precise descriptions and including a city plaza, on its right a church and next to it a rectory and a town hall. Similar towns were built for the Indians, the *reducciones* and *congregaciones*, although the motive for building these towns was mainly to simplify taxing and forced labour, and to convert the inhabitants to Catholicism.

As such, the governance of Spanish colonies was more decentralized than the English and French colonies. There was a viceroyalty, who ruled the whole of the Spanish Americas on behalf of the Spanish Crown, but for many towns, this was a distant ruling and there were checks and balances in the form of the *audiencia* and from the missionaries. The *audiencia* was a type of court of appeals, which controlled the actions of these viceroyals. The viceroyal was also required to consult such *audiencia* before making any major decisions. Furthermore, the nobility could approach the Spanish monarch directly, bypassing the viceroyalty. The clergy also became a countervailing power, sometimes protecting their congregation from the abuse of the Spanish rulers, and at other times working together with the Spanish rulers in oppressing the indigenous population in return for favours. All of the mutual dependencies resulted in a system of *patronage,* the logical consequence of a government system with a strict hierarchy on one side and checks and balances on the other side.

In the early 1800s, Spain and Portugal were conquered by Napoleon; the Spanish king abdicated and the Portuguese king fled to Brazil. The Spanish opposition organized a guerrilla attack against the French occupation and in order to further cooperation they established the first national assembly in 1810. Together with representatives from the Latin American colonies, they wrote a liberal constitution that reduced the role of the king, gave primary power to the legislative council, replaced suffrage based on property with universal suffrage, and reduced the role of the church and nobility in favour of the commercial class. The constitution also called for a rationalized administration based on new provinces and municipalities. When Napoleon was defeated, the former Spanish king was released and returned to Spain. He initially promised to accept the constitution, but once reinstalled he quickly rejected it. This was an affront to the citizens who had composed it, and it dashed expectations in the Americas for a better future under Spanish rule. In Latin America, it resulted in the wars of independence in which royalists and liberals fought against each other. An important difference from the process of independence of the English and French colonies was that independence in Latin America was led by people of Spanish origin and not by the indigenous population. It resulted in the independence of many previous viceroyalties in the Americas, but also in 50 years of civil wars and subsequent international wars. The outcome was not decentralized nations with a major role for regions and municipalities, but rather very centralized states and nations. Some nations turned into monarchies, but most became military regimes, which is understandable given the military background of the Spanish colonizers migrating to the Americas. It is only in the last 30 years that the military regimes have been replaced by democracies.

These are some of the characteristics of the former Spanish colonies:

1. A palace type, hierarchical government in Spain itself, with little separation among the executive, legislative and judiciary functions.
2. Colonial governance was more decentralized, with relatively strong governance in the cities and regions and mission posts in the rural areas.

3. The Spanish who conquered and ruled the Americas primarily had military training and were of nobility. This, together with the fact that the wars of independence were initiated by the Spanish colonizers and their descendants, partly explains the emergence of the military regimes after the wars of independence.
4. The government system was as hierarchical as the French presidential system and English colonial rule. There was a caste-like social stratification with five classes: people born in Spain and of nobility on top of the hierarchy, and the slaves at the bottom of the hierarchy. In between, were the people born in the Americas from Spanish nobility, people born from mixed marriage and the indigenous populations.
5. The system resulted in dramatic inequality, under which the descendants of the colonial power also suffered. The end of the colonial era resulted in a half a century of civil wars, revolutions and *coup-d'états* in which *criolos* and *mestizos* fought the *peninsulare* and the big land and mine owners.

Regional government

As we have seen, the general tendency for states is to centralize its government, but most countries also have a subnational government. This section focuses on this intermediate level of government between the local and the national levels of government. This level includes the departments (especially in French-speaking countries, but also in Paraguay and Uruguay), *provincia* (in some Spanish-speaking countries), *muhafazah* (in Arabic countries), *ostan* (Persia/Iran), *oblast* (Russian), regions (in many English-speaking countries), *Länder* (e.g. Germany), *Amter* (Denmark), *Wilayat* (Afghanistan and Algeria), *voïvodships* (Poland) states (US), *concelhos* (Portugal), counties (Scandinavian and Baltic countries), *kraje* (Czech Republic), prefectures (Japan), *län* or *landsting* (Sweden), *Suurlahoeet* (Finland), territorial authorities (New Zealand), districts (Bangladesh, Ghana), *comunidades autónomas* (Spain) and *eparchy* (Greece). The general term is 'regional government'.

'Province' comes from the Roman Empire in which an area on behalf of (*pro*) the central government of the empire is controlled (*vincere*). The classic origin is still influential because provinces are often considered areas outside the capital city, which are administratively controlled on behalf of the national government. In some countries, the capital city is still a separate entity in addition to the provinces (Belgium, Romania). One would expect provinces to be smaller than national states, but the largest provinces in the world, namely Xinjiang in China (1,660,000 km²) and Quebec in Canada (1,542,056 km²), comprise an area larger than that of many a nation (cf. the Netherlands 41,526 km², France 674,843 km² or even Peru 1,285,220 km²). Only a few, very small, countries operate without such regional government (e.g. Iceland, Aruba).

The area controlled by regional government can be distinct in terms of culture (specific dialect, customs and habits); historical background, such as a duchy or a county; economic development, mainly rural or urban; or in geographical terms.

Classic ideas about provinces continue to influence the present-day position of regional governments in unitary states. Their main function is to steer and control developments within the region on behalf of central government because the nation is too large to be governed entirely from the capital, and to assist (especially small) local governments that are unable to develop the policies required by law on their own because they lack the expertise. Small localities often have problems in hiring the required specialized personnel to issue permits, control pollution and ensure public safety. In such cases, provinces can assist. Regional government has the advantage of *economies of scale*. By combining local policies, regional governments can reduce the costs of service provision to the set of member municipalities, especially in case of technical services, sanitation, water and sewer systems.

In theory, the need for regional government depends on a number of factors, namely the size of countries, the distance between the centre and the periphery and the difficulty of communication among them, the heterogeneity of countries, the average size of municipalities, variations in the severity of problems, the composition of regional economies and cultural diversity. Such factors provide a rational explanation for the necessary variation in tasks, responsibilities and authority of regional government.

As sound as this may appear from a rational point of view, the argument lacks explanatory power in practice. Given the huge variations in the size, function, power and responsibility of the regional level in different countries, other reasons seem more likely than the rational ones mentioned above. Third- and fourth-level governments are found even in the smallest countries and neither changes in the average size of municipalities nor the other factors mentioned have affected the position of the regional-level governments up to now. As an example, the factors mentioned in the literature cannot explain why, for instance, Gabon has more provinces than South Africa, or why very distinct countries like the Netherlands, Rwanda and Uzbekistan have the same number of provinces.

A second merit of regional government is related to *spillover effects.* Decisions made in one municipality often impact the citizens in neighbouring municipalities. Every decision made in a city can have an extraterritorial impact and the possible inconsistency of such decisions among different municipalities, not to mention consistency between local and higher law, can affect residents' rights in a negative way. In fact, there might be something like a tragedy of the commons (see Chapter 1) concerning local government when every municipality wants to have its own new housing estate, golf course, industrial area, theatre and other services. Regional government can coordinate and conduct planning on a regional level, and thereby prevent inefficiencies, generate positive spillover effects, internalize the external effects caused by uncoordinated policies and increase efficiency by bringing about policy coordination. In this way, regional governance serves to rationalize local policy making.

There are a number of arguments against regional involvement and in favour of transferring its power and authority to the central level. The existence of regions could inhibit the *possibilities of redistributing* resources from richer to poorer regions. Instead of a tragedy of the commons at the local level, a destructive competition between regions could emerge, for instance in order to attract investments. Furthermore, a powerful regional government collecting its own taxes would make *macroeconomic policy* less feasible. By definition, regional government poses an additional layer between national and local government. Some see this as positive in the sense of being the cartilage between the national and local levels, but others see it as a cause of *increasing complexities in designing a satisfactory transfer system* between governmental levels and as *increasing the difficulties of collaboration* between governmental levels.

Given the pros and cons of regional governments, their functions, roles and responsibilities vary as widely as their names. Tasks that are performed in one nation by municipalities or by national government are handled by the regional government in other nations. In federated countries, the regional levels often have more authority (e.g. in Canada, Belgium, Argentina, Germany, India, Russia, UAE) while in unitary states they have a subordinate position in relation to central government.

An international comparison of the position of regional government points to the predominance of politico-historical factors, path dependencies and institutional resilience as the more important elements explaining the number and size of such governments.

Recently scholars tried to measure the power of regional governments in different countries using a Regional Authority Index based on formal legal criteria. This index is based on two dimensions of regional authority: self-rule and shared rule. The index points to the differences in power and authority of regional governments in different states.

Self-rule involves the authority exercised by a regional government over those who live in its territory; the extent to which a regional government is autonomous rather than de-concentrated; the range of policies for which a regional government is responsible; the extent to which a regional government can independently tax its population; and the extent to which a regional government is endowed with an independent legislature and executive.

Shared rule involves the authority exercised by a regional government or its representatives in the country as a whole; the extent to which regional representatives co-determine national legislation; the extent to which a regional government co-determines national policy in intergovernmental meetings; the extent to which regional representatives co-determine the distribution of national tax revenues; and the extent to which regional representatives co-determine constitutional change (Marks et al., 2008, p. 115).

Using this index, it becomes clear that the power and authority of regional government in federal states such as the USA, Russia, Germany, Australia and Italy are much higher than in unitary states such as Japan, Poland and the UK. Unfortunately, the index has only been applied to OECD and European countries.

Local government

The municipality is, without a doubt, the governmental level closest to the people. The local level ultimately delivers the public services, although higher government levels may have planned them. Furthermore, it may be difficult for an ordinary citizen to participate in the policy-making process at national or regional level, but it is much easier to participate in the town or village, either directly through a local council or through communication with the mayor.

There are two main purposes of local government: effective and efficient service delivery and providing a forum for citizen input into service delivery in order to enhance its quality. As Anwar Shah wrote:

Local governance ... includes the diverse objectives of vibrant, living, working, and environmentally preserved self-governing communities. Good local governance is not just about providing a range of local services but also about preserving the life and liberty of residents, creating space for democratic participation and civic dialogue, supporting market-led and environmentally sustainable local development, and facilitating outcomes that enrich the quality of life of residents. (Shah, 2006, p. 2)

Sometimes, these services refer only to technical areas, as in France, and at other times public service delivery includes housing, libraries, social care, public order and safety. Even within Europe, countries differ in the extent to which national or subnational governments are responsible for education, health services, housing, infrastructure, local economic development, the provision of welfare, public order and safety, social integration, culture and recreation and sports, to mention just some of the policy areas in which local authorities could be autonomous. The tasks decentralized to municipalities in a majority of European countries concern basic education, sports, social services, urban planning, local infrastructure, culture, environment, water supply, public transport, waste management and to a lesser extent (parts of) health care, housing, local economic development, sewage and public order and safety (Council of European Municipalities and Regions, 2011).

The goals of providing a democratic forum and of service delivery are rarely completely accomplished. In order to understand this, we first have to acknowledge the huge differences between municipalities. Some are metropolitan areas with a population exceeding 15 million inhabitants, like Bangkok, Beijing, Tianjin, Shanghai, Delhi, Kolkata, Bogotá, São Paulo, Buenos Aires, Dhaka, Istanbul, Moscow and Los Angeles. As of 2013, there were 924 identified urban areas (urban agglomerations or urbanized areas) in the world with populations of 500,000 or more, totalling nearly two billion people (Demographia World Urban Areas, 2013). Europe alone includes 71 metropolitan areas with more than half a million inhabitants in each. These are the urban areas faced with the problem of increased urbanization and expansion. At the other extreme are the small often rural municipalities, with sometimes no more than a few hundred inhabitants, facing the problem of inadequate capacity for service delivery because of institutional and personnel constraints.

Local governments all over the world and even within countries face challenges which can be grouped into four dimensions:

- *Contextual conditions* are found in the judicial situation, the socio-economic situation of the country involved, historical determinants as outlined above in the colonization and its aftermath, urbanization trends, et cetera.
- *Structural conditions* refer to the position of local government vis-à-vis other governments; for instance, the degree of decentralization, in terms of the delegation of tasks local government is responsible for, but also in terms of financial autonomy.
- *Institutional conditions* refer to the size of local government, its internal organization, its financial situation (budget), the availability of a robust database on key economic variables, personnel, financial management and the quality of the infrastructure.
- *Human resource conditions* refer to the quality of leadership, the availability of skills in economic and policy analysis, in budgeting, financial management and procurement, well-trained staff for budgeting and personnel management, and skills in auditing, survey design and evaluation.

That both small and large municipalities face these challenges does not imply that they face them to the same degree or that all four dimensions are equally important for every local government. In particular, local governments in developing countries face a number of impediments that inhibit their effectiveness. For instance, they lack financial resources to improve their situation, and they are financially dependent on local taxes and government grants, which are often insufficient to meet the most urgent needs.

Centralization and decentralization

If one thing stands out, it is that throughout history there seems to be a natural tendency towards a dominant central government and centralization within this central government with consequent neglect for capacity building or transferring powers and authorities to the local level through decentralization. This tendency follows the Iron Law of Oligarchy formulated by Robert Michels in 1911. He argued, 'It is organization which gives birth to the dominion of the elected over the electors, of the mandataries over the mandators, of the delegates over the delegators. Who says organization, says oligarchy,' and, 'Historical evolution mocks all the prophylactic measures that have been adopted for the prevention of oligarchy' (Michels, 1915, p. 423).

In the nineteenth century, such inevitability of leadership was challenged in, for instance, anarchism, a word derived from the Greek *anarchos*, meaning 'without rulers', propagated, in ancient times in Taoism by Liezi, and later on in Europe by the Jacobins, and philosophers like Rousseau, Godwin, Proudhon and Kropotkin. They believed in either complete liberty (Rousseau), the spread of individual knowledge and the subsequent redundancy of state power (Godwin), the organic system of society with its inherent harmonious development towards perfection (Comte), the evolution of man towards a state of perfect adaptation, involving a reduction of conflicts and thus, less need for hierarchy (Spencer), or a system with public ownership of means of production and democratic control of all organizations, without any government authority (Bakunin).

Political philosophers like Bagehot, Mosca and Pareto argued that the masses must accept that they are led by a minority and must follow the idea of state and nation, that they have to accept a political formula in which leadership is central, that even in socialist organizations – emphasizing equality – there is a tendency towards oligarchy because of the division of labour, the need for technical expertise and the success in elections. Idealistic notions of democracy described by Aristotle would be false because democracy can exist for the people, of the people, but never by the people (Michels, 1915). The main arguments have remained the same: leadership is an inevitable element of organization and unison, in order to counter threats and to protect property rights, for successful production and socio-economic development, and often such leadership tends to concentrate and centralize power.

One indicator of the degree of centralization is the level of public expenditure at the local level compared to the national level. Only in Scandinavian countries do local-level public expenditures and taxes exceed those of central government. Even if the localities spend substantial amounts of money, how much responsibility do they have, can they make independent policy decisions and are they limited by national laws and regulations?

This tendency is understandable from the point of view of the Iron Law of Oligarchy, but it is unusual given the assumed advantages of transferring powers and responsibilities to the local level. In 1957, Stigler argued that the closer a representative government is to the people, the better it works. He argued that people should have the right to vote for the kind and amount of public services they want, which is only possible at the local level. In 1972, Oates wrote 'each public service should be provided by the jurisdiction having control over the minimum geographic area that would internalize benefits and costs of such provision' (p. 55) because local governments understand the concerns of local residents; local decision making is responsive to the people for whom the services are intended, thus encouraging fiscal responsibility and efficiency (cf. Shah, 2006, p. 4). Within the EU, the *subsidiarity principle* has been adopted: political decisions in the EU must always be made at the lowest possible administrative and political level, and as close to the citizens as possible.

Recent research in decentralization and centralization

The apparent contradiction between the theory and practice of centralization and decentralization has made this subject one of the key themes of Public Administration. Its merits are widely debated, based on theoretical arguments and investigated through empirical research.

Decentralization concerns the devolution of power and responsibility over policies from the national level to the local level. This is supposed to be advantageous since it would result in tailor-made policies adapted to the needs of the locality, and would stimulate policy experimentation, as opposed to the one-size-fits-all, supply-based policies of central government. It would result in more efficient and effective service delivery because local officials are more knowledgeable about local circumstances, and locals can participate in policy making. Furthermore, it would increase the information on which public policies are based, since local politicians would know their constituents better than authorities at the national level, and would be better informed about the local circumstances. It is said to increase policy stability, because it tends to increase the accountability of governments as well as the checks and balances. Decentralization would be a means for overcoming the limitations of centrally controlled national planning by delegating greater authority to officials working in the field, closer to the problems. It would induce administrative efficiency, because it can cut through red tape and may increase officials' knowledge of and sensitivity to local problems; it may result in better penetration of national policies to remote local communities, greater representation for various religious, ethnic and tribal groups in the policy process and greater administrative capability at the local level. It can provide a structure in which local projects can be coordinated; it can enhance civic participation and it may neutralize entrenched local elites, who are often unsympathetic to national development policies. It may result in a flexible, innovative and creative administration that is more effective in its implementation because of simplified monitoring and evaluation; it can increase political stability and national unity and reduce diseconomies of scale. Centralization can result in over-regulation; decentralized institutions and policies are supposed to be more flexible and able to respond quickly to changing circumstances and customers' needs. Since they know what actually happens, they could be more innovative and may generate a higher morale, more commitment and greater productivity, especially in organizations with knowledge workers (cf. de Vries, 2000; Osborne 1993, p. 253). In other words, some scholars perceive decentralization to be the panacea for all governmental issues.

Other scholars point to the drawbacks of decentralization, arguing that it would pose *a threat to the principle of equality before the law* in equal circumstances. It would be unfair if farmers in one local community had to conform to environmental protection standards that were not required in a neighbouring community. Education standards, social security and taxes should be the same in every community. Decentralization may also result in a situation comparable to the problem of the *tragedy of the commons*. This would occur if every locality delivered the same services in competition with one another, and thus ruin the market (the development of manufacturing and industrial areas is a visible example of the tragedy of the commons). Another issue is the free-rider problem occurring between municipalities; for instance when a relatively large, poor central municipality finances and subsidizes a theatre, library or sports centre and the residents of the relatively rich suburban neighbouring municipalities are the main users, the latter group profits without sharing the costs. Central control of these common property resources might be necessary because it would place decision making about the distribution of costs and benefits into the hands of an external governmental agency.

A third argument against decentralization is that many local governments *lack the administrative capacity* to deal with complex policies. Given the historical and enduring neglect of building local governance capacity and the tendency towards centralization as outlined in this chapter, this argument make sense, especially in those developing countries that were exploited as colonies and in small rural areas that do not have the capacity for effective and efficient service delivery. Historical developments and the subsequent absence of capacity in local governments are not the only reasons that argue against the effects of decentralization. In the developed world, some people simply prefer the superiority of central provision of collective goods. The Thatcher administration in the UK, for instance, asserted that most services are more efficiently provided centrally because local government is incompetent and wasteful and there are too many local authorities that strongly resist any improvement in their efficiency.

Unfortunately, empirical research has not yet produced definite results about the pros and cons of decentralization. A meta-evaluation on research on decentralization, published in 2013, concludes that in terms of all of the presumed merits of decentralization, there are mixed, inconclusive or even negative results (cf. Local Development International, 2013). The conclusion is that much depends on the features of the context in which decentralization takes place, the policy area decentralized, the capacity of local government, and whether sufficient attention was given to the design and implementation of decentralization. This calls for new research into the extent to which the realization of the supposed merits of decentralization depends on the way intergovernmental relations are institutionalized, the local capacity, and the historical and cultural context (cf. Treisman, 2007).

These outcomes ensure that the subject of decentralization will remain a key theme in Public Administration in the years to come. The key questions concern the nature of the policy areas that are suitable for decentralization: how the capacity of local governments can be enhanced in order to effectively and efficiently handle the transfer of authority and power to them; whether the supposed merits of decentralization are universal or dependent upon cultural, socio-economic, technological, and historical variation between countries and regions, and the institutions needed to make decentralization work; and whether decentralization as an alternative for the hierarchical relations between central, regional and local government is also a solution for the centralization of power within central government.

A second more pragmatic research field that has recently developed concerns capacity building. What will it take to better equip regional and especially local government in different parts of the world to improve their service delivery and to enable them to implement decentralized policies in an effective and efficient way? In many countries, public administration capacity at the local level is weak and that weakness poses a threat to the achievement of the goals of public policies. In order to assess the capacity of local governments, one needs to have insight into their functions – what they are supposed to do – and insight into their ability to perform their tasks.

The actual functions of local government vary all over the world, especially with regard to the variety of policy areas they are responsible for, but two abstract dimensions can nonetheless be distinguished that capture the basics of local government capacity: one is service delivery and the other is promoting good governance principles. In the literature, one can find many factors explaining the varying capacity of local governments. As mentioned above, four basic conditions regarding local government capacity concern the contextual, structural, institutional and human resource conditions.

Countries and regions vary to the extent that one or the other condition fails to be optimal in enabling positive decentralization effects. Part of Public Administration's research is aimed at finding the degree of fit between what local governments are expected to do and what they are able to do, and, in the case of a misfit, trying to establish such a fit. In case of deficient knowledge and skills (human resources conditions), the means to accomplish that fit can be found in training and technical assistance programmes, but if the problems are concentrated at an institutional, structural or contextual level, training individual local officials may be less effective, and the question arises as to what other instruments are available to improve those conditions, what inhibiting and catalysing factors are involved and how improvement in the institutional, structural and contextual issues can be accomplished.

Conclusions

This chapter described the features and purposes of the three basic layers of government: central, regional and local. It began by suggesting that path dependency theory can help us understand the organization; one needs to investigate how the organization developed and seemingly minor choices can nonetheless have enormous consequences.

It then applied path dependency theory to the establishment of governments in former colonies by distinguishing three forms of colonization based on the colonial powers: the French, the English and the Spanish. There are differences in the dominance of the head of state, the head of government or parliament and in the degree to which the colonizer actually governed the localities in the colonies or neglected the institutionalization of local government. The three types of colonization were similar in that they were highly hierarchical, caused huge inequality in the colonies and promoted the idea to the newly independent states that a centralized government was necessary in order to develop.

The resulting government structures seem to be dependent on the type of colonization (settler or exploitative) as well as on the features of the government system of the three European powers as established in their respective constitutional frameworks at the time of independence.

A common tendency in all cases was that when the colonizer was primarily exploitative, the first decades of independence in the former colonies were characterized by unrest and civil wars, resulting in highly centralized one-party or military regimes, which only gave way to democratic regimes after some decades and, in many Latin American countries, after a century.

The tendency towards centralized government, when theories suggest that a decentralized government will perform better, has resulted in a long debate within Public Administration about the merits of decentralization, the key theme of this chapter. Many benefits can be expected from transferring power and authority from the central to the local level, but the debate is far from finished since expectations have not been supported by the outcomes of empirical research.

Further reading

Elliott, John H. (2007). *Empires of the Atlantic world: Britain and Spain in America, 1492–1830.* New Haven: Yale University Press.

Herbst, Jeffrey (2014). *States and power in Africa.* Princeton: Princeton University Press.

Munck, Ronaldo (2013). *Rethinking Latin America: Development, hegemony, and social transformation.* London: Palgrave Macmillan.

Treisman, Daniel (2007). *The architecture of government: Rethinking political decentralization.* Cambridge: Cambridge University Press.

Waites, Bernard (2012). *South Asia and Africa after independence: Post-colonialism in historical perspective.* London: Palgrave Macmillan.

Chapter 4

What is the role of a bureaucracy?

The external structure of government, as described in the previous chapter, sets the context for the internal structure of government, which is the topic of this chapter. Depending on the institutionalization of central, regional and local government and their intergovernmental relations, these levels vary in terms of how they are organized, or as some would argue, bureaucratized, while others would say capacitated. This chapter addresses the organization of the public sector, with a special focus on the merits of bureaucracy as a key theme in Public Administration.

What is a bureaucracy? What are its features and why does the public sector all over the world opt for this form of organization, despite the criticism that surrounds it? Through history, bureaucracy has been criticized, especially in the nineteenth century. In a comedy by French writer Honoré de Balzac (1898), bureaucracy was described as a giant machine operated by pygmies; Karl Marx (1858) wrote that 'the bureaucracy takes itself to be the ultimate purpose of the state'; and in the twentieth century, Albert Einstein said, 'Bureaucracy is the end of all sound work' (Hillwatch, n. d.) There must be *some* positive effects of bureaucracy; otherwise it would have disappeared long ago. Economist Joseph Schumpeter wrote that bureaucracy is not an obstacle to democracy, but an inevitable complement to it (1950). And German sociologist Max Weber defined bureaucracy as an ideal type furthering the efficiency and predictability of governmental actions (1946).

In order to understand the merits of a bureaucratic organization, we need to provide a brief introduction to organizational theory that distinguishes different types of organizations, including the bureaucracy. This chapter continues by discussing whether public organizations are distinct from private organizations. While some scholars doubt such differences and suggest that public and private organizations are similar in all but their *insignificant* parts, others argue that public and private organizations are similar in all but their *significant* parts.

This chapter concludes by addressing criticisms levelled at the 'bureaucratic phenomenon', as French scholar Michel Crozier (2009) once described it, in order to understand why bureaucracy is one of the key themes of Public Administration. As in the previous chapters, we begin with some explanations of terminology in order to define and delineate the crucial terms used in this chapter.

Terminology

Organization

An organization can be defined as any cooperation between people trying to achieve a common goal. Hence, a group project, a government agency or a ministry or even a supermarket involves some degree of organization. An organization can be private or public, depending on its funding, accountability and the nature of its output, i.e. public or private.

When the organization is funded from taxes or from the profits of natural resources owned by government, and when someone or some group (of politicians) in the organization is accountable to the public or (other) government for the functioning of the organization, and the output is a collective good or service, i.e. non-rivalrous and non-excludable, it is a *public organization*.

When the organization is funded from the profits from non-collective (rivalrous and excludable) goods or services, the ownership of the organization is in private hands, and the goods or services provided are rivalrous and/or excludable, it is a *private organization*.

There are also a number of organizations that combine these features: semi-public organizations having some, but not all three, characteristics of a purely private or public organization. Examples include some universities, private sanitation companies contracted by the municipality, a privately owned lighthouse, a non-governmental organization like a welfare organization, a food bank, a labour union or an employers' organization. It is not always easy to determine the extent to which an organization is public or private.

Line and staff

Large organizations consist of line and staff organizations. The line employees directly contribute to the goals of the organization. In a university, this would include teachers, professors, department chairs, deans and associate deans.

The *line organization* has established hierarchical relations within the organization and reflects the authority coming from the top to the bottom and accountability from the bottom to the top; it reflects the direct relationship between superior and subordinate(s).

The whole organization might be a ministry or government department. Within the ministry, the director general supervises all affairs of the ministry and is accountable to the minister. Below the director general, there might be several directorates; each directorate will have its own director who is responsible for the affairs of the directorate and accountable to the director general. Each directorate might have a number of departments. Each department will have a department head who is responsible for the affairs within the department and accountable to the director of their directorate, and may have a number of bureaus with responsible managers who are accountable to the department heads. An organizational chart represents the line organization and reflects its structure and complexity. Figure 4.1 is an example of an organizational chart of a relatively simple line organization.

The *staff organization* has supporting and/or advisory functions within the organization, such as administrative assistants, a human resources department, an IT department; or in universities, secretaries, administrative offices (i.e. enrolment, advisory and bursar), the education office, public relations, international studies, the dean's office, et cetera.

There are two types of staff: support staff and advisory staff. The former assist employees in the line by reducing their workload, by doing secretarial work and by handling material provisions. They mostly have only *derivative authority*, such as a professor's secretary inviting

Figure 4.1 *Line organization*

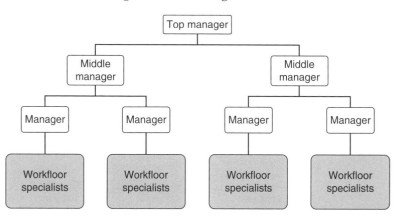

a student for an appointment with the professor. Because the secretary acts on behalf of the professor, the invitation is compulsory. The advisory staff in an organization advise the line on organizational or substantive issues like legal, personnel and financial issues, facilities, developments, the position of the organization in its environment, strategy, coordination and/or monitoring. In some organizations, the staff have no authority over the line, but in other organizations they can have more than just *advisory authority*. They might have *compulsory authority*, which is required before the line can make a decision, sometimes they have *concurrent authority*, in which the line cannot take a decision without the consent of the staff, and at other times they have *functional authority*, giving the staff the authority to make decisions regarding their field of expertise. Figure 4.2 provides

Figure 4.2   *The staff in a partial organizational chart*

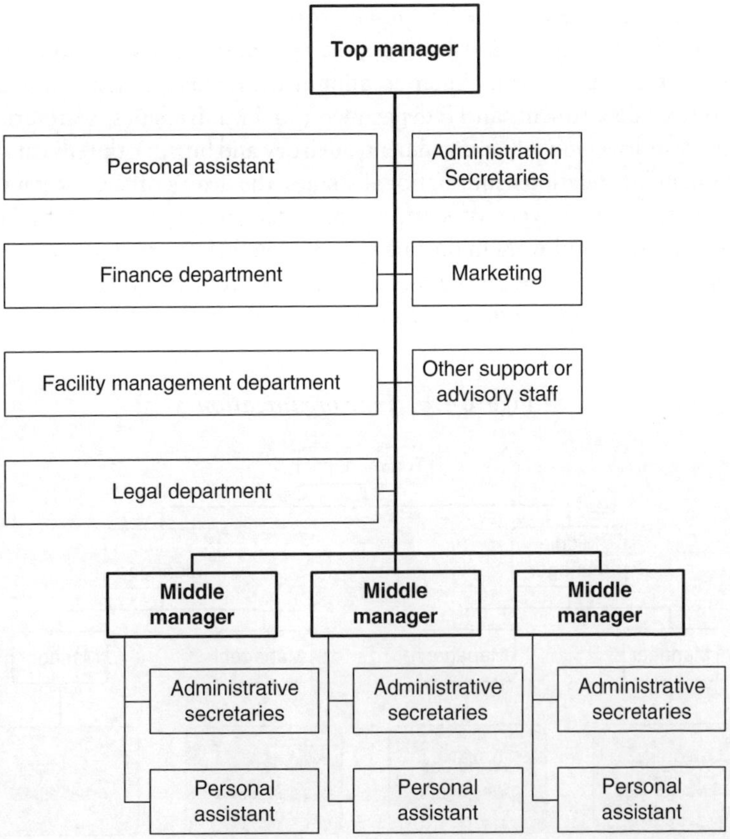

an example of the staff included in a partial organizational chart, in which the only line is between the top manager and the three middle managers – in bold.

Divisions

Larger organizations might be separated into a divisional structure in which every division is self-contained with its own line–staff organization and each division has individual departments, i.e. financial, legal, personnel. In this case, the division remains accountable to the head of the organization, and the head is responsible for its functioning. The important difference between a division and a department is that the former has more *delegated authority*, i.e. is allowed to make decisions independently, is responsible for its own finances and resources, and is less dependent on the internal and external workings of other divisions and thus more flexible in its operations. In the military, this distinction is evidenced by the army, navy and air forces. A multinational company might have a European, Asian, African and American division. Within central government, each ministry can be seen as a division of government. Whether regional and local governments are divisions of central government depends on the power and authority allocated to them, as outlined in the constitution. If they only implement policies decided upon by central government, if they are accountable to central government for their performance and if central government is responsible for their functioning, they are similar to divisions of central government. If they are autonomous, not accountable to central government and central government is not responsible for their internal and external functions, they are separate organizations.

Management

Every unit in an organization needs to be managed; the activities and the employees need to be organized and coordinated in order to achieve the goals of the organization effectively and efficiently. Management is responsible and accountable for accomplishing this effective and efficient coordination and organization. In large organizations, top management, middle management and lower management can be distinguished based on the unit's position in the line.

Henri Fayol, a nineteenth-century French mining engineer, is one of the classic writers on management and is viewed as a founding father of modern management theory. He focused on the role of management in increasing the efficiency of organizations, and distinguished six tasks for management in general:

1. Planning: developing a design for what the unit has to do, how to do it, and who should do what, when and how. We would now call this a SWOT analysis: strengths, weaknesses, opportunities and threats.
2. Organizing: optimally allocating material, resources and people to accomplish the tasks of the unit.
3. Steering: commanding or directing in order to make the plan work and assigning tasks to everyone involved.
4. Coordinating: communicating what the manager expects from the employees and what the employees can expect from the manager.
5. Ensuring output: ensuring that the unit delivers what it is expected to deliver.
6. Controlling: monitoring and evaluating the unit's performance.

Fayol's recommendations for improving the efficiency of an organization emphasize the role of management. He also suggests that the content of the tasks should be the main criterion for structuring an organization. A breakdown of an organization into divisions, directories and departments must ensure that the work done in each of the units focuses on a specific and coherent part of the task to achieve the goals of the organization. Fayol believed that management should have the authority to give orders, which employees within the unit are required to obey, and that each employee should receive orders from only one manager. Fayol had a particular interest in employee motivation. He suggested that treating employees with respect and fairness, emphasizing equity and creating a team spirit and *esprit de corps* increased productivity because employees are motivated by more than just money (cf. Fayol, 1917).

This chapter here includes a discussion of Fayol, as opposed to one of the many other classic organization theorists, because Fayol addresses two classic themes in Public Administration. First, management as the answer to the threats and opportunities any organization faces, partly because of the dynamics in its environment, but especially because of the internal division of labour into separate units in organizations. Second, his emphasis on the dual focus of management in assigning tasks and motivating personnel in order to improve performance of the unit in relation to the organizational goals. The next chapter addresses this second aspect of management. This chapter focuses on the first aspect and the dilemmas involved in the inevitable structuring of organizations into separate units along line and staff.

Basics of organizational theory

Organizational theory studies organizations to identify, describe and understand what they do to solve problems arising within their own organization and between the organization and its environment, and how they can and do maximize their efficiency and effectiveness. Such theories explore the structure of organizations, the division of work within organizations, the coordination required, the supervision and delegation of power and authority, organizational behaviour and organizational ethics. This chapter focuses on the first four dimensions.

The inevitability of organizational problems

That organizations will experience problems is inevitable and aptly described in the model designed by American scholar Larry E. Greiner (1972). He predicts that every organization that grows will experience the same crises during its growth (such as the crisis of leadership, the crisis of autonomy, the crisis of control, the crisis of red tape and the crisis of complexity/identity). The solutions to the crises (direction, delegation, coordination, collaboration and network solutions, respectively) will increase further growth but eventually result in a new crisis in need of a new solution, inevitably causing new problems.

In the early stages of an organization, one creates growth by exploiting the creativity of the developers. No hierarchy is needed; the few people in the organization just do their thing and their actions make the organization thrive. When the organization grows, it becomes likely that some of the new organizational members start to do things that are not in line with the original goal of the organization, that might be damaging for the organization and that impede further growth. At such a moment, Greiner predicts a crisis, and further leadership growth is needed. Steering directs and coordinates the actions of each employee, and planning clarifies the division of labour, structure and an optimal allocation of resources.

In addition to growth, however, the establishment of leadership causes the next crisis, in which the employees will experience too little autonomy to do their job optimally. The decision-making processes may take too much time and communication from the top may be too uniform for the growing organization; the result is suboptimal function-ing of employees and units within the organization. This is the crisis of autonomy, often solved by delegating power and authority down into the organization from the top management to the middle management of units lower in the organization. Although such delegation is effective at the time in that it will probably increase growth, it also results in the next crisis, which is a crisis of control. Too much delegation will cause less coordinated action and perhaps compartmentalization.

Compartmentalization occurs when cooperation between units becomes secondary to cooperation within units. Cooperation in the organization as a whole may be hampered and can even transform into competitiveness in which units become concerned primarily with their own affairs as opposed to the organization as a whole. Serving the interests of one's own unit can even work against the goals of the whole organization. *Alienation* goes one step further and implies that people working in a unit lose sight of the unit's role in the organization as a whole and have no clue about their own contribution to the overall goals of the organization. Establishing units in a growing organization is inevitable, since a manager should manage no more than eight to ten employees – the *span of control* – but the division of organizations into units can have potential side effects.

The new challenge is that further growth requires increased coor-dination. It implies instituting rules and regulations that are explicit about who is required to do what, how, when and where. The inevi-table consequence of such rules and regulations is increased paper-work, guidelines, reporting and thus a new crisis in terms of red tape. The solution for that problem is to diminish regulations and increase more informal collaboration. This will result in a subsequent crisis of overconsultation and deliberation, creating the need for increased commoditization. This process continues, implying that the solution to a current organizational problem will result in a temporary improve-ment, but will inevitably lead to the emergence of a new problem.

Solutions in varying organizational structures

The internal evolution of organizations is one dimension of organi-zational theory. Just as important is how the organization functions in its environment. Environments can be more or less dynamic and complex, and ideally there should be a fit between an organization's structure and the characteristics of its environment in order for the organization to anticipate and react adequately to externalities. *Henri*

Mintzberg (1993) became famous by pointing out that there is no ideal organizational structure as such, and that the optimal organizational structure depends on its environment. An organization in a dynamic and complex environment will need to be different from an organization in a stable and uncomplicated environment. He distinguished five structures based on the dominance of top management, what he called the strategic apex, middle management (middle line), workforce (operational core), advisory staff (techno-structure) and support staff.

In a simple organization top management is dominant over the workings of the whole organization. In a division structure middle management is dominant, while in a professional organization the workforce is dominant. When the support staff are dominant Mintzberg foresees an adhocracy and when the advisory staff are dominant a (machine) bureaucracy is the result. According to Mintzberg (1980), the five structures are determined by the dominance of certain types of coordinating mechanisms, i.e. direct supervision, standardization of work processes, standardization of outputs or of skills or by mutual adjustment. Based on these mechanisms, five types of organizational structures can be distinguished. If direct supervision from the top management dominates, it results in a simple structure. If middle management dominates, it results in a divisional structure. If the workforce dominates, this results in professional bureaucracy. If the advisory staff dominate, this results in a machine bureaucracy. If the support staff dominate, this results in an adhocracy. According to Mintzberg, top management (the strategic apex) tries to retain control over decision making and thus drives centralization. Support staff (the techno-structure) aim at standardization in work processes. The degree to which they succeed determines whether an organization structures itself as a machine bureaucracy. The workforce tries to resist such influences and promotes autonomy and decentralization. The degree to which it succeeds determines whether an organization will become a professional bureaucracy.

Autonomy is also sought in middle management by favouring limited decentralization and coordination restricted to the standardization of its outputs. When it succeeds, a 'divisionalized form' results. The support staff attempt to gain influence by placing their expertise to the fore and by promoting voluntary collaboration in which mutual adjustment is crucial. If they succeed, the organization adopts the 'adhocracy' configuration (cf. Mintzberg, 1980, p. 329).

Additional determinants of the type of organization include the age and size of the organization (as Greiner also suggested), the degree of formalization, regulation, and elaboration of the administrative techno-structure, the complexity and dynamics of the environment, and power factors, such as external control on organizations (Mintzberg, 1980, pp. 327–328).

This brings up an important distinction about the role of management. Fayol and many other organization theorists give management a premier role in the construction and success of their organization. Greiner's model views decisions as forced upon management by the inevitably emerging problems, which management can anticipate and react to in a limited number of ways. Mintzberg further minimizes the independent impact of management decisions on the organizational structure and judges the likelihood of a specific organizational structure to be contingent, i.e. determined by factors out of the control of management. The power and authority the management can exert depends on its position in the type of organization that emerges.

The specifics of a public organization

Are public organizations different from private organizations, and if so, how? In classic organization theory, this distinction is not considered relevant. Frederick Taylor developed 'scientific management' for business, but he believed his main principles were applicable to public administration as well, adding that this was specifically the case since the average public employee did little more than one-third to one-half of a good day's work (Fry & Raadschelders, 2008, p. 56). Others suggest that 'Organizations are organizations, whatever they do' (Pugh & Hickson, 1976, p. 5). Opinions about this vary. In the 1950s, Wallace Sayre said – and in 1979 Graham Allison (1992) repeated – that 'public and private management are fundamentally alike in all unimportant respects' (p. 457).

Earlier public and private organizations were distinguished based on three criteria, i.e. funding, accountability and the type of goods and/ or service provided. How do these distinctions influence the organization and management of public organizations vis-à-vis private organizations? Its dependency on collective revenues such as taxes means that a public organization has very little power to increase its financial resources as compared to private organizations. As discussed in Chapter 2, one of the difficulties of collective goods is paying for them. In general, people do not like to pay taxes – even if they make use of the goods and services those taxes fund. Public organizations face tight budgets, but they have very little influence over increasing revenue. Raising taxes to increase organizational budgets is not within the purview of the public organization. Politicians outside the public organization make the decisions about public revenues and expenditures. This has consequences for the financial situation of many a government as was shown in Table 1.1. Most governments in the world collect fewer financial resources than they need for their expenditures and are unable to balance their budgets. If a private company had a financial deficit every year, it would close down or go bankrupt. This is not the case for public organizations. This can be reassuring for them, but it also poses the permanent challenge to public managers of managing with insufficient means. Limited public revenues pose an especially serious issue in developing countries. In these countries, governments are unable to provide basic collective goods and services, such as clean drinking water, education and health services, because they lack the financial – and consequently, human – resources to do so. This precarious situation calls for creative and innovative solutions, found especially in an adhocracy and professional bureaucracy, and this, in turn, poses a dilemma for the accountability characteristic of the public sector, and often results in a machine bureaucracy.

Accountability is structured with a political layer above public organizations that make the decisions that bureaucrats prepare and carry out. The political layer is held accountable for the workings – and especially the failings – of the public organization for which it is responsible. Because the political layer cannot oversee everything that happens inside the organization, it has to rely on organizations to follow procedures, on a standardization of work processes and thus on a relatively large advisory staff (techno-structure) to assure that everything inside the organization functions in conformity with these standards. The result is often that public organizations begin operating as machine bureaucracies. The likelihood of this is furthered by another basic element of public affairs, namely that everyone is equal before the law and that collective goods are non-excludable. This requires procedures, laws, rules and regulations, that apply to the public sector, that increase the likelihood that caution and precision, i.e. features of a machine bureaucracy, are prioritized over efficiency, speed, innovation and creativity, i.e. features of an adhocracy or professional bureaucracy.

The political layer is different from the ownership layer of a private company. Owners of a private company typically have experience and knowledge about the business and its organization and maintain a top management or leadership position inside the organization. In the public sector, the political layer is above the organization, but it is still outside the administrative apparatus. It often lacks the necessary inside knowledge and experience in public organizational matters, although this might vary among different regime types. The information asymmetry between the political layer and the administrative apparatus is likely to be greater than in private organizations, increasing the necessity of procedures and standardization of work processes. On the other hand, the political layer is closer to the organization in the public sector than the stakeholders in a private company. The political layer steers organizational developments directly by proposing new policies (to be prepared and implemented by their organizations), by proposing expansion or downsizing of the organization, or by shifting financial means inside the organization from one directorate or unit to another.

This would not be an issue if the interests of the political layer coincided with those of the administrative apparatus. German sociologist Max Weber (1994) pointed out that political and administrative interests diverge. According to Weber, politicians are primarily concerned with being elected, often based on their charisma, ideals and promises, whereas administrators are appointed based on knowledge, experience and professionalism. Hence, politicians find their legitimacy in the support of the people, based on a political spoils system in which power and conflict dominate, while administrators find their legitimacy in their knowledge and experience; that is, a merit system, in which rationality and efficiency dominate. Politicians are partisan, often generalists, knowing a little about a lot of things, while administrators are expected to be neutral, specialized and deeply knowledgeable about a few things. Since politicians' prime goal is to be re-elected, they want to achieve many goals in a relatively short time, while administrators are focused on their career, which calls for a long-term perspective. More recent scholars have suggested additional differences between politicians and public administrators, such as their emphasis on optimizing outcomes or procedures, prioritizing effectiveness or efficiency, trying to establish change or continuity, and in viewing their position as a calling or an occupation.

These differences between the political leadership and the administrative management and organization of the public sector makes life inside public organizations more complex than in private organizations, where the interests of the owner or leader are not, by their nature, different from those who do the work in that organization.

This complexity increases because the goods provided by the public sector are collective goods. The provision of collective goods does not lend itself to the development of a one-on-one customer–provider relationship, such as buying a hamburger or a television set. Instead, in the provision of collective goods there is a multitude of groups involved, consisting of market forces, individuals, labour unions, employers, organizations and interest groups, each with its own preferences, requests and issues. All of these groups lack an 'exit option', because it is almost impossible to escape from the contribution to or provision of collective goods by one's government. The alternative to exit is influencing the provision of collective goods by participating in the decision making and implementation of collective goods. By their nature, collective goods affect the entire population, which makes their provision complex and necessitates meticulousness on the part of the public organization. This increases the need for proper procedures and the standardization of work processes, and thus the likelihood of a machine bureaucracy, even though the population itself might prefer a professional bureaucracy or even an adhocracy, focusing on personal attention, client orientation, entrepreneurship, innovation and creativity. The conclusion is that public organizations are, by their nature, (somewhat) different from private organizations.

One could argue, and many scholars have done so, that the differences between private and public organizations are relative instead of absolute. The motivation for this argument is based, in part, on the notion that public organizations could learn from practices and innovations taking place in private organizations – and vice versa – in order to improve their functioning. The arguments for and against this distinction are based not only on research and scholarship, but also partly on ideology and bias. Public organizations have a bad image. Quite simply, one could ask oneself three questions:

1. Does it fundamentally matter whether an organization is dependent on a budget based on taxes or on pizza sales?
2. Does it fundamentally matter whether an organization is led by a politician or a business person?
3. Is there a fundamental difference between an organization that sells hamburgers and one that makes laws?

If the answer is 'no' on all three accounts, then there are no fundamental differences between public and private organizations. If the answer to all three questions is 'yes', then such differences apparently exist.

And if the answer is that it depends on the kind of resources compared, on the character of the politician and the business person, and on the kind of good provided, then the differences are relative.

What aspects of the organization are most affected by this public–private debate? Above, it was argued that public organizations have features that result in the natural tendency to become (machine) bureaucracies, although others have argued that the bureaucratic phenomenon is not limited to public organizations and that it is as common in the private sector. The next three chapters address whether this matters for recruitment, careers and human resource management in general and for public administrators' motivation, ethics and integrity.

There has been a substantial amount of scholarly research on this issue. Fottler (1981) studied the differences between the public and the private sector based on their funding sources. The publicness of the resources has an impact on management's values, incentives and constraints. Wilson (1989) emphasized the constraints on public organizations and argued that management in the public sector has more limited incentives to motivate employees, less control over the inputs and organizational resources and little opportunity to improve economic efficiency. Bozeman (1987) compared the public and private sector based on our second criterion – political leadership – and investigated the effects for organizations affected by varying degrees of political control. He found significant differences in the possibilities for management change and employee motivation. Allison (1992) argued that although public and private managers use management tools identical in name, the actual meaning and effect of such tools are different in public and private sector organizations. Bozeman and Loveless (1987) also compared public and private organizations according to the third criterion and concluded that the one sector is not consistently more productive than the other one.

The essence of bureaucracy

The previous sections argued that public organizations show a natural tendency to become bureaucracies, but bureaucracies are not a recent phenomenon. According to Finer, the first elements of bureaucracy were evident in the Egypt of the pharaohs and the China of the Han Empire. Both were known for their hierarchy inside the line with a centralization of the organization aimed at lessening discretionary functions from the top echelons downwards (Finer, 1997, part I, p. 476). The

Egyptian bureaucracy, known for its professionalism, was especially notorious for its reliance on written documents and paperwork, under the adage '*if there is no evidence of something on paper, it does not exist*'. Every act and agreement, person, piece of land and building was documented on paper and copied several times, which became the only way of proving its existence. The Chinese bureaucracy was renowned for its recruitment of public administrators based on examinations. It is said that a Chinese family felt the same happiness if one of its members passed the examinations as the Greeks experienced when one of their people won at the Olympics. The more examinations passed, the higher one would climb in the hierarchy of the public administration. As early as AD 124, an academy was started by Confucianists to train students for official posts within public administration, and by the end of the first century this academy had enlisted 30,000 students (Finer, 1997, part I, p. 489). A second feature of bureaucracy found in this early Chinese Empire was the establishment of a nested administration in which the acts of each administration were controlled by other administrations. Such checks and balances were deemed necessary to prevent and control the potential abuse of the powerful functions within the administration. Later on, during the Ming dynasty, the bureaucracy succeeded in taking all power and leaving the emperor helpless within his palace, unable to write anything without the consent of his chief administrators.

The remnants of these classic forms of bureaucracy are still visible in the modern concept of bureaucracy as described by German sociologist Max Weber in what he called the ideal type of bureaucracy (Weber, 1921, 1978). Weber did not necessarily believe bureaucracy to be an ideal form of organization in the normative sense, but it is an ideal type that characterizes a bureaucracy in its purest form. Weber acknowledged the advantages as well as the drawbacks of such an organization. The advantages have to be considered in the context of Weber's time.

Europe of that time was emerging from an era in which many public functions were sold to the highest bidder. The sellers tried to earn a quick return on investment by getting as much money as possible out of the function and charging citizens heavily for their services. This resulted in administrative arbitrariness in which the outcomes of requests depended on the functionary involved – and the amount of money needed to convince the functionary – as opposed to the rules.

People from respectable families and nobility typically occupied the senior public posts, regardless of their ability to fulfil the duties of those posts. In Europe, instead of being knowledgeable and experienced it was deemed more important to be loyal to the state, to come from a family whose members had been loyal for generations, to actively participate in the state religion, to support the political party that supported those in power, to be the same race and class as the rulers and to be male with a 'proper' education that included accepted etiquette. This slowly changed during the nineteenth century as senior public functions were opened up to people who proved their knowledge and skills, especially in law, through a university degree and to people who were able to make a glorious career through the public service by proving their capabilities in organization and management.

Weber interpreted these developments through the lens of his ideal types as conceptual models for understanding their long-term consequences, and developed eight characteristics of the pure type of bureaucracy. According to Weber, the actual state of public administration never came near his ideal type of bureaucracy, but a tendency towards the pure form was evident in various systems.

In its purest form, Weber argued, eight elements (listed in Table 4.1) constitute the ideal type of a bureaucracy.

Several researches have investigated the precedence of Weberian-type bureaucracies in the world. At the end of the twentieth century, American researchers Peter Evans and James Rauch (1999) investigated 36 countries and found that the public sector in countries like Kenya, the Dominican Republic, Guatemala, Nigeria, Argentina, Syria, Haiti, Ecuador, Uruguay, Chile, Peru and Portugal is hardly organized to the Weberian principles, whereas in countries like Singapore, Korea, Taiwan, Pakistan, Hong Kong, Malaysia and Spain the Weberian system is to a much higher degree approximated in the public sector.

Table 4.1   *Weber's eight characteristics of a pure bureaucracy*

1. A formal hierarchy within the organization.
2. A strict division of tasks and authority based on written job descriptions.
3. The implementation of tasks based on written documents.
4. Recruitment based on formal examinations and careers based on experience within the administration and seniority.
5. The separation of the functionary and the task.
6. The insignificance of the individual functionary compared to the task to be performed.
7. A fixed salary independent of one's performance.
8. The functioning as a goal in itself as opposed to the means to personal profit.

Nowadays, the Quality of Government Institute of the University of Gothenburg in Sweden collects comparative government data.

Amendments to the Weberian bureaucracy

Bureaucracy is one of the key themes in Public Administration, and scholars widely debate its merits, the distinction between politics and administration, and the dilemmas involved in each of the eight Weberian characteristics of bureaucracy. This debate involves still undetermined issues. This section addresses some of them.

The structure of the bureaucracy

The first issue is that a bureaucracy needs, and is even defined by, an abundance of rules, regulations and written procedures. The advisory staff have a dominant position in such an organization, as seen in Figure 4.3.

The million-dollar question is what happens when the structure is out of balance and when the abundance of procedures starts to impede the effectiveness and efficiency of the functioning of the organization. Robert Merton (1957) was one of the most influential writers on this subject, suggesting that ritualistic behaviour could become the norm in order to ensure conformity to procedures, and that a displacement of goals was likely when the organizational goal is no longer serving society but acting in accordance with the regulations. Martha Feldman and Jane Dutton pointed to the paradox of

Figure 4.3 *A visualization of a bureaucratic organization*

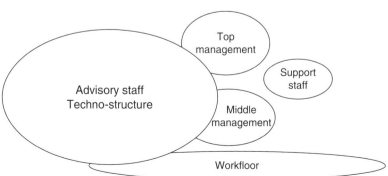

policy analysis, in which analysts produce study after study, always gathering and sharing information, without ever using it in decision making, just because it is their job, they earn a salary for doing it and because it is consistent with the rational–legal type of organization that a bureaucracy is.

Politicians and bureaucrats

The *distinction between the political layer and bureaucracy* is also widely studied. The classic idea is that politicians have the power to make decisions, and public administrators are limited to preparing and implementing these decisions. Critics have pointed out that the concepts of 'political layer' and 'public administration' suggest a distinctiveness that is not visible in practice and that through time, the distinction has become less valid for describing what goes on in government. They point out that the differences are exaggerated since many politicians have a background in public administration and many senior public administrators have previously been politicians, thus making relations between the political and administrative layers more similar to relations between entrepreneurs and their businesses.

In theory, public officials only prepare and execute decisions made by politicians, but in practice they do more than that. They also make decisions themselves. As Edward Page remarked, 'To compile a list of cases in which the civil servants have made policy would be arduous work and tedious reading' (Page, 1985, p. 6).

Instead of strict hierarchical relation, struggles between the bureaucracy and the political layer over decision-making power are common. In this process, bureaucrats see an increase in their power. First, because of the increasing complexity of policy issues and the increasing dominance of technical rationality, whereby politicians become dependent on the expertise of public administrators; and second, because of the latter's means to obstruct, delay, vacillate, hesitate and regulate (Kettl, 1993, p. 414). Weber himself also acknowledged the danger of a trained and specialized public administration that is more likely to get its way than an elected politician, who is not a specialist.

Other scholars have pointed to the negative side effects of public administration that is expected to be neutral and loyal to whatever politician is elected and placed over their organization. Just after the Second World War, Germany debated a duty to resist, obliging civil servants to turn down orders from politicians which clearly offended the constitution of the state. At the opposite end of the spectrum, in England, just after the same war, scholars warned against the obstructive force that public administration could pose for a possible socialist government in case the Labour Party won the elections. All of this points to the dilemma of minimizing partisanship of public administration and maximizing loyalty and neutrality, while simultaneously maximizing individual responsibility, political responsiveness and accountability of the civil service (cf. de Vries, 1999).

The strict hierarchy inside bureaucracies

The goal of a strict hierarchy within an organization, based on written job descriptions in which the lines of authority are fixed, is to make processes run smoothly and to make them verifiable and accountable with clear lines of communication so everyone knows their role and expectations, including unequivocal responsibility for successes and failures. As discussed in the previous chapter, i.e. Michels' Iron Law of Oligarchy, such hierarchy is also inevitable. The negative consequences of a strict hierarchical organization are clear. The side effects of the one-directional, top-down approach are twofold. First, the top of the organization may disregard advice from those who implement the policies, resulting in the neglect of problems in implementation. Something that may be desirable from the top managers' point of view might not be feasible in terms of implementation. This might also be the case because of the arduous and lengthy process of communicating problems and recommendations of the so-called street-level bureaucrats all the way to the top of the organization – after which it has to go down the chain of command again in order to resolve the problems – often without considering sensible suggestions from the bureaucrats that could improve the functioning of the organization. In other words, hierarchical organizations are rarely known to be learning organizations. Second, the strict authority relations can and do result in conflicts between different units, all of which try to alter the division of responsibilities in such a way that is profitable for their unit. Third, being subordinate in a strict hierarchical structure may result in less motivation, fewer feelings of responsibility except for the task assigned and, ultimately, even in indifference and cynicism.

Extensive documentation

Extensive documentation of what has been done and what needs to be done poses a similar dilemma. On the one hand, it enhances the transparency of the work and the possibility for controlling, directing, monitoring, and installing checks and balances to ensure that the actions and implementation have been carried out as described. On the other hand, it takes (sometimes a lot of) time, time taken away from the actual work which can result in inefficiency when the documentation becomes a goal in itself. When separate functions have formal job descriptions, describing and prescribing what functionaries should do as well as what they should refrain from doing, the result can be alienation and a failure to see the big picture and the contribution of one's work in relation to the organizational goals.

The next chapter will deal with other side effects of a Weberian bureaucracy when it discusses human resource management, i.e. recruitment based on examinations and careers based on experience and seniority. It will also address the separation of functionary and tasks and salaries based on performance. These side effects are more related to the individual work environment.

Bureaucracy in different regimes

The last issue addressed is whether bureaucracy fits all the four regime types mentioned in Chapter 2, or rather what aspects of bureaucracy tend to dominate in different regime types. The question is not an issue of fit between bureaucracy and regime type because bureaucracy is viewed simultaneously as a threat and a necessity in all regimes.

Ferrel Heady (1996) argued that in former colonies, the administration will almost certainly resemble the colonial power administratively, even though independence was forcibly won and political strings have been cut (Heady, 1996, p. 318). According to Heady, there are differences between colonies that were fortunate to have a colonial power with a good record of administrative institution building and those less fortunate. This might explain the variation between such countries in terms of their skilled manpower regarding management capacity, developmental skills, technical competence, corruption et cetera (pp. 318–320).

Nonetheless, regimes vary to the extent that bureaucracies can prosper. This issue has been extensively investigated for club-type regimes, namely the bureaucracy in one-party states such as China and the previous Soviet Union and in (previous) military regimes such as in Egypt, Argentina and Thailand. Within such regimes, bureaucracy seems to thrive, especially its hierarchical characteristics.

Every type of regime has its own tools for controlling the bureaucracy to ward off the threat it poses. In club-type regimes, the party or the military might pose a kind of parallel bureaucracy, resulting in a potential overload of administrative controls. Temple-type regimes or religious states, such as Iran, solved the problem by positioning clerics inside the bureaucracy in order to ensure that its acts conformed to the interests of the religious leaders. In forum-type regimes, such controls are practised by agencies such as the audit office, ombudsman and a state council; and in palace-type regimes, the head of state is likely to place friends and family as advisory staff inside the bureaucracy. The only bureaucracies relatively free of such controls and checks and balances are those in very poor countries, where the costs of staff in addition to the line are unaffordable. There is no overt consent to the increased risk of corruption and fraud, failure to comply with procedures, or abuse of discretion because of the absence of procedures, but such side effects are necessarily assumed to be inevitable.

Scholarly literature on relations between bureaucracy and democracy (the forum type) has pointed to the dilemmas at stake, especially regarding recruitment procedures. Recruitment, as suggested by Max Weber, does not guarantee that the members of the bureaucratic apparatus are representative of the population as a whole, or that they are neutral. Such recruitment can easily result in a kind of bureaucratic elite corps, which is too far removed from the interests of the people and can pose a threat to democracy (Kaufman, 1981). Scholars have, in fact, found differences between the ideology of top officials and the population, the former being somewhat more right-wing conservatives (Aberbach et al., 1981, p. 124). For a democracy, representativeness will suffer at the hands of a Weberian system of merit recruitment based on knowledge, experience and capabilities. Recruitment is also an issue in other regime types, where loyalty based on party membership, a military career or kinship to the ruler replaces expertise and experience as the most important criteria.

In fact, all of the features of bureaucracy as originally described by Max Weber have been criticized for their negative side effects and the dilemmas they pose for effective and efficient organizations.

One of the main research areas in Public Administration is how to retain the benefits of the features of bureaucracies, while simultaneously avoiding the negative side effects. Can effective organizations be built without a strict hierarchy? Is it possible to transform bureaucracies into learning organizations? How can organizations motivate functionaries to work more effectively and efficiently and to increase their performance? How can compartmentalization, alienation and indifference be prevented and individual responsibility, political responsiveness and accountability be increased?

Table 4.2 *The features, rationale and side effects of bureaucracy*

Features mentioned by Weber	Rationale	Side effects
A formal hierarchy within the organization	Clear responsibilities which make processes run smoothly by controlling, directing, monitoring, settling inevitable conflicts and ensuring efficient communication throughout the organization	Top of the organization may disregard advice from those who implement policy which prevents learning Conflicts between different units
A strict division of tasks and authority based on written job descriptions	Complete transparency about what functionaries are supposed to do and refrain from doing	Compartmentalization, alienation from the greater picture
The implementation of tasks based on written documents	Rule of law is dominant and it prevents bureaucratic arbitrariness	Conformity to rules and regulations becomes a goal in itself instead of a means to achieve substantial goals
Recruitment based on formal examinations and careers based on experience within the administration and seniority	Employing knowledgeable and skilled people in the public sector	Representativeness of public service becomes a problem since diversity in recruitment and careers might be jeopardized
The separation of the functionary and the task	Outcomes of processes depend on rules and regulations and not on the personality of the public servant	Achieved at the expense of individual responsibility, political responsiveness and accountability
The insignificance of the individual functionary in relation to the task	Neutrality and loyalty of public servants; the personal interests of the individual functionary are irrelevant to decision making	Indifference on the part of the functionary and denial of democratic rights to functionaries
Fixed salaries independent of performance	Security for the public servant and prevention of abuse of the function by the functionary	A lack of motivation to work effectively and efficiently
The function viewed as a goal in itself as opposed to a means to make a personal profit	Adherence to functioning is central; abuse of the function for personal benefit is prevented	Improving job performance is not sought

Recent research

In the early 1980s the bureaucratic phenomenon had encountered so much criticism out of research in Public Administration, but also in societies at large, that the side effects of its features were seen as out-weighing their rationale. It resulted in a quarter of a century of research and practice in *reforms in the public sector*. Behn summarized the criticism which resulted in NPM aptly: 'Their argument is quite simple: The traditional method for organizing the executive branch of government is too cumbersome, too bureaucratic, too inefficient, too unresponsive and too unproductive. It does not give us the results we want from government. And today, citizens expect government to produce results. They are no longer tolerant of inefficiency or ineffectiveness. Thus, we need a new way of doing business, a new paradigm for the management of government' (Behn, 1998, p. 33).

At first the solution was sought in varying types of public sector reforms introducing, for instance, centralization in England because local governments were seen as inefficient organizations in comparison to central government in the eyes of the then prime minister Margaret Thatcher, and in other countries decentralization because their central governments expected local governments to be able to handle problems more efficiently than central government. Still other governments introduced austerity measures reducing the size of the public sector through deregulation and a reorientation of core tasks, through privatization and by putting public organizations at arm's length, i.e. turning them into semi-independent agencies that had their own governing boards and could operate relatively independently of ministers and governmental departments, but nonetheless which had clearly mandated statutory objectives.

The reforms aimed at taking responsibility from the politicians and bringing it into the administration, under the label 'let managers manage'. Later on in the 1990s the concept of NPM became better defined through the work of Osborne and Gaebler, 'reinventing government' as discussed in Chapter 2, and the European variant thereof as described by Christopher Hood. The reforms aimed for a lean and mean government, through outsourcing tasks to the profit sector, decentralization to local government and deregulation in order to reduce bureaucracy.

The emphasis shifted from due process to output management. New Zealand was the frontrunner in the application of NPM in introducing annual performance agreements between chief executives and their minister, the introduction of flat hierarchies, the application of accrual accounting practices, the disaggregation of the large bureaucracies in small single-purpose agencies, contracting out service delivery to private-enterprise and not-for-profit organizations, and full privatization. Public Administration as a discipline followed the trend by giving the arguments for the desired reforms, by publishing about best practices. The main aim of such research was to find alternatives for bureaucracy by introducing the entrepreneurial administration and customer orientation, out of the idea that citizens are mainly customers of services delivered; by introducing competition inside the public sector; by introducing performance measurement and pay-for-performance practices; and by simplifying rules in order to abandon what was called paper pushing or red tape. All the features of a Weberian bureaucracy had to be abandoned in favour of the private sector model in which increased productivity and efficiency dominated. These reforms spread over the world, induced by international organizations like the OECD, the World Bank, the UN, the Asian Development Bank, Inter-American Development Bank, the IMF and USAID.

This lasted until approximately the turn of the millennium, after which the dilemmas became increasingly visible and the one-sided emphasis on outputs became heavily discussed. This resulted in new ideas for reforms, such as the *Neo-Weberian State*, in which the features of Weberian bureaucracy became re-evaluated. This theory suggests reaffirming the crucial role of governments as the main facilitator of solutions to the new problems. Central are the administrative law in preserving its basic principles and a public service with a distinct status and culture. The Neo-Weberian state constantly needs to adapt and to consult with citizens, to modernize relevant laws, to professionalize itself, and to encourage a greater orientation on the achievements of results rather than merely the correct following of procedure.

The different views on the directions reforms should take illustrate that it is not easy to find a way out of the dilemma between the reasons why bureaucracies are organized the way they are and the negative side effects of that specific way of organizing the public sector.

Conclusions

This chapter began by discussing the structure and dilemmas of public organizations. Concepts such as line organization, top management, middle management, staff organization, support staff and advisory staff were explained. It continued with an introduction to organization theory, and the merits of alternative organizational structures as responses to the threats and opportunities any organization faces. Given the three features of public organizations – budgets based on taxes, political leadership and accountability and the provision of collective goods – this chapter argued that a public bureaucracy will most likely emerge as the dominant form of public organization. It presented Weber's eight characteristics of public bureaucracies in their purest form and concluded by exploring a number of dilemmas that bureaucracies face.

The solutions, i.e. conformity, predictability and good governance, in which laws and regulations (as opposed to the whims and desires of individual administrators) that are intended to address the dilemmas of bureaucracy can result in negative side effects. One of the key themes in Public Administration is investigating how bureaucracies work, understanding the dilemmas they face and finding ideals in the dilemmas.

In recent decades, the general mood has been towards reducing paperwork, loosening strict hierarchies, changing one-directional communication into deliberation and limiting the role of advisory staff. Perhaps other innovative practices are possible and perhaps we need to change how we frame questions and dilemmas in order to find solutions. Regardless of answers to these questions, it is clear that bureaucracy will remain a key theme in Public Administration for some years to come.

Further reading

Balla Steven J. & Lodge, Martin (2015). *The Oxford Handbook of Classics in Public Policy and Administration*. Oxford: Oxford University Press.

Gormley Jr., William T. (2014). *Taming the bureaucracy: Muscles, prayers, and other strategies*. Princeton: Princeton University Press.

Heady, Ferrel (2001). *Public administration. A comparative perspective*. New York: Marcel Dekker.

Rainey, Hal G. (2009). *Understanding and managing public organizations*. New York: John Wiley & Sons.

Shafritz, Jay M. & Hyde, Albert C. (eds) (2012). *Public Administration: Classic Readings*. Boston: Wadsworth.

van der Meer, Frits M., Raadschelders, Jos C. N. & Toonen, Theo A. J. (eds) (2015). *Comparative civil service systems in the 21st century*. Basingstoke: Palgrave Macmillan.

Chapter 5

Who works in government?

Like all organizations, ranks at all levels and in all areas of public bureaucracies have to be filled. Individuals need to be recruited, socialized and trained, gain experience and make careers, and they have to be managed in order to make the apparatus function well. Working in the public sector is the topic of this chapter. This chapter argues that despite the dominance of bureaucracy as the main organizational model, the way it actually functions varies all over the world. And within the public sector, working conditions, tasks and functions, and the requisite knowledge, skills and attitudes vary depending on where one is positioned in the organization.

This chapter introduces the internal operation of public sector organizations. It discusses recruitment with its variety of criteria, working conditions, socialization, training, capacity building and career advancement through the hierarchy. It moves from the basic level of implementation, through lower management and middle management in staff and line functions, to top management and leadership.

This chapter proceeds in this manner not because hierarchy is the sole subject of interest, however. It also examines lateral relations, as in who the official works for. Who is the client, who is the principal and who is the agent?

The internal operation of the public sector can be understood, in part, by the formal structure of the organization. Equally important to the internal operation is the informal structure of the organization; the organizational culture is embedded in the societal culture in which it functions, and is influenced by its own long-term development, in which path dependencies are important. Previous chapters addressed the formal structural organization as well as the importance of path dependencies. This chapter focuses on the informal organization including the cultural dimensions of organizations, which determine how the formal organization is interpreted and managed.

One example of the impact of cultural differences can be found in the *discretion* of public administrators. Discretion refers first to *the quality of behaving or speaking in such a way as to avoid causing offence.* Some countries, such as New Zealand and Sweden, have traditions that support 'free and frank' advice to political superiors as a dimension of political non-partisanship, while in other countries, such as Mexico and Korea, the converse is more traditional in that civil servants are not encouraged to give contrary advice to ministers (cf. Matheson et al., 2007, p. 20). Similar differences are evident in the second meaning of discretion, *the freedom to decide what should be done in a specific situation, if the rules are not completely clear*. There are dramatic differences between organizations and between countries in the extent to which public administrators are trusted to do what the organization expects them to do, and in the extent to which every decision needs to be monitored and approved by a higher or adjacent official. The third meaning of discretion concerns *protecting confidential information* and organizations vary in whether they view specific information as confidential or are more transparent.

Before this chapter describes one of the most famous cultural theories, it discusses some relevant terminology.

Terminology

Culture

In cultural anthropology, culture is sometimes viewed as the entirety of the achievements of a society. Kroeber and Kluckhohn (1952) found over 160 definitions of 'culture' and developed a more specific definition:

Culture consists of patterns, explicit and implicit, of and for behaviour acquired and transmitted by symbols, constituting the distinctive achievement of human groups, including their embodiment in artefacts; the essential core of culture consists of traditional (i.e. historically derived and selected) ideas and especially their attached values; culture systems may on the one hand, be considered as products of action, on the other as conditioning elements of further action (Kroeber & Kluckhohn, 1952, p. 357).

This definition complicates the meaning of culture in some ways. The pyramids and sphinx are part of ancient Sumerian, Egyptian and Sudanese cultures since they are achievements of those societies to honour the Gods and their deceased rulers as representatives of those Gods. As products of society, they are a cultural heritage. In addition to physical aspects such as these, culture also incorporates intangible aspects, such as beliefs, ideas, values and norms which guide, even condition, behaviour. States can have a national culture that distinguishes them from other states, as argued in Chapter 3 with the example that Spanish colonizers would marry natives while English settlers would not. While structural patterns might have determined these different patterns of behaviour at the beginning of colonization, later on they became matters of course and, as such, a cultural feature that distinguished the English from the Spanish, and ensured cohesiveness within both groups.

In addition to national culture, more levels can be distinguished. Culture characterizes relations between states, for example, the common use of the French language and the axiom that diplomats remain polite, even if there are hostilities. Culture characterizes (groups of) states, as seen in the role of religion, values and habits; it is co-determinative for individual behaviour, evidenced in the choices people make, what they do and what is not done; and culture is important at the level in between, namely in organizational behaviour. It is this level of culture that this chapter focuses on.

Edgar Schein (1984, p. 3) defines organizational culture as 'the pattern of basic assumptions and beliefs that are shared by members of an organization, that operate unconsciously, and that define in a basic "taken for granted" fashion of an organization's view of itself and its environment' and as 'that a given group has invented, discovered or developed in learning to cope with its problems or external adaptation and internal integration, and that have worked well enough to be considered valid and, therefore, to be taught to new members as the correct way to perceive, think and feel in relation to these problems'.

These assumptions and beliefs have a number of features. First, they refer to the nature of relations between the organization and its environment, especially whether this relation is dominant, submissive, harmonious or conflictual. Second, they refer to the nature and existence of truth and reality and how truth and reality reveal themselves. Third, they address whether humans are basically evil, good or neutral, selfish or social, and thus to be trusted or to be controlled. Fourth, there are specific assumptions and beliefs about the nature of human activity in terms of whether it is passive or active, fatalistic or self-determined. Finally, culture refers to basic ideas about human relationships: are they competitive or cooperative, individualistic or communal, and what kind of authority is prominent in each? (Schein, 1984, p. 6) Such basic assumptions about relations, truth and reality determine actual behaviour and the expectations of such behaviour. How strongly they influence behaviour depends on the strength of the culture.

Culture can be stronger or weaker, dependent on the homogeneity and stability of an organization and the duration and intensity of the shared experiences of a group. As a result of path dependencies, central, regional and local government administrations in many countries have a relatively long history of shared experiences, are more or less stable and homogeneous and are thus more likely to have a strong culture. Any discussion about culture includes issues of how to identify it, whether it can be measured at all, whether and to what extent organizational culture affects the organization and management, and whether a strong or weak culture is preferred. A strong culture can become obsessive, inhibitive of change and cause intolerance towards nonstandard behaviour. A weak culture can make an organization unmanageable if organizational members do not cooperate in order to achieve the organization's goals.

Management

Like culture, management can be defined in numerous ways, depending on the task and the object of management. With regard to its object, 'management' can be combined with a number of prefixes, such as self-, people-, project-, process-, resource-, sport-, facility-, transition-, innovation-, knowledge-, quality- or even 'total-quality-'. As a task, definitions of management emphasize nearly every job possible, for instance the well-known POSDCORB functions of planning, organizing, staffing, directing, coordinating, reporting and budgeting, but one could emphasize many other tasks such as motivating, facilitating, marketing, visioning or creating. Denhardt and his colleagues distinguished 12 functions describing what managers in public and non-profit organizations should do, including external awareness in identifying issues that affect the work unit, keeping subordinates informed, representing the unit, coordinating, planning, guiding, budgeting, managing materials and personnel, supervising, monitoring and evaluating. He also distinguished ten characteristics of how these functions are executed effectively, namely through a broad perspective, strategic view, environmental sensitivity, leadership, flexibility, action orientation, results focus, communication, interpersonal sensitivity and technical competence (Denhardt et al., 2002, p. 8). The diversity in focus results in almost as many definitions of management as there are scholars writing about management. For example, Henri Fayol (1949, pp. 5–6) said, 'to manage is to forecast and to plan, to organize, to command, to coordinate and to control'. This later resulted in the POSDCORB functions. According to the management guru Peter Drucker (1955, 1999), 'Management is a multi-purpose organ that manages business and manages managers and manages workers and work'. Mary Parker Follet viewed management as the art of getting things done through people (Barrett, 2003, p. 51), and Harold Koontz defined management as the art of getting things done through and with people in formally organized groups. Perhaps the best definition is from Henri Mintzberg, who stated very simply that *management is what managers do*. According to Mintzberg, this is often varied, fragmented, unplanned and uncoordinated, which is quite different from what management theories prescribe (Mintzberg, 1973).

What management does and how it does it is dependent, in part, on culture, the dynamics of the environment, characteristics of the organization and its goal(s), the position of management in the organization, the available resources and the type of people working in the unit of the organization that is managed.

Leadership

Most of what has been said about varying definitions of management can also be applied to definitions of leadership. There are almost as many different definitions of leadership, prefixes to the noun 'leadership' and varying functions of leadership as there are persons who have attempted to define the concept (Bass, 1981). Some view leadership as a dimension of management, in the sense that managers should exhibit leadership in their conduct. Others view leadership as an influence process that enables managers to motivate their people to willingly do what must be done, and to do it well (Cribbin, 1981). Still others see leadership in terms of position in an organization; that is, a leader is someone who has subordinates. The highest formal position in the organization is the leader, because the leader can alter the probability of what others in the organization do by influencing them or by exercising power. Last, but not least, leadership can be understood as an action. You show leadership by your conduct, and it can be moral, visionary, motivating, enabling, et cetera. This variation in definitions focuses on the dimension one wants to emphasize in distinguishing good leadership from bad leadership, resulting in a simple definition: *a leader refers to someone who has followers* and *leadership refers to features of behaviour that induce people to follow*.

This chapter examines organizational culture and its impact on management and leadership in the public sector. By working through the different stages of recruitment, socialization, career making, middle management, top management and leadership, we can better understand the different dimensions of management and leadership in public organizations. Before describing those stages, one of the most widely used theories on organizational culture is addressed.

Cultural dimensions

Around 1980, Dutch management scholar Geert Hofstede developed his theory of organizational culture. At the time, he worked for IBM, which had multiple divisions in a large number of countries. Hofstede conducted a survey and gathered data from approximately 60,000 employees in 50 countries and three regions. On the basis of that research, he was able to distinguish four cultural dimensions that he later extended to five. These dimensions point to differences regarding power distance, individualism (as opposed to collectivism), uncertainty avoidance, masculinity (as opposed to femininity), and the fifth, the degree of Confucian dynamism (as opposed to short-term orientation).

- *Power distance* refers to 'the extent to which less powerful members of institutions and organizations expect and accept that power is distributed unequally' (Hofstede, 1997, p. 28). It has to do with loyalty, obedience and respect shown by the powerless, or subordinates being treated and expected to be treated as equals by the powerful. Indicators for power distance within organizations are the extent to which managers tend to consult their staff before making decisions, wage gaps, centralization, status, office furnishings and the acceptance of (huge) salary differences. It suggests that a society's level of inequality is endorsed by the followers as much as by the leaders (cf. http://geerthofstede.nl/dimensions-of-national-cultures). According to Hofstede, the power distance was especially high in former Spanish colonies such as Guatemala, Panama, the Philippines, Mexico, Venezuela, and Ecuador, as well as in Arab countries and exploitation colonies such as Malaysia, Indonesia, India and West Africa. Low levels of power distance are prevalent in OECD countries with Latin OECD countries experiencing a culture of higher power distance than Anglo-Saxon OECD countries.
- *Individualism* and *collectivism* refer to how people define themselves in relation to others and whether they are loosely or tightly integrated in groups. The way to distinguish individualism from collectivism is to ask whether people are competitive, whether they are inclined to set goals without considering others' interests,

whether the ties between them are loose. A comparison of nation-states revealed that individualism is more common in OECD countries but, for instance, also in South Africa and India, the two main former English colonies. Hofstede found the most collectivist countries in Latin America in particular – the former Spanish colonies, not Portuguese Brazil. Hofstede argued that differences in wealth, climate and history are related to a more individualistic or collectivist culture.

Uncertainty avoidance is the comfort sought in predictability, rules and regulations and stability. It indicates the extent to which culture programmes its members to feel either uncomfortable or comfortable in unstructured situations (cf. Shi & Wang, 2011, p. 99) and whether people emphasize order and consistency over innovation. Uncertainty is preferably avoided; for instance, by (over)regulation in written and unwritten rules, maintenance of strict codes of behaviour, and a belief in the absolute truth (cf. Jandt, 2006). People in Latin and Catholic countries seem to score much higher on uncertainty avoidance than people in Confucian cultures, with people in Judaic and Muslim cultures in the middle.

Masculinity and *femininity* refer to the expected role of women vis-à-vis men and gender relations in general, and also to their ascribed features, with males seen as more task oriented and goal oriented, assertive and competitive and focusing on material success, and females seen as people oriented, modest, caring and emphasizing interpersonal relationships. In Hofstede's research, Japan was the most masculine, while the Scandinavian countries were most feminine.

Confucian work dynamism refers to a long-term or a short-term orientation in life. A short-term orientation involves a preference for rapid results and quick fixes to problems, while long-term orientation is about having a grand purpose, commitment, organizational identity and loyalty to the organization. In the latter case, traditions are important, people plan ahead, and work is a lifelong commitment to the organization and its goals, while in the short-term orientation, job-hopping is more likely, and commitment, organizational identity and loyalty play a limited role. Being a temporary employee or having tenure does not matter to those with a short-term orientation; as soon as one can find a better job, one quits and goes. A long-term orientation is more common in South East Asia, while it is rare in Central Asia and OECD countries (cf. Hofstede, 1980; Hofstede & Bond, 1988).

The importance of Hofstede's research lies in his identification of the five dimensions, which are particularly useful in distinguishing organizational cultures but less instructive in comparative research. First of all, his research was done over 40 years ago, and second, many scholars have criticized cultural theory for assuming that cultural dynamics are bound by national borders. As argued above, culture is evident on all levels, and culture can also vary over organizations and even within organizations over time. Political leaders, for example, are sometimes assumed to have a short-term orientation (until the next election) while public administrators are assumed to have a more long-term orientation since their work in public administration is their professional life.

Hofstede's model was extended in the GLOBE (Global Leadership and Organizational Behavior Effectiveness) project conducted in the mid-1990s. The GLOBE researchers measured culture at different levels and presented the results in the form of quantitative data based on responses of about 17,000 managers from 951 organizations functioning in 62 societies throughout the world (Shi & Wang, 2011, p. 94). The basic premise of the study was the same as Hofstede's, but the researchers extended the number of dimensions by categorizing masculinity–femininity into separate dimensions, including assertiveness, a humane orientation and a performance one, and by distinguishing two types of collectivism, in-group and institutional collectivism. The research pointed to important differences between regions: in Latin America, managers are not averse to self-protective leadership; in South Asia, an outstanding leader should be willing to make personal sacrifices; Arab countries score relatively high on uncertainty reduction, future orientation, power distance and institutional collectivism, and low on gender egalitarianism and assertiveness; and Eastern Europe and Central Asia would be characterized as team-oriented, future-oriented and paternalistic, with large consultative bodies and a tendency towards high power distance. Results were published in the *Journal of World Business* in 2002 and 2012 (House et al., 2002; Dorfman et al., 2012).

These cultural dimensions can easily result in the mistaken idea that differences only exist between cultures. One of the outcomes of the GLOBE project points to the existence of universal values. All over the world, leaders are expected to show integrity, be inspirational, visionary and performance-oriented, and leaders who are non-participatory, malevolent, autocratic or self-centred are despised.

Also, almost worldwide, the charismatic, value-based type of leadership – stressing high standards, decisiveness and innovation, motivating people around a vision, creating a passion among them to perform, and doing so by firmly holding on to core values – seems to be the most appreciated form of leadership (Center for Creative Leadership, 2014).

The remainder of this chapter focuses on the impact of organizational culture on work in the public sector, starting with differences in recruiting, and continuing with working, managing and leading in the public sector.

Moving through the organization

Recruitment

Recruitment involves the process of inducing suitable candidates to compete for appointments in the public sector and then selecting them. What is meant by 'suitable', how does one get those individuals to compete for the job, what is the process and who makes the final hiring decision? Recruitment in a Weberian bureaucracy presumes that examinations will determine who enters the public sector. This system is not always used in practice. In fact, the opposite is more likely; in spite of recruitment procedures, governments use nepotism, cronyism and favouritism to select friends and friends of friends. It is one of the prerogatives of politicians to appoint their friends, family and fellow party members into high public positions as a favour for proven loyalty and to ensure further loyalty. Similar issues are evident in terms of diversity in the public sector, especially regarding gender. In Korea in 2005, less than a quarter of all public servants were female and in Japan, only one out of five public servants was female. In the Netherlands, one out of three public officials is female. This is rather different from countries like Mexico, Finland, the UK, Portugal and Ireland where the majority of public servants are female.

Differences in cultures are especially visible in recruitment for (senior) management functions. Recruitment for these positions may be position-based, open to both internal and external candidates, or career-based, in which only people already holding public office at a lower level can apply for higher level posts. Countries also vary in the number of positions that are mainly political appointments or merit-based, i.e. based on knowledge, expertise and seniority.

According to Weber, careers depend only on experience and seniority. If someone has ample experience and knows how a unit within an organization works, it makes the most sense to promote this employee to unit manager. This is not how this typically occurs in practice. If we look at opportunities for men and women, Finland is the only country with a majority of senior managers who is female. In all other countries, opportunities for females to make careers within the public sector are minimal. In Mexico and the UK, a majority of the public sector workforce is female, but females only account for 30% of senior management. In the Netherlands, Belgium and Switzerland, this proportion is even lower at 15%, and in Japan and Korea it is at or below 3% (cf. Organisation for Economic Co-operation and Development, 2007). This phenomenon is known as the glass ceiling, the invisible career barrier for women, which is absent for men. Recruitment processes are often not as rational as Weber presumed and the opportunities that are available in the public sector depend on national and organizational culture, as discussed above.

Recruitment for most high-level management positions in countries like France, Japan, Mexico, Turkey and Korea is mostly career-based, while in Anglo-Saxon countries with a Westminster system, such as the UK, Sweden and the Netherlands, recruitment for most senior management positions is open to outsiders as well as insiders.

Major differences also exist in the degree of political involvement in staffing senior positions. Recent research into varying practices of political appointments in the public sector was conducted on behalf of the OECD (Matheson et al., 2007), acknowledging this dilemma:

> [P]olitical involvement in administration is essential for the proper functioning of a democracy. Without this, an incoming political administration would find itself unable to change policy direction, but public services also need protection against being misused for partisan purposes, they need technical capacity which survives changes of government, and they need protection against being used to impair the capacity of future governments to govern. (Matheson, 2007, p. 5)

There are countries such as the USA, France, Sweden and South Africa where all senior management functions are subject to political intervention, while in countries like the UK, New Zealand, Korea and Denmark the career system dominates. There are also hybrid systems where some candidates are selected based on administrative selection criteria such as merit and experience, but the final hiring decision is a political one. In 2003, Mexico switched from a politicized system to a merit system by dramatically reducing the number of political functions. But there seems to have been some truth in the story of the father asking his friend – a high public official – a favour in getting his son a job inside the public sector. The friend asks whether he is searching for a senior director post. 'No, that would be too much for a young guy.' 'A director's post then?' 'No, let him start at a much lower level,' the father replies. 'That is difficult,' the high official says, 'because in that case, he has to go through the exams'.

Working conditions

Cultural variation is also visible in working conditions and especially in public sector wages. In some Central Asian countries, individuals can still buy a position in the public sector, for instance as a police officer, and although they are hardly remunerated officially for their work, they can still make a 'decent' living. In Uganda, it is believed impossible for public officials to live on their official salary even if they have a full-time job; thus, they sometimes have to find less honourable means to supplement their wages. At the other end of the spectrum, in Pakistan, basic salaries of public officials are below those in the non-governmental sector, but they receive several benefits in addition to their salary including fuel charges paid up to 94% of their basic salary. They also receive a generous housing allowance and a transportation allowance, and the two highest grades receive fully maintained staff cars for official and private use. The lower grades receive a laundry allowance for the maintenance of their uniform. Senior officials are granted an allowance for entertaining official guests at their office or residence. A senior post allowance is given in order to maintain a certain minimum gap between the highest paid and the lowest paid; and a domestic staff allowance is provided for the higher grades. Previously, this allowance was only provided if domestic help was actually hired; nowadays, it is part of the base salary (Faiz, 2006).

Research in Latin America has showed that the wage gap between the public and private sector seems to have been dependent on the public sector position or grade, with lower positions in the public sector earning more than comparable employees in the private sector, and higher officials in the public sector earning less than their counterparts in the private sector. In many OECD countries, benefits include retirement, social security and guarantees for lifelong employment. In yet other countries, benefits include medical insurance and school fees. In the USA, public officials receive pension contributions that are 30–50% greater than the pension contributions paid by private employers.

Table 5.1 presents a comparison of public and private sector wages. According to this table, public sector officials earn an income that is above the national average and higher than the wages in the manufacturing sector, but lower than wages in the financial sector; in addition, wage differences in these sectors reflect the general income inequality across countries.

Table 5.1   *Wages in the public sector compared to other sectors*

	Ratio of average public administration wage to per capita GDP	Ratio of public sector wages to financial sector wages	Ratio of public sector wages to manufacturing wages
Africa	1.3	0.7	1.8
Asia and Pacific	1.4	0.9	1.4
Europe	1.4	0.7	1.3
Western Hemisphere	1.4	0.8	1.3
Middle East and Central Asia	1.2	0.5	1.3
European Union	1.3	0.7	1.3
Low-income countries	1.9	0.7	1.4
Middle-income countries	1.4	0.6	1.4
High-income countries	1.2	0.8	1.3

Source: IMF, *Evaluating Government Employment and Compensation* (Clements et al., 2010, p. 13)

Chapter 7 elaborates on income inequality in general which is much lower in developed countries than in developing countries. In using such statistics, one must remember that secondary working conditions and benefits differ from country to country (cf. Organisation for Economic Co-operation and Development, 2008, p. 37; Organisation for Economic Co-operation and Development, n.d.).

Instructions and socialization

How do public officials, public administrators, civil servants and bureaucrats begin their work in the public sector? They might spend their first days getting acquainted with the formal organization, the position of the unit in the organization, the task of that unit and their own position regarding that task. They probably receive instructions from their manager or an experienced colleague about their job. They are introduced to their colleagues and begin work. In addition to doing their job – perhaps being nervous about doing a good job – and getting trained in actually doing a good job, new employees explore their environment. In addition to the formal organization and their position in that organization, they are interested in the informal organization, i.e. the organizational culture. What do their colleagues do? How do they do it? Do they consult one another? Are there conflicts between them? Do they seem stressed? Do they make the newcomer feel welcome? When do they arrive in the office and when do they leave? How do they start their working day? Do they have lunch breaks and do they have lunch at home or at the office, and if it is the latter, do they lunch together, only with colleagues from their own unit or also with colleagues from other units? What are the relations between the colleagues? Are they all males or females or is there a balance? Are their people from different racial backgrounds, age groups, et cetera? How do they communicate? Do they laugh or are they formal and reserved? What type of managers does one have to deal with? Do they chitchat or are they distant and authoritarian? Are they interested in you or only in how you do your job?

A little later one becomes interested in whether one has good colleagues, honest or corrupt, friendly or hostile, lazy or hardworking. It becomes important to know how colleagues and managers react to mistakes, whether there are staff meetings and what is discussed. Can you contradict your colleagues and manager or is that simply not done? In other words, newcomers try to get socialized in the system.

Socialization is the process through which people are integrated into society or an organization through exposure to the opinions and actions of other members of the society or the organization (cf. Sobis & de Vries, 2011). Social psychologists (Goslin, 1999) are interested in socialization as the process that influences an individual's cognitive development until maturation. There are two approaches to the concept. Primary socialization is learning and internalizing social roles and statuses of the groups to which individuals belong, the first group being the family. Secondary socializing agents include play groups and work groups who continue the process through the experience of rewards or punishment to induce proper behaviour.

Social psychology theories build on this idea and advocate active socialization by the organization in order to create professionalism among newcomers by establishing a psychological contract between the newcomer and the organization. It is different from the normal contract that defines the duties, the pay and the legal arrangements. Schein defined the psychological contract as

> "the unwritten expectations operating at all times between every member of an organization and the various managers and others in that organization... . Each employee has expectations about such things as salary or pay rate, working hours, benefits and privileges that go with a job... the organization also has more implicit, subtle expectations, for instance that the employee will enhance the image of the organization, will be loyal, will keep organizational secrets and will do his or her best" (Schein, 1980, p. 22).

Employees can be socialized in a 'right culture'; their behaviour can be latently steered. Such socialization is almost entirely brought about by middle management. Social psychologists usually name them 'experienced organizational members'.

The *contents of such socialization* can vary in terms of 'mental programming', the number of topics to be included, and the relative importance of each. Most scholars agree that it should at least involve the following four topics: (1) acquiring knowledge about the formal features of an organization (i.e. goals, strategy and organizational structure) and its informal features (i.e. organizational culture and power relations); (2) this results in acceptance; learning to function within groups, learning how to do the job and acknowledging the skills and knowledge needed; (3) it also results in the incorporation of work group values, attitudes, norms and understanding which promotes good friendships; that leads to (4) establishing personal change and learning with regard to identity, self-image and motives for doing a job.

Such socialization results in clarity and congruence about what the new employee and the organization can reasonably expect from one another. In social psychology, this is called a *psychological contract* – something that essentially exists in each individual's head, the 'individual beliefs, shaped by the organization, regarding terms of an exchange agreement between individuals and their organization' (Rousseau, 1995, p. 9).

Herbert Kaufman (1960) presented one of the classic examples of such socialization in his description of recruitment and socialization in the forest service in the USA, which aimed at hiring forest rangers who knew what they could expect from the agency and what it would expect from them. He described how the agency did this: self-selecting potential entrants through realistic recruitment campaigns, entrance tests and socialization which concentrated on the technical and administrative aspects of work, a probationary year under the guidance of appointing officers, and through conference, education and training camp attendance. These measures ensured newcomers became acquainted with – and even built an identification with – the agency, and had an intrinsic readiness and ability to conform to its expectations.

In psychological schema theory, it is assumed that such socialization changes how employees process information, use the prior knowledge emphasized during the socialization process, and select criteria in determining what they attend to and how they construct meaning. Intensive socialization provides search criteria which act as pre-existing templates to manage cognitive overload and speed up problem solving (cf. Overell et al., 2010).

Careers

Advancing up in the organization involves acquiring more managerial tasks and a higher managerial position. In addition to one's own tasks, one becomes involved in arranging tasks for other employees in the organization and making decisions. This might seem like the individual is gaining power and responsibility, but more often one becomes more dependent.

Mid-level managers are responsible for ensuring that their units deliver what they are expected to deliver. It includes a division of labour, i.e. planning and dividing it among people, plus hiring new employees, perhaps firing ill-functioning personnel and managing the unit's budget. Managers are more involved with other units in the organization, and will become accountable to the top management for the performance of the unit and perhaps to some degree also to the public. Performance with regard to the content of one's job is the first prerequisite for a mid-level manager.

Simultaneously, one becomes a principal responsible for the effective and efficient functioning of members of the unit and an agent who receives orders from higher management to change focus, procedures, work flows, processes, et cetera. At the same time, the manager is dependent on decisions made by top management as well as on the quality of one's unit. Dealing with this power and these dependencies, choosing when to exercise power and when to refrain from using power, when to be flexible and when to stand firm, are therefore key features of managerial work.

Mid-level management is difficult and requires arduous work because the resources, personnel, equipment and finances needed to accomplish the unit's task are usually insufficient to do the task correctly, efficiently and effectively. In its administrative aspects, one has to use all the elements of the POSDCORB model: plan, organize, staff, direct, coordinate, report and budget. While these take up a significant part of a manager's day, they do not often reflect the reality of managerial work: tasks falling behind schedule, employees getting sick or pregnant, reorganizing, slow funding, employees not doing what they are supposed to do, making time-consuming mistakes or suddenly being moved to a different task or getting a different job, and budget and reporting information arriving too late or never. If management was as easy as the POSDCORB model suggests, it would be straightforward. Therefore, a second key feature of managerial work is dealing with uncertainty, complexity, organizational dynamics and contingencies, and being able to make decisions about what to do when things go differently than anticipated.

An additional problem in the public sector – and especially the public sector in developing countries – is that mid-level management is often management without means. For instance, recruiting, hiring and retaining qualified staff and creating the conditions under which they can do their job effectively is one of the biggest challenges for mid-level managers. Resource dependence in such functions is inherent to the position. This means that others who can provide those resources can exercise power. In the public sector, mid-level managers first depend on those resources in their unit, the quality and experience of the employees and the functioning of the unit. But resources also originate, in part, from decisions made higher up in the organization, from the environment of the organization, and on the success that competing departments and units have in increasing their resources. Because of this dynamic, some scholars view power in organizations as crucial (Pfeffer & Salancik, 1978).

Mid-level managers are not helpless. They have several tools, but their success in applying them depends on their managerial skills. One of the key themes in Public Administration is the necessary skills of managers and leaders.

A basic skill that managers must have is understanding. They must understand themselves – in terms of their own strengths and weaknesses; their staff – their motivation, needs and desires; their unit as a whole – its goal(s), culture and how its people interact; the organization – its structure and the position of their unit within it; and the system in which the organization functions – its funding, its relation to the public and to the environment (Denhardt et al., 2002, pp. 3–4). Without this understanding, managers will have a difficult time achieving anything or influencing organizational behaviour.

Another vital skill is the ability to deal with power dependencies and with uncertainty and complexity. Unit and staff managers need to be informed and able to put things in perspective in order to understand the organization. The latter is facilitated by a good education in, for instance, Public Administration. Being informed in the specific organization one works in can be accomplished by watching and listening, reading reports, participating in meetings, asking questions and communicating. Communicating involves transmitting messages and listening to information provided by others, using various communication channels, talking face-to-face and in group meetings, communicating electronically and verbally and nonverbally, but also being able to read between the lines, because not all information received is actually what the sender intended to convey. Recent research on managers in EU countries pointed out that managers spent much of their time gathering information and keeping up to date through telephone/email and meetings with colleagues. This was their second main daily activity, surpassed only by the time spent on their own projects and directly followed by the time spent on administrative work.

Administration, information gathering and project work are not the only requirements of the manager. Information has to be shared with the unit as well as with top management, and the extent to which this occurs varies in practice. A couple of years ago, research found that the top management of a regional Dutch police force had developed a strategic plan establishing priorities in policing. A year after the plan was developed, the policemen in the streets were still unaware of these priorities. Planning, allocating tasks, coordinating, staffing and reporting are only effective if the information is shared with those involved.

The same goes for the interpersonal role of managers, which should be effective in motivating the unit and addressing the needs and desires of the staff. The extent to which managers fulfil such interpersonal tasks varies, in Hofstede's terms, according to their masculinity/femininity and their ideas about power distance (not only of the organization, but also of individuals). In some organizations personal matters are simply not discussed, while in other organizations managers care about the personal lives of their employees, exchange information about personal lives, and consider personal circumstances when planning, assigning work and evaluating employee performance.

The manager also has to represent the unit in meetings with higher management and laterally with other mid-level managers in order to protect the unit's interests. Finally, a mid-level manager needs to convey orders, new strategies and new tasks, as decided by higher management, to the unit as a liaison.

At this point, a reference to Chapters 2 and 4 is necessary. Those chapters distinguished between public and private goods and public and private management. This distinction also affects mid-level managers in the public sector and distinguishes them from mid-level managers in the private sector. Allison described the characteristics that can specifically impact the work of public managers in contrast to the work of private managers. He mentions, among others, that the time perspective in government is dictated by the political agenda and is thus shorter than in the private sector, as is the length of service of politically appointed managers. He also sees difficulty in measuring performance in the public sector, as well as conflicts between the civil service and political appointees, as a major distinction between the public and private sectors. Furthermore, Allison points to the different criteria for successful actions, emphasizing equity in the public sector and efficiency in the private sector, and the unique and more open position of the public sector in relation to the public, press and media, pressure groups, and the legislative branches (cf. Allison, 1992).

Not all scholars in Public Administration accept the validity of this contrast. In the lower ranks in particular, the differences are not believed to be as definite. As a result, there have been numerous calls for transferring private sector practices to public administration under the guise of NPM (see Chapter 2). In daily work, this resulted in applying pay-for-performance schemes in which employees are paid on the basis of their performance, instead of receiving fixed remuneration, and in the outsourcing and privatization of the some of the functions of government as well as in public–private partnerships.

This transference requires a substantially different approach from mid-level managers; it must focus on efficiency instead of precision and effectiveness, on creativity as opposed to conformity, and on external communications and viewing citizens as consumers as opposed to internal communication and viewing the political level as the consumer.

From a comparative perspective, it is questionable whether such change can be successful in every country, irrespective of its dominant culture. Especially in masculine, collectivist countries with a high power distance, a high-risk avoidance and a long-term perspective, the practices of NPM may conflict with the existing public sector culture.

Cultural differences might explain why the NPM reforms found their pioneers in OECD countries that scored low on masculinity, collectivism, power distance and uncertainty avoidance, such as Australia, New Zealand and Scandinavian countries. Such innovations are also likely to encounter institutional resistance in countries with a strong Weberian tradition of organizing the public sector according to the ideal type of bureaucracy to the greatest degree possible, because of the conflicts between the rule of law and the rule of commerce, between precision and efficiency, and between public service motivation in the public interest and a private sector motivation at the service of profit maximization.

Top management and leadership

Characteristics of good leadership

Many books have been written about the characteristics of good leadership. Recent empirical studies and theoretical models in Public Administration have tried to determine the best leadership practices that contribute to achieving organizations' major objectives. In the middle of the twentieth century, social scientists developed 'great man' theories focusing on leaders' typical traits and personality. These traits were sought in a leader's personality, background, who he or she is, what he or she possesses, his/her behavioural traits and the degree to which those traits fit the environment. Although research is inconclusive in finding a relationship between personality features and good leadership, personality does matter in practice in being accepted as a leader. This applies to such *features* as height (tall people seem to have a natural advantage), weight (for instance in Nauru in the Pacific), strength (preferring men over women), appearance (colour of hair), lineage (being of noble birth or from a certain tribe) and gender (in many cultures, males are preferred as leaders above women).

The same goes for *possessions*, such as wealth, intelligence and control of means of production, e.g. being a successful business entrepreneur. Although research does not point to a causal relation, people are inclined to think that if someone has proven successful in their personal affairs, he or she is likely to be successful in caring for society.

Later, the actions of a good leader are deemed to be important: do they show the right combination of decisiveness, democratic procedures and inclination to delegate; is there a balance between task orientation and people orientation, and between steering, supporting and facilitating? Finally, research has shown that different situations demand different behaviour from leaders. A leadership trait may be very important in one specific context, but not in another (Fiedler, 1964). This depends on the structure of tasks and the power of a leader, but also on the type of staff, the history of the organization, the culture of the organization, the quality of the relationships between leaders and their followers, the nature of the changes needed and the accepted norms and culture within the organization. 'Situational leadership' theory has suggested the nature of the task in terms of uncertainty and the nature of the followers in terms of their maturity are central variables in defining the required type of leadership (Hersey & Blanchard, 1979). According to this theory, it is not leadership itself that determines the success and productivity of an organization, but the fit between the characteristics of leader and what is required given the specifics of the context and the people, i.e. followers, the leader has to work with.

Recent research on leadership and management

One of the main themes in recent research is how leaders, managers and staff cooperate and work together and how this affects the performance of each individual, each department and the organization as a whole. This research involved developing novel theories on leadership, management and followers, as well as the pursuit of transformational leadership – also in management – that supports and even initiates administrative reforms.

Transformational leadership

In one research approach, leaders are viewed as determinative forces of organizational and societal change and reform, conforming to Sidney Hook's saying that, 'all factors in history, save great men, are inconsequential'. According to this approach, leaders are essential in giving the organization direction and meaning and in bringing about organizational change. This research focuses on leadership tasks, leadership roles, leaders' formal position and authority, interpersonal roles, information roles and their decision-making roles in transforming organizations. One of the claims is that organizational change occurs and is successful if, and only if, there are transformational leaders who are able to change the organizational culture, are willing to adopt best practices in order to achieve results and who master organizational resistance to change. Such leaders are said to be characterized by charisma, i.e. they provide vision and sense of mission, instil pride, gain respect and trust; inspiration, i.e. they use symbols to focus efforts and express important purposes in simple ways; intelligence, i.e. they promote rationality; an employee orientation, i.e. they are sensitive to individualized considerations, giving personal attention, treating each employee individually, coaching and providing subordinates with advice; and being frontrunners in addressing and communicating high expectations.

Leadership substitutes and neutralizers

Recent research, however, also argues that the importance of leadership traits is context dependent and that the behaviour of followers is as important as leadership. This has resulted in a second approach which searches for leadership tools that not only direct and steer and reward and punish but result in a close relationship between leaders and followers. This personal relationship is based on trust and care, with attention to the emotional aspects of working in the public sector. It allows the employees some autonomy, can result in trust between leaders and followers, and can eventually result in self-managed teams. It involves increasing performance by giving more responsibilities to the staff and inducing them to be cooperative and helpful towards one another. The role of managers in this view is to coach the individual employees and the self-managed and semi-autonomous teams. This stream of research points to the need for theories about followers instead of theories about leaders and the identification of *substitutes* and *neutralizers* for leadership. 'Substitutes' refers to the importance of the characteristics of employees, i.e. the skills, knowledge and competence needed for doing their work as professionals who require little supervision. Two requirements for such professionalism are that (1) the professionals know the organization in which they are working and their own duties and roles very well and preferably even better than their managers do, and (2) that detailed regulations and policy documents exist. 'Neutralizers' concern the characteristics of the tasks, making a distinction between complex and risky tasks, in which leadership and management are indispensable, and simple, repetitive tasks that employees can master without extensive training or direction.

Ideas about effective leadership and management in relation to organizational performance are changing from emphasizing general characteristics of both groups to focusing on the required features as a function of the characteristics of the employees and tasks to be managed and led.

Back to the classics

There are scholars who return to and investigate ancient wisdom in different cultures as found in the writings of Kautilya, Lao Tse and Confucius, in religions such as Shinto, Islam, Judaism, Christianity and Buddhism, and in practices of traditional leadership and early writings on the leadership and management of public administration. They investigate whether we perhaps took a wrong turn or if we have missed something important for present-day Public Administration (cf. Drechsler, 2013b, 2015). One of the results of this retrospection is the development of the idea of the neo-Weberian state in Europe, promoting the return to the classic ideas of Max Weber. In the theory on the neo-Weberian state, the role of the state is reaffirmed as the main facilitator of solutions to the new problems of representative democracy as the legitimating element, of administrative law in preserving the basic principles, and of the idea of a public service with a distinct status and culture in contrast to private services. The theory adds 'neo' elements, such as a necessary shift from internal to external orientation, consultation with and direct representation of citizens' views, a modernization of the relevant laws, a greater orientation towards the achievements of results rather than merely correctly following procedures, and a professionalization of the public service (Drechsler, 2005b; Pollitt & Bouckaert, 2004).

Conclusions

This chapter addressed the internal operation of public organizations and focused on the people working inside such organizations. The previous chapter argued that the bureaucratic organizational model is dominant in the public sector; this chapter pointed to differences in recruiting, working conditions and career advancement. Cultural differences are a crucial consideration, and they greatly influence how the public sector operates and how the public service works in different parts of the world. A key theme in Public Administration is investigating the actual nature of cultural dimensions and assessing their impact and the level of government they influence.

The same questions can be asked about management and leadership. What are the crucial dimensions of management and leadership, and how do they affect the working and performance of public organizations?

A substantial amount of research has been done and many possible answers have been provided to these questions. They are key themes in Public Administration because the answers are not unequivocal. In spite of all of the research, discussions continue about the nature and impact of culture and leadership; on what is needed to advance from lower management through middle management and top management to leadership; and on what is needed to perform in each of these positions in an effective way.

Another basic question is to what extent leaders dominate and exert power to steer their organization, its culture, its performance and the environment of the organization, e.g. society. If they are dependent on developments in society and if they have to adapt to the type of organization they are leading, its culture, its employees and its environment, leaders need effective instruments for soft steering. Such instruments need to attain, for instance, a personal relationship between leaders, managers and employees, and need to enable the creation of self-managing teams by searching for substitutes and neutralizers for management and leadership.

What management instruments work best and what leadership traits are needed depend on numerous factors, including the motivation of public sector officials. The different types of motivation are the central topic of the next chapter, which focuses on what goes on inside the minds of public administrators.

Further reading

Bovaird, Tony & Löffler, Elke (eds) (2009). *Public management and governance*. London: Routledge, Taylor & Francis.

Denhardt, Robert B., Denhardt, Janet Vincent & Aristigueta, Maria P. (2002). *Managing human behavior in public and nonprofit organizations*. Thousand Oaks, CA: Sage.

McMahon, J. Timothy (ed.) (2010). *Leadership classics*. Long Grove, Ill: Waveland press Inc.

Rainey, Hal G. (2009). *Understanding and managing public organizations*. New York: John Wiley & Sons.

't Hart, Paul (2014). *Understanding public leadership*. London: Palgrave.

Yukl, Gary (2010). *Leadership in organizations*. (7th edn/Global Edition). Upper Saddle River, NJ: Pearson Prentice Hall.

Chapter 6

What motivates government officials?

This chapter addresses what goes on inside the minds of public officials. What motivates them to work for government and what do they strive for within the context described in the previous chapters? Are they personally motivated to provide collective goods in an effective and efficient manner, in order to contribute to the basic function of government and to solve collective problems, and are they personally engaged to help citizens and make their society a better place? Or is their work for government motivated by less noble factors, such as earning a decent salary in exchange for as little effort as possible, and an opportunity to establish a swift career, thus increasing their income, status and power? Or do they see their function in the public sector as a means to further their personal interest, resulting in an abuse of their position with corruption and fraud as the consequence?

How have these questions been answered in the past? In many countries, being asked to work in the public sector is seen as an honour. Being entrusted to become a public official is seen as being able to meet the high expectations from political rulers as well as the citizens in resolving collective problems, and so indicative of a person's dedication and integrity, skills and knowledge, loyalty and trustworthiness. Such a job gives a person a feeling of being able to make a difference for society and to contribute to the public good instead of only advancing selfish interests. Obtaining such a position is something to be proud of, for the person involved as well as his or her family. No additional motivation is needed as there is an inherent gratification in being asked to assist in making society a better place.

In economic reasoning another viewpoint dominates. The idea of rational *homo economicus* (economic man) implies that everyone's behaviour is guided by the desire to maximize their own benefits, that people prefer more to less (of something desirable), although the question 'more of what' varies among people (cf. Chapter 7 of this book). In a democracy, politicians want to maximize the votes they get during elections in order to increase their influence. In a free market system, private business wants to maximize profit and sales volumes. What do public administrators try to maximize? Does eighteenth-century philosopher Adam Smith's quote apply to the work of public officials, '*It is not from the benevolence of the butcher, the brewer, or the baker that we expect our dinner, but from their regard to their own interest*'? (Smith, 1776, Book 1, Ch. 2., I. 2. 2) If so, what does it imply for the functioning of government?

The application of economic reasoning to the public sector has resulted in a theory that suggests that public officials are budget maximizers; they strive to maximize the growth of their department or organization in order to increase their own opportunities for career advancement, higher salaries and increased status and influence. Political reasoning views public officials as power maximizers; they try to maximize information asymmetry between them and their (political) leaders in order to prevent political decisions that would be prejudicial for them individually or their organizations. Sociological reasoning has resulted in an alternative for the *homo economicus*, namely the *homo reciprocans* who needs and wants to cooperate and compromise with others in order to improve the environment in which he lives, and who in order to balance what is best for himself and society:

> [C]omes to new social situations with a propensity to cooperate and share, responds to cooperative behavior by maintaining or increasing his level of cooperation, and responds to selfish, free-riding behavior on the part of others by retaliating against the offenders, even at a cost to himself, and even when he could not reasonably expect future personal gains from such retaliation (cf. Bowles et al., 1997, p. 370).

The least noble motivation for working in the public sector is to view it as a means to maximize personal profit by abusing one's position through fraud and corruption. Public officials provide public goods and services to citizens, such as permits, garbage collection, health care and education, and they collect taxes and can impose fines, which puts them in a power position vis-à-vis citizens. One way to abuse such a position is to take advantage of it by asking for a personal remuneration in exchange for a swifter permit, a lower fine, lower taxes, more frequent garbage collection, extra attention in school or higher placement on a waiting list in a hospital. In some parts of the world, a doorman of a ministerial department can even make a good living by accepting gratuities for directing citizens to the right office or locating someone in a ministry who could assist them.

Although corruption is different from maximizing a budget or acting as an economic man, what all of these theories have in common is that they consider individuals to act mainly in a self-centred and egoistical manner with little regard for the common good, i.e. the provision of public services. This chapter argues that this self-centric view of public officials is one-sided, and while it may be present, it is only one of a number of possible types of motivation to work in the public sector. It also argues that in the design of the public sector, many precautions can be and have been built into the system to prevent unethical behaviour. Finally, it points to recent Public Administration research aimed at finding ways to counter such self-centred behaviour and to promote administrative integrity.

Terminology

Job motivation

Job motivation concerns the disposition of employees to acquire a certain job and to put a certain amount of effort into the tasks involved on that job. Ideally, all employees would be fully engaged and would put their time, knowledge and skills into the job without needing to be ordered around. A number of different factors can encourage such motivation. Scholars hypothesize a causal relationship between organizational rewards in terms of wages, and collegial support, organizational commitment and job engagement (cf. Saks, 2006).

A proper reward is the first factor. Working in an organization is a form of social exchange in which efforts put into the job are exchanged for remuneration, either in the form of fixed wages or through pay for performance. Such rewards do not have to be limited to wages. Other rewards include the gratification of making a career, the feeling of contributing something of value or contributing to the common good and the satisfaction of seeing the visible effects of one's work. Being proud to do such work and getting recognized for one's contribution – by colleagues, managers or the public – can also be a type of reward.

Factors that influence work motivation can also be found in job-related conditions, such as the skill variety required, the significance of the task, task identity, positive feedback, the status involved in being responsible for the task and the autonomy required by the task.

A third group of (de)motivators can be found in contextual conditions, the interpersonal relations with colleagues and managers, the extent to which they are cohesive, or adversely the degree of bullying, discrimination, corruption and fraud. Additional contextual conditions include job security, physical surroundings, i.e. one's own desk or office, and the number or quality of support staff.

The degree to which each factor is deemed important might be as culturally dependent as leadership and management styles. Nonetheless classic theorizing suggests a general hierarchy in the factors that determine work motivation. In the 1940s, Abraham Maslow proposed a hierarchy of needs with five levels. In the first level, employees work primarily because of the need to earn money to buy food (wages). If that need is satisfied, they strive for safety (job security) – level 2. After that, they seek belonging (task identity, organizational identity) – level 3. Subsequently, they desire esteem (pride) – level 4. If all previous needs are satisfied, they pursue self-actualization – level 5, as seen in skill variety, task significance, autonomy and responsibility, professional development, et cetera. Most of the research in the field of work motivation is done in organizational psychology, and research outcomes have shown that Maslow's hierarchy of needs is weak in predicting job motivation.

Maslow's hierarchy was the precursor to other theories that seem to explain job motivation somewhat better and relate job motivation to management style. Frederick Herzberg (1959) distinguished between motivators (satisfiers) and hygiene factors (dissatisfiers). The first do determine job satisfaction and are about achievement, recognition, growth possibilities, the content of the work, the level of responsibility and career advancement. The latter do not as such promote job satisfaction, but if they are absent or insufficiently available this can result in demotivation. These are determined by the company policy and administration, the kind of supervision, interpersonal relations, working conditions and salary.

Herzberg criticized leaders and managers trying to increase job satisfaction by only removing the factors that make for dissatisfaction. This theory is still in use, but was severely criticized for not distinguishing between different types of employees, some of whom are intrinsically motivated (by the contents of the work) and others who are primarily externally motivated (by the working conditions and salary).

This distinction was made in the most popular theory, the one developed in the 1960s by Douglas McGregor. He distinguished management styles based on Theory X and Y. Theory X assumes that employees want to put as little effort into a job as possible in order to earn their salary, and they need constant external incentives to perform, such as continuous supervision, controls and orders. These incentives in the form of rewards and punishments force people to do what is expected through threats or intimidation. In terms of Maslow's hierarchy of needs, level 1 is emphasized because individuals only work for money; they are unwilling to maximize their cognitive, emotional and physical resources in the performance of their work; and they are cynical and inefficient.

In Theory Y, managers expect employees to be self-motivated and – within the right conditions – employees will do their utmost to do their work and improve upon it. Doing a fine job is a sufficient reward in itself. In terms of Maslow's hierarchy, levels 4 and 5 are emphasized since employees are engaged in their work. The specialness of working for the public sector with a public service motivation is sufficient to have public officials doing their utmost to work as efficiently and effectively as possible.

William Ouchi added Theory Z based on Japanese management systems. Theory Z emphasizes the job motivation produced by creating loyalty between employees and their organization. In this theory, the organization not only takes care of its employees by giving them a job for life, but it takes care of their housing, entertainment, sports clubs, et cetera, in order to establish a strong and long-term connection between the employee and the organization. In terms of Maslow, levels 2 and 3 are emphasized. Employees are committed to their organization and its goals.

Job motivation of employees, including public officials, cannot be reduced to one dominant type and cannot be reinforced by just one motivating factor. However, motivation can easily turn into demotivation if one or a couple of motivating factors is completely absent.

Morality

Morality relates to the values and norms people adhere to at the individual level. Values are about moral principles, prescribing the general boundaries of one's actions, whereas norms are the more pragmatic translation of such principles into habits, traditions and laws, i.e. formal and informal standards of behaviour maintained by a society at large or by its government. Many norms are established in written documents, such as laws and regulations, but norms can also be orally transmitted from generation to generation, resulting in varying mores like 'be honest', 'don't steal or kill', 'show respect to the elderly', 'wash your hands before eating', 'walk the talk', 'show courage and wisdom', 'be humble and moderate', or in other cultures 'show character', 'be ambitious', and in completely individualized societies 'do it your own way'.

Moral principles are more abstract. An example of a moral principle is the classic golden rule as laid down in many a holy scripture, emphasizing reciprocity: '*Hurt not others in ways that you yourself would find hurtful*', as it is formulated in Buddhism, or similarly: '*Do to others what you would want them to do to you*' as it is formulated in the Bible, or as Confucius is said to have said: '*Never impose on others what you would not choose for yourself*', or in the Quran '*Wish for your brother, what you wish for yourself*'.

A general moral principle aimed at prescribing the boundaries of one's freedom is the harm principle as formulated by John Stuart Mill in his book *On liberty*: '*The only purpose for which power can be rightfully exercised over any member of a civilized community, against his will, is to prevent harm to others*' (Mill, 1859, Ch. 1, I. 9).

Moral principles can also emphasize equality, such as the two justice principles John Rawls formulated in his book *A theory of justice*. They read, '*Each person is to have an equal right to the most extensive total system of equal basic liberties compatible with a similar system of liberty for all*,' and '*Social and economic inequalities are to be arranged so that they are both: a) to the greatest benefit of the least advantaged, and b) attached to offices and positions open to all under conditions of fair equality of opportunity*' (Rawls, 1971, p. 302).

A third type of moral principle emphasizes the mutual connection between individuals and their relation to society, as in the Kantian principle '*One should act only according to that maxim by which one desires that it should become a universal law*,' and '*One should treat humanity always as an end and never as a means only*,' (Kant, 1785/1993, p. 30) or as given in the dignity principle as laid down in the Universal Declaration of Human Rights, which states in article 1, '*All human beings are born free and equal in dignity and rights. They are endowed with reason and conscience and should act towards one another in a spirit of brotherhood*,' and as in the communitarian principle as formulated by Amitai Etzioni in his book *The new golden rule*. It reads, '*Respect and uphold society's moral order as you would have society respect and uphold your autonomy to live a full life*.' (1996, p. xviii).

Public Service Motivation and morality of public officials in reality

So, like every organization, the public sector needs public officials who are engaged and place a high value on morality. Since the seminal work of Perry and Wise in 1990, job engagement in public administration is widely investigated under the label of Public Service Motivation (PSM). PSM is an 'individual's orientation to delivering service to people with the purpose of doing good for others and society' (Hondeghem & Perry, 2009, p. 6) and it consists of three dimensions: (1) intrinsic job motivation, or job engagement, (2) compassion, the desire to help other people, and (3) self-sacrifice, a willingness to invest in charity (Cowley & Smith, 2013).

In reality the scores for these PSM indicators vary, and no country has a majority of public officials who adhere to all three dimensions. In many countries, especially countries with a low GDP per capita – but also in many OECD countries – intrinsic work motivation and the disposition to self-sacrifice, as measured by being active in charity, is rather low. Even in countries with a very high GDP per capita, such as Norway, Sweden, Switzerland and Canada – in which public sector officials need not worry about their income – only slightly more than half of the public officials are predominantly intrinsically motivated. The only indicator that reveals rather high scores for public sector employees is the indicator for compassion. A majority of public officials show a disposition to help others, in poor as well as affluent countries. Nonetheless, PSM measured along these three dimensions is more frequently found among public officials than among private sector employees (cf. Cowley & Smith, 2013).

What does the research reveal about the morality and integrity of public sector officials? Morality is especially important for them because government designs and decides on laws and regulations (behavioural norms), imposes them on people, applies them in its policies and upholds them in its institutions; therefore, the individuals working inside government should be exemplary in abiding to the rule of law. Not all public administrators exhibit such morality, as seen in several indicators of corruption of public officials. The World Bank conducts comparative research into how governments control corruption, conventionally defined as the exercise of public power for private gain. That research points out that there are huge differences in the degree to which governments are able to control corruption.

There are regional differences, especially related to wealth and state of development, with high-income OECD countries scoring best. There are also differences within regions. For instance, Northern and Western Europe scores better than Southern and Central Europe; the Chilean, Uruguayan and French Guyanese governments are perceived as less corrupt than other Latin American governments; Botswana, then South Africa and Namibia, which follow closely, hold relatively similar positive positions in Africa, as do South Korea, Japan and Singapore in Asia. Their research also shows a division within the Middle East with governments experiencing relatively less corruption in the countries in the centre of the region, and countries in the northern and southern parts of the Middle East (Yemen, Iraq and Syria) exhibiting relatively more corruption.

Types of bureaucrats based on their motivation and morality

These variations in motivation and morality among civil servants have formed the basis of a substantial amount of research in Public Administration, and some of this research has included attempts to classify different types of officials within the bureaucracy. In the 1960s, Anthony Downs suggested a classification related to job motivation. He did not include a classification for individuals who are purely public service motivated, because, in his view, there are no employees who act without some self-interest. This is similar to what was written in the introduction to this book:

> [G]overnment is based on a duality of power struggles and ambitions of individual rulers, their attempts to stay in power, and their willingness to start political conflicts over that power, and the justified need for a government of a population that accepts that power – through which that power is transferred into authority – because the people get something back in return, namely public goods.

According to Downs, the following types of public officials can be distinguished:

- Purely self-interested officials, motivated almost entirely by goals that benefit themselves rather than their bureaus or society as a whole. These are further divided into two sub-types:
  - Climbers pursue increased power, income and prestige.
  - Conservers are predominantly concerned with maintaining their own security and convenience.

- Mixed-motivated officials have goals that combine self-interest and altruistic loyalty to larger values:
  - Zealots are loyal to relatively narrow policies or concepts, such as the building of aeroplanes. They seek power for its own sake and only effectuate policies to which they are loyal.
  - Advocates are loyal to a broader set of functions or to a broader organization than zealots, and they are impartial when it comes to decision making regarding the policies they adhere to and decisions inside the organization. They become less impartial and support their organization and policy area when it comes into conflict with other organizations.
- Statesmen are loyal to society as a whole and they enjoy having influence on important issues (cf. Downs, 1967, pp. 5–6).

As for morality and corruption, Transparency International distinguishes between grand corruption and petty corruption. Grand corruption consists of 'acts committed at a high level of government that distort policies or the central functioning of the state, enabling leaders to benefit at the expense of the public good' (Transparency International, 2011). At the end of 2010, this type of grand corruption became visible with the publication of embassy cables by WikiLeaks. According to this information, many heads of government and state and their friends all over the world stashed billions of US$ in Swiss banks, originally public money that could also have been used to solve society's problems. Such incidents are not concentrated in one specific part of the world, but can be found globally.

Petty corruption is 'the everyday abuse of entrusted power by low- and mid-level public officials in their interactions with ordinary citizens' (Transparency International, 2011). Examples include bribery, embezzlement, patronage and nepotism. Bribery seems to be most frequent among that group of public officials that is expected to uphold the law, namely the judiciary and the police. In this regard, it is interesting that police detectives featured in television series and mysteries have been used as examples to distinguish between types of bureaucrats on the basis of their morality. Thus, in 2001, William Gormley (2001) distinguished moralists, pragmatists and rogues, based on their inclination to disobey orders, tell lies, break the law, look the other way and abuse the power inherent to their position (cf. Sobis et al., 2011).

Dividing public officials along the two dimensions of motivation and morality does not necessarily result in an overlap. The detectives in mysteries and TV series all have a high public service motivation and are mostly successful in solving murder cases, irrespective of whether they are moralists, pragmatics or rogues. In the public sector, the troublemakers are those public officials who only have their narrow self-interest in mind and simultaneously act like rogues.

Consequences of deficient motivation and morality

When some public administrators in some governments lack motivation and morality, this can be detrimental to all levels of government. First of all, it is bad for the effective and efficient provision of collective goods. Public goods will not be provided according to the needs in society, but according to the desires of public officials promoting the work of their own department. In an organization with corruption or low morale, scarce resources are not utilized optimally but wastefully. If some individuals bribe officials to move higher up a medical waiting list, the wait time for others on the list is automatically longer. A study in the Philippines found that corruption delays and reduces the vaccination of newborns, discourages the use of public health clinics, reduces satisfaction of households with public health services and increases waiting times at health facilities. In Ghana, it was found that due to corruption most people do not have access to quality health care because of inadequate facilities, roads are in deplorable states, and funds are not available to build schools and hospitals. And in Nigeria, due to widespread poor service delivery and corruption, 53% of Nigerians have no access to clean drinking water and electricity service is uncertain – in spite of the fact that government has spent billions on these issues. In addition, the infant mortality rate is still high, life expectancy is still low (between 47 and 51 years) and adult literacy is still very low (cf. Kayode et al., 2013).

Public officials who break the law damage citizens' trust in government and their willingness to transfer their authority to government to make binding decisions on their behalf. Ultimately, this will reduce citizens' inclinations to subject themselves to such a government.

Personal and departmental interests of public officials at each level of government may distort the substantive arguments about the optimal division of tasks and responsibilities between the branches. Budget-maximizing dispositions among public officials could prevent the transfer of power and authority between governmental levels, and can thus frustrate decentralization efforts.

Self-interest, low motivation and questionable morality also affect the environment inside bureaucracies, which was the key theme of Chapter 4. In large organizations, as public organizations typically are, no one knows exactly what is going on at each level, and therefore information exchange and communication are vital. In the 1960s, Anthony Downs pointed out that the communication process is extremely vulnerable to the proclivities of each official to screen information so as to benefit him- or herself as well as to serve the formal functions of his or her bureau (1967, p. 10). Public officials can suppress or minimize information that is unfavourable to their own performance or abilities and only distribute favourable information. They can de-emphasize information that is likely to displease their superiors and exaggerate information that would make their superiors happy. They can select what information goes higher in the organization; this information might suggest that present policies should be continued, or if the officials are 'climbers', that more resources should be devoted to their bureaus. Downs concludes, 'All officials are motivated to suppress information indicating that their own functions or bureau sections should be diminished in importance or given fewer resources' (p. 11).

With regard to management and leadership – the key theme in the previous chapter – low motivation and morality of employees call for more controls, more hierarchy and more reporting, thus increasing what is generally seen as the downside of bureaucracies and promoting a kind of leadership and management that unfavourably alters how leaders, managers and staff function and cooperate, and how this, in turn, affects the performance of each individual official, each department and the organization as a whole. This poses a dilemma in balancing such controls, the necessity to steer and direct unmotivated and immoral employees and the feasibility of using substitutes and neutralizers for leadership.

Last but not least, low motivation and morality adversely affect other colleagues who may be highly motivated and moral. Low morality, self-centred dispositions and corruption may be seen as infectious diseases which could easily spread through an organization if not treated. If your non-performing colleague has the same salary as you, but gets away with living the easy life, driving nice cars and living far beyond what he or she could afford on his or her wages alone, it becomes tempting to copy his or her behaviour or to leave the organization that allows such conduct. In the end, it results in Gresham's law, namely, '*Bad money drives out good money*' (Selgin, n.d.). This saying has become famous, because the word 'money' is interchangeable with many other words, such as 'motivation' and 'morality'.

Solutions for improving motivation and morality

Because of the negative consequences of low morality and motivation, there has been substantial research in discipline and action in the practice of public administration in order to effectively strengthen motivation and combat corruption. This section presents some of the most common instruments used for achieving these goals. It begins with four suggestions aimed at directly improving the motivation and morality of individual public servants, and continues with solutions that indirectly impact individual behaviour through establishing an institutional, organizational and societal context that furthers the motivation and morality of the individual.

Codes of conduct

The first step is to clarify what is expected. In practice, this is often outlined in codes of conduct as broader sets of principles that are designed to inform specific laws or government actions and written to guide behaviour by exemplifying the fundamental principles and values of public service (cf. Gilman, 2005). They are meant to inform public administrators about what is expected of them, to focus public administrators on doing the right things for the right reasons and to act as a professional statement expressing the public service's commitments to a specific set of moral standards (Gilman, 2005).

Countries all over the world have produced such documents. The code of Hammurabi in old Sumer, written down about 4,000 years ago, is considered the first code of conduct, and it suggests that low morality and motivation in public office is not a new problem. This code states that:

> If a chieftain or a common soldier, who has been ordered to go upon the king's highway for war does not go, but hires a mercenary and if he withholds the compensation, then shall this chieftain or soldier be put to death, and he who represented him shall take possession of his house. (Constitution Society, n.d., p. 8)

Clearly, there must have been individuals in these early times who flouted the moral code by letting others do the work and keeping the remuneration themselves. Hammurabi wanted his code to be for all time, making his inscriptions a code of conduct for his successors:

> If such a ruler have wisdom, and be able to keep his land in order, he shall observe the words which I have written in this inscription; the rule, statute, and law of the land which I have given; the decisions which I have made will this inscription show him; let him rule his subjects accordingly, speak justice to them, give right decisions, root out the miscreants and criminals from this land, and grant prosperity to his subjects. (Constitution Society, n.d., p. 39)

Nowadays codes of conducts are found in many countries but they differ enormously in content. There are even variations within countries with common heritage, countries in the British Commonwealth, for example. In 2007, New Zealand adopted a code of conduct that could be printed on one page. It stated that anyone working in public services organizations must be fair, impartial, responsible and trustworthy. It elaborates that fairness required citizens to be treated fairly and with respect, and that public servants should be professional and responsive, must work to make government services accessible and effective, and must strive to make a difference to the well-being of New Zealand and all its people. Impartiality meant that political neutrality was required to enable citizens to work with current and future governments, carry out the functions of the organization, unaffected by personal beliefs, support the organization to provide robust and unbiased advice and respect the authority of the government of the day. As for acting responsibly, 'We must: act lawfully and objectively use our organization's resources carefully and only for intended purposes treat information with care and use it only for proper purposes and work to improve the performance and efficiency of our organization.' And trustworthiness was specified as follows:

> We must: be honest, work to the best of our abilities, ensure our actions are not affected by our personal interests or relationships never misuse our position for personal gain, decline gifts or benefits that place us under any obligation or perceived influence, avoid any activities, work or non-work, that may harm the reputation of our organization or of the State Services. (State Services Commission, 2007)

In South Africa, the 1997 Code of Conduct for Public Servants requires all employees to comply with its terms, and it emphasizes the faithfulness of employees to the republic and the honour of the Constitution by putting the public interest first, showing loyalty to the government of the day, and by promoting the unity and well-being of the South African nation. Other aspects of motivation and morality elaborated in this code of conduct are service to the public, relationships among employees, the performance of duties, and personal conduct and private interests. With regard to the latter, it even states that during official duties, employees must dress and behave in a manner that enhances the reputation of the Public Service and act responsibly as far as the use of alcoholic beverages or any other substance with an intoxicating effect is concerned (Public Service Commission South Africa, n.d.).

One of the more recent codes of conduct was produced in 2013 by the College of Policing in England, and it aimed to support each member of the police in delivering the highest professional standards in their service to the public. It emphasizes nine principles: accountability, integrity, openness, fairness, leadership, respect, honesty, objectivity and selflessness, which according to this college should 'underpin every decision and action across policing'. It also advises the police force not to use illegal drugs, not to consume alcohol when on duty and not to engage in sexual conduct or other inappropriate behaviour when on duty (College of Policing, n.d.).

The oath of office

Codes of conduct are based on ideas from the Enlightenment which assumed that if you tell people what is expected of them, they will act accordingly. Many view this assumption as naïve. A somewhat stronger commitment is having public officials swear an oath of office. Swearing an oath of office is believed to be more binding because it is a personal commitment of the official in relation to a deity and/or to his or her conscience. Breaking an oath is therefore more serious than violating a code of conduct. If the pledge is part of a ceremony, it can create a feeling of pride in belonging to the profession and can be a double-edged sword.

Like the code of conduct, oaths of office have been around for a very long time. In ancient Greece, it was tradition to swear an oath of office. The military swore the Athenian oath and medical doctors were required to swear or promise according to the Hippocratic oath. Individuals applying for citizenship, public offices, offices in the judicial sphere, assemblies and councils had to swear an oath of office. Even the individuals who managed the formulation of oaths had to swear an oath. Although the exact wording varies, in many countries heads of states, heads of government, members of parliament, judges and military service members have always been required to swear or promise that they are loyal to the state, its constitution and to the head of state, to promote the general welfare of the population, and to defend the integrity and independence of their state. Oaths of office are increasingly needed for public officials in general. In Costa Rica, public servants must answer the question: 'Do you swear before God and promise the Country to observe and defend the Constitution and the laws of the Republic and faithfully fulfil the duties of your office?' In Germany, federal officials have to state: 'I swear to protect the Basic Law for the Federal Republic of Germany and all valid laws within the Federal Republic and to fulfil my duties of the office faithfully ... so help me God/so I promise.'

Ethics training programmes

Socio-psychological experiments among students have concluded that promising not to cheat just before making a test does, in fact, diminish the amount of cheating during the test. The same experiments also point out, however, that these effects are temporary and do not affect the propensity to cheat on a test administered a couple of months later; so the promise should be repeated on a regular basis. This is one of the reasons why many organizations send their employees to ethics training. This is partly a component of the socialization process of newcomers, but it helps these employees understand and manage the ethical dilemmas they will be confronted with in their position.

This idea also has its roots in ancient civilizations. In its style and format, Confucian readings are indicative of this early concern with teaching and training. According to Confucius, this was especially needed in the field of virtue, emphasizing the importance of being steadfast in allegiance or duty and getting to know oneself for the sake of others, thereby positively influencing motivation and morality. Nowadays, there are numerous training institutes and training programmes in nearly every country that strive to improve the motivation and morality of their public servants.

In Japan there are said to be between 100,000 and 200,000 people a year who participate in the ethics training workshops held by ministries and government offices. This translates to one or two persons out of every three national public officials in regular government service receiving some sort of training pertaining to ethics every year (Takada, 2012). As their ethical board puts it, 'Merely providing the knowledge is not going to be sufficient from now on. It is becoming more and more important to help public servants develop their ethical mindset to one that encompasses the behavior, attitude and work ethics that are more appropriate for someone serving the public' (Takada, 2012, p. 103).

China started an 'Ethics in Government' campaign in 2011 requiring public servants to receive systematic and compulsory training in ethics over the following five years, according to the State Administration of Civil Service. *China Daily* wrote: 'The ethics campaign ... will be "of great significance" in lifting public confidence in the government and in civil servants as well as in consolidating the Party's governance position' ('Civil servants to be taught ethical behavior', 2011).

Ethics training has transformed from a cottage industry to a major enterprise (cf. Menzel, 2007). Still, there is cause for scepticism about its effectiveness. The emphasis in most training is on discussing practical cases, pragmatics, rules, laws, regulations and compliance. Moral reasoning and virtue theory, which are needed to fundamentally change the mindsets of officials, are rarely addressed. These subjects are emphasized in many ethics courses in Public Administration.

Changing the costs and benefits

Given that personal interests induce low job motivation and corruption, some governments have tried to influence the benefit–cost ratio in a way that makes ill behaviour less profitable and more risky. They do this by passing and upholding strict laws and sanctions. This is also a practice that dates from ancient times – recall the soldier in the code of Hammurabi.

Singapore is known for its tough punishment of corrupt officials in the public and private sectors: dismissal, imprisonment, repaying ill-gotten gains plus an equal amount in fines, reversal of the rule of evidence placing the burden on the accused to prove that he or she did not act in a corrupt manner, forbidding exchanging 'red packets' at Chinese New Year as an excuse for bribes, being considered guilty even if the accused had no power, right or opportunity to return a favour to the bribe giver and the prosecution of Singaporean citizens for corrupt offences committed outside Singapore (Hin, n.d.). The idea is that such punishment will make potential offenders think twice before committing the offence.

It is also possible to change the cost–benefit ratio into a positive reinforcement by rewarding employees who are highly motivated and exhibit highly moral behaviour. This can be done by setting targets and production quotas and basing wages on how much work each employee personally completes (pay for performance). Managers can provide additional remuneration to employees who are highly motivated by letting them advance through the pay grades more rapidly, providing them with bonuses, allowances and promotions, and awarding them with honours such as 'employee of the month'.

In spite of the effectiveness of such measures, it can have a downside when taken to the extreme, as in the former Soviet Union under Stalin. A pay-for-performance model in its extreme form resulted in gross inefficiencies, manipulation of figures, overproduction, continuous negotiations over wages, quotas and skills, and an irrational division of labour, in which skilled and motivated people refused to work when their production was dependent on the production capacity of machines, instead of on their own efforts.

Changing the work environment

The previous four policies are aimed at directly influencing the individual employee. There are also indirect measures that attempt to increase job motivation and morality through adapting the work environment, i.e. the context in which individuals work. This primarily concerns the role of managers and leaders, who are increasingly required to show exemplary behaviour, act as role models for their employees and address such issues regularly in staff meetings.

Second, the role of colleagues is important. An organization could respect and reward whistle-blowers – employees who report unacceptable situations inside their organization or the malpractice of their colleagues. One can require employees to promise to report the misconduct of fellow officials and even hold colleagues, or the whole department, responsible for the misconduct of individual officials. One of the main problems is that this type of reporting is often seen as snitching instead of concern and care, and has a negative impact on the interpersonal relations within teams.

Many governments have opted for formal internal and external controls. Internal controls involve the (re-)introducing of checks and balances, in which decisions are not made by one individual official but with the approval of a number of officials or different departments. A disadvantage is the resulting red tape and increased paperwork and the time it takes for decision making.

External controls can be established through an ombudsman, auditor, external accountant, counsellor, fiduciary, confidential officer for integrity or through civic integrity watchdogs and consumer organizations.

At a higher level, solutions are sometimes sought in reorganization. If corruption is perceived to be widespread in central government, decentralization might mitigate this issue. If corruption is perceived to be high at all government levels, privatizing service delivery might be considered.

Recent research into motivation and morality

It is hard to avoid the conclusion that motivation and morality are high on the agenda of many governments. Some governments have been successful in combating corruption and others have been successful in achieving high performance. Nonetheless the search for effective and efficient instruments to accomplish the goal of both high job motivation and high morality continues because, as was argued earlier, most instruments for solving serious dilemmas end up creating different serious dilemmas.

Recent developments in Public Administration follow two strands. What both have in common is that they suggest that the primary problem of the public sector is that its role is too often criticized and minimized, resulting in low motivation and morality. The second problem is that the public sector is too inert and closed. The solutions for the public sector would be, first, to regain its leading position in solving societal problems by improving its performance, and, second, to increase its integrity by opening up and giving a more significant role to citizens and their shared interests, thus improving the transparency, accountability and professionalism of the public service. This could have multiple effects; internally it would make low motivation and morality among public servants more obvious and transparent and would itself be a source of increased motivation and morality for public servants, and externally it would provide more public goods and services that citizens need based on their shared interests, as opposed to what the public sector wants to supply based on the self-interests of its employees.

Performance measurement

In order for governments to regain their leading position, many agree that public sector performance needs to increase. In order to achieve this, performance measurement and management systems have been introduced in the public sector resulting in increased empirical research into how to manage performance in an optimal way and alternative ways to measure performance.

Performance can be measured in relatively simple ways, for instance by measuring the timeliness of the public sector in answering letters and handling requests for permits, by the percentage of crimes that are solved, the number of students earning a diploma, the amount of police on the streets, et cetera. It can also be done in a more sophisticated way by benchmarking or comparing governments, organizations and departments for efficiency – usually viewed as the ratio between inputs and outputs, and effectiveness – usually measured by the ratio between process and outcomes, however difficult this is. In this research, performance is considered a result of individual motivation, competence and the ability to perform as allowed within an organizational structure; but performance management is the ability to increase the motivation to perform and to improve competences by pointing to training needs, and can result in furthering the organizational reform needed to improve on the conditions for optimal performance.

Performance measurement and management systems might appear to be straightforward and simple, but there are many dilemmas involved. For instance, the introduction of a pay-for-performance system as an alternative for fixed remuneration. The more one produces, or the more output, the higher the pay. One of the problems is measuring this type of performance because not all tasks are easily measured, and performance is not only dependent on individual motivation and competence but also on how the organization is structured. As for measuring performance, there is a saying: 'what is relevant is difficult to measure and what is measured is often not that relevant'. This idea when combined with another common saying 'what you measure is what you get', can easily result in the pursuit of irrelevant goals, just because they can be measured. For instance, if universities receive funding based on the number of graduates, there is a risk that they will even let students graduate who haven't earned the required credit. Measuring the quality – the knowledge, skills and attitudes – of graduates would be more relevant, but it is also more difficult.

Another dilemma is what to measure: inputs, throughputs, outputs, outcomes or feedback. If one just measures output and tries to maximize it, this could negatively impact quality care and could result in more standardization and less attention to the details of cases, less attention to regulations and decreased customer orientation.

The international financial crisis in the first decade of the twenty-first century was said to have been caused by financers who were only concerned with maximizing output, i.e. the number of mortgages and loans, because output determined their bonuses. It resulted in high-risk loans and mortgages which led to increased default and the ultimate bankruptcy of a number of financial institutions. Similar issues appear when focusing on minimizing inputs – the costs of providing collective goods and services. Minimization of inputs can result in faulty processes, output and outcomes, and can negatively affect learning and improving or feedback on one's work. The same goes for one-sidedly maximizing processes, outcomes and feedback.

Unfortunately, the search for performance improvement is not always directed towards improving the effectiveness and efficiency of the whole system – from input to throughput, output, outcomes and feedback. Too often, performance measurement and management is only focused on one part of the system, and the secondary effects on other parts of the system are ignored. Moreover, it is challenging to simultaneously measure and manage those values that are crucially important to the public sector.

A subsequent problem is that even if one successfully measures performance, how is this success translated into public policies, the performance of individual officials, departments or to the functioning of organizations, because actual performance is often contingent, i.e. dependent, on the circumstances while the performance measures are mostly *a-contextual*.

Notwithstanding these issues and dilemmas, performance measurement and management have increased dramatically in public sector organizations all over the world. Partly this is due to new possibilities in the technological infrastructure of generating and analysing performance data as well as the research done to make performance measurement more sophisticated and the institutionalization of performance management due to the popularity of NPM which emphasizes the presumed benefits: enabling budgeting, control, steering, learning and evaluation by management and increasing the motivation of individual officials by performance-related rewards. It has resulted in extensive monitoring of and reporting on the performance of the public sector (cf. Van Dooren & Van der Walle, 2008). On the one hand, this serves to increase insight into the performance of public officials, departments and organizations, but on the other hand, it also increases the administrative burden and sometimes fails to provide a valid picture of what is going on. Performance measurement is, therefore, not always sufficient as a tenable argument for a system of pay for performance. The merits of performance measurement and management are still widely investigated in Public Administration. At present performance management is conceived as consisting of three phases in establishing: (1) detectors, the information gathering and measurement of performance, (2) directors, the setting of targets and standards, and (3) effectors, incentives to modify the behaviour of employees in order to make them meet the targets and standards (Hood, et al., 2001; Walker et al., 2010).

Alternatives to performance measurement and management by way of extensive monitoring, reporting and monetary incentives have also been explored. One path of research suggests that leaders and managers can stimulate their employees through 'soft steering', i.e. better socialization through which managers and employees know what to expect from one another and what is expected of themselves, and through which an internalized public service motivation can be established.

Good governance

With regard to enhancing the morality and integrity of the public sector, a current debate focuses on the concept of good governance and what constitutes good governance. The concept was originally viewed as an alternative for government. According to scholars in the late 1980s and early 1990s, government had to accept that society cannot be steered or controlled hierarchically, and that government functioned badly anyway. Governments needed to be replaced by societal actors and their goals accomplished through non-hierarchical societal networks. From this line of thinking emerged the idea of New Service Delivery. Its focus is on a government that serves instead of steers, and controls society by helping citizens articulate their shared interests (Denhardt & Denhardt, 2003). Citizens and their public needs were to be at the forefront, and civil servants were expected to build relations based on trust, collaborate with citizens, focus on community values, professional standards and citizen interests, and aim for shared leadership (Denhardt & Denhardt, 2003, p. 553 ff).

Since the second half of the 1990s, the role of government and the creation of good institutions by government returned to the agenda when scholars realized that there had to be a government to create security, protect property rights, reduce societal problems and take back a leading role in controlling and steering societal developments; how this is managed is crucial. This resulted in criteria for good governance, such as governance on the basis of democracy (voice and accountability), legality (rule of law) and political stability, and that governments should act effectively, based on regulatory quality and control of corruption (Kaufmann et al., 2003).

The idea that how a government acts, i.e. the internal process, as opposed to what governments actually do, i.e. their external workings, is critically important to the good of society and constitutes the main hypothesis of the theory of good governance. The hypothesis is increasingly disputed (Kettl, 2002) because it aims to optimize processes and throughput, i.e. what governments need to do to put their internal organization in better order, while according to its critics good governance should be about output and outcomes for society, which are dependent on more than throughput and internal organizational processes (Grindle, 2004).

Conclusions

This chapter addressed what goes on inside the minds of public administrators, especially regarding their motivation and morality. It started with the specialness of the public sector and the necessary commitment and trustworthiness of public officials. After discussing terminology, it explored several theories on job motivation and morality, distinguished types of administrators according to two dimensions and presented an overview of public service motivation and integrity inside government all over the world.

Subsequently, it was argued that the three indicators of public service motivation – intrinsic job motivation, compassion and a willingness to invest in charity – are indeed more frequently found among public officials than in the private sector. Nevertheless, there are substantial differences in the extent to which public officials possess the right attitudes, and many solutions have been suggested and applied for improving job motivation and morality. These solutions produce many other dilemmas, resulting in a trade-off of one problem for another. As a result, explaining what determines the motivation and morality of public officials, and evaluating the feasibility, effectiveness and efficiency of instruments meant to improve motivation and morality, remains one of the key themes in Public Administration.

Some solutions include performance measurement and management, including pay for performance as an alternative for fixed remuneration, and establishing good governance by emphasizing the need for democracy and rule of law, by making processes transparent and administrators accountable and diminishing fraud and corruption within the public sector.

These solutions can also be seen as an initial example of policy making, in which serious problems are addressed by formulating goals and finding instruments to achieve those goals. This chapter addressed an internal organizational problem, and analysed possible solutions. It demonstrated the complexity of problem solving in terms of defining goals and applying appropriate instruments. The instruments vary in effectiveness, and some even produce serious negative side effects.

Further reading

Berman, Evan M. & Bowman, James S. (2012). *Human resource management in public service: Paradoxes, processes and problems*. Thousand Oaks, California: Sage.

Condrey, Stephen E. (2010). *Handbook of human resources management in government*. San Francisco: Jossey Bass.

Denhardt, Janet V. & Denhardt, Robert B. (2003). *The new public service: Serving, not steering*. London, New York: Routledge.

de Vries, Michiel S. & Kim, Pan Suk (eds) (2014). *Value and virtue in public administration*. London: Palgrave.

Huberts, Leo (2014). *The integrity of governance*. London: Palgrave.

Menzel, Donald (2012). *Ethics management for public administrators*. London, New York: Routledge.

Pollitt, Christopher & Bouckaert, Geert (2011). *Public management reform. A comparative analysis –new public management, governance, and the neo-Weberian state*. Oxford: Oxford University Press.

Walker, Richard M., Boyne, George A. & Brewer, Gene A. (eds) (2010). *Public management and performance: Research directions*. Cambridge: Cambridge University Press.

Chapter 7

When do public decisions result in optimal outcomes?

Understanding the internal processes of government is especially important because governments make decisions that affect all of us, and these processes partly explain why public decisions are made in the way they are. A classic example is the decision by King Priamos of Troy to bring in the wooden horse that was left behind by the Greeks, who had seemingly retreated after years of siege. Priamos might have had good intentions, i.e. acquiring a beautiful trophy that would make its citizens proud of their victory, but it proved to be a devastating decision for the city; the Trojan horse was filled with Greek soldiers who conquered Troy during the night. Was this decision made due to the fact that Priamos was king and the government structure allowed him to make the decision on his own? Was the government organization perhaps structured in such a way that sound guidance from his advisors could not reach him, or did it reach him but he ignored it? Was it perhaps due to a Trojan culture in which power distance, masculinity, collectivism, uncertainty proneness and short-term strategy dominated? Or was it something inside the head of this king – personal pride, elation, and disregarding the public interest – that made him decide as he did?

This chapter provides a basic understanding of decision making in the public sector. Not all decisions involve life and death, as in the case of the Trojan horse, but even minor public decisions affect citizens. Politicians decide on laws and regulations based on the advice of their civil servants and their political culture. The individuals who work in public administration often provide the analysis and possible alternatives for resolving social problems. The decision process is not over once a law is passed; the law still has to be implemented, and this implementation involves a number of additional decisions that are often left to public administrations. When a king, president or prime minister decides to go to war, the decision might be based on the advice of those surrounding him, but once the decision is made the combat strategy and actual fighting is carried out by the military.

Decisions are about which issues to address and which issues to ignore, how to accomplish behavioral change, and what should be compulsory and what should be prohibited. The Code of Hammurabi was one of the first documents describing how decisions should be made in different circumstances. It included guidance on property ownership, marriage and divorce, debts and contracts, criminal justice, inheritance and monogamy. For instance, a man could not be convicted of theft unless the stolen goods were found in his possession, and a debtor did not have to pay rent for a year if his crop failed because of storms or droughts. Nowadays, governments make similar decisions about pensions, marriage law, social benefits, infrastructure, taxes, health care, education, crime, etc., thus deciding who gets what, when and how (cf. Lasswell, 1950).

This chapter focuses on the process of decision making. It discusses decision making before policy making because each phase of the policy-making process is shaped by public decisions. Public decision making involves defining collective problems. It involves determining whether a problem is critical enough to require the development of a public policy. It is about deciding public policy content and goals and the instruments used to achieve those goals. It concerns who is responsible for implementing the policy as well as the amount of human, financial and material resources allocated to implementation.

This chapter addresses the factors that are important in decision-making processes and why decisions sometimes succeed and at other times fail in achieving their goals. Human variables, institutional context and societal and political context contribute to the difficulty of making rational, let alone optimal, decisions. Despite good intentions, mistakes and suboptimal decisions are the most likely outcome, and the situation in public administration is no different. Public Administration as a science has tried hard to understand what goes wrong and to provide solutions for these problems.

Decision making is one of the key themes in Public Administration because it is the focus of substantial research. This research focuses on the impact of substantial and strategic rationality, the potential and limitations of technical decision support, and the role of knowledge versus vested interests in such processes. The chapter begins with some words on terminology.

Terminology

Public decision making

Decision making can be defined as the intentional and reflective response to perceived needs (Kleindorfer et al., 1993, p. 3). Public decision making differs from individual decision making in that it targets societal needs as opposed to personal needs. Such decisions involve more than just the consequences for an individual's life. By definition, public decisions include many individuals since they concern adopting laws and developing, defining and executing public policies. These decisions can involve the allocation of resources for education, health care, social housing, infrastructure, the police, fire brigade and army. Governments make decisions about steering and guiding the behaviour of individuals and societal groups as well as providing for the safety, security, socio-economic development and well-being of the populace. Decisions can be focused on children, consumers, interest groups, stakeholders, government agencies, schools, hospitals, business leaders, et cetera; government is heavily involved in steering its society and its people, and this results in thousands of public decisions every day.

Public decisions are made by (groups of) public officials acting in the public interest, including politicians, judges, policy makers, teachers, firefighters, police officers, benefit officers, et cetera; and examples of public decisions include those made in educating and grading students by teachers, those made in warning, fining or arresting lawbreakers by police officers, and those made by firefighters in deciding the best way to extinguish a fire.

Rationality in decision making

When is a decision rational? Kenneth Arrow described rationality in decision making as preferring more of something desirable to less, as maximizing some utility function under a budget constraint, and as completely exploiting information and using sound reasoning in making and acting upon required decisions (p. 390). Business people act rationally when they prefer more profit over less profit, collect all the information needed, and analyse this information in a sound way in order to make the right decisions and to act accordingly. In lotteries, ordinary people prefer a larger prize and higher probability of winning over a smaller prize and a lower probability of winning, and they act rationally when they compare different lotteries and choose

the former. Politicians act rationally when they prefer more supporting votes over fewer and make decisions that increase the number of
supporting votes. According to Downs (see Chapter 6), statesmen try
to maximize their influence on important issues. In the same sense,
environmentalists prefer a clean industry over a less clean industry and
will support decisions that accomplish this. Classic socialists judge
political decisions based on their effects on income distribution, and
they prefer more equality over less equality, while liberals tend to
prefer more equality in individual opportunities over less equality in
individual opportunities.

In order to understand what decisions will be optimal in each of
these situations, people need to be well informed and make sound use
of that information in their reasoning. This is not as straightforward
as it seems. Especially in public decision making, the outcomes of decisions are determined not only by the decision maker but also by the
decisions made by other actors, while the decisions of all the actors
together determine the actual outcome for each of the actors involved.

A complicating factor in this regard is that multiple types of rationality, or utility functions, exist. Max Weber distinguished *instrumental
rationality*, which is the calculated choice to achieve what one wants to
achieve; *substantive rationality*, where value orientations such as those
found in religious, ethical or aesthetic motives dominate one's decisions; *affect rationality*, in which feelings and emotions dominate one's
decisions; and *traditional rationality*, in which decisions are especially
determined by customs and habits and the desire to maintain the status
quo. Later scholars added other types such as *social rationality* where
reference groups determine decisions and *legal rationality* where decisions are determined by what the law prescribes.

Different rationalities can result in the same decision, for example attending church, mosque or temple. Some might attend because
they view this as a means to an end, i.e. going to heaven in the after-
life (instrumental rationality). Others might attend services or pray
because this is an end in itself (substantial rationality). Still others
might attend because of the emotions and feelings that such attendance
evokes (affect rationality), because they are brought up in this tradition
by parents and grandparents (traditional rationality), because they live
in a neighbourhood where everyone attends and in which there is social
control (social rationality), or because it is obligatory, being prescribed
by law (legal rationality).

More often, however, varying rationalities result in different preferences, conflicting interests and multiple and contrary optima of public

decisions for the different stakeholders. This can be seen in the relatively simple decision of whether to build a paid parking lot near a shopping centre. The interests of the entrepreneurs/shopkeepers, residents, commuters, environmental interest groups, automobile club, the administration, and political parties are likely to collide, and a second-best, compromise decision about which nobody is completely satisfied may result. Kenneth Arrow's 'impossibility theorem' would apply in this case, namely, no rank-order decision system can be designed to satisfy all 'fairness' criteria simultaneously. Even when participants vary in their preferences, a decision by a group of decision makers will reflect the preferences of each of its participants, and there will be no dictator who imposes his or her preferences on the other participants. According to Arrow this type of 'fair' decision making is, by definition, impossible.

Optimizing decision-making processes

It is no wonder that one of the main issues in decision-making theory is what is an optimal public decision. The classic answer is that a public decision is optimal if it maximizes expected utility by maximizing the positive effects for society and minimizing negative effects. An optimal decision is possible if the decision maker acts by way of so-called *synoptic rationality*. This implies that the decision maker compares as many alternative options as possible based on as many criteria as possible, determines the magnitude of the effect of each alternative on each criterion, calculates the probability that the effect will occur, and weighs each criterion according to its importance. In this case, one can calculate the 'expected utility' of each alternative, rank them according to expected utility and decide on the optimal option; that is, the one with the highest expected utility. Being fully informed, considering as much information as possible and calculating the costs and benefits of each alternative would, in this way, result in optimal decisions.

Given the multitude of rationalities, it is not surprising that this process has many problems. Stakeholders may agree on the alternatives, and perhaps also on the criteria and the effects of each alternative on every criterion as well as on the probability that such effects will occur, but when it comes to weighing the different criteria, disagreements arise.

Furthermore, there are technical issues. Information about certain effects, probabilities and alternatives might be unavailable and decision makers may be unable to compare more than a limited number of alternatives and criteria. A technical problem is how to weigh, for instance, the effects of alternative locations of a parking lot, when one criterion is measured in monetary terms (financial costs), another in the number of places (in square metres), a third is measured in units of time (waiting time) and still another in decibels (noise produced). These measurements are contestable and dependent upon economic, political, ideological and cultural features, as well as the issue of how to weigh options when the costs are paid by one societal group while the benefits are accrued by another. This issue of weighing criteria has been dealt with by numerous scholars, especially with regard to decisions involving the redistribution of resources when those who benefit are not those who bear the costs.

According to economist Wilfredo Pareto, a decision is optimal when there is no alternative decision which could improve the outcomes for some societal groups without deteriorating the outcomes for others.

In his classic *A theory of justice*, John Rawls suggested an ethical solution to the distribution issue. According to Rawls, distributional justice is crucial and a public decision is optimal if it provides the greatest benefit to the least advantaged members of society, and if it optimizes the equality of opportunity among the citizenry. Although one might assume that on the basis of the first part of this rule, a redistribution of incomes is always required to level out income differences, this is not necessarily the case. Politicians with differing ideologies adhere to Rawls' theory because just as huge income differences can be disadvantageous for the poor, so can complete income equality since it could disincentivize economic growth and result in lower income for all. Furthermore, the second part of his proposal fits rather well within neo-liberal notions of justice.

Many other, different guidelines for optimizing decisions have been proposed. It is partly because of the existence of such very different decision guidelines that the optimization of public decision making is far from easy. Some have concluded that the ideal has to be considered unattainable and should be abandoned in favour of alternative models of decision making. Others have argued that although optimal decision making might be unfeasible, one should keep trying to develop instruments to approximate the ideal and find solutions for the limitations of such decision-making processes. This chapter addresses arguments made by two contending parties and provides an overview of the research in order to find solutions to improve public decision making.

Factors inhibiting decision making for optimal outcomes

Before discussing recommendations for improving decision-making processes, this section presents a brief overview of the factors that underlie problems in decision-making processes. These are found in (1) individual deficiencies for rational action, (2) the institutional context in which public decisions are made, and (3) societal structures in which conflicts of interests and power disparity impact public decision making.

The individual decision maker

The first constraint to optimal decision making is the limited ability of individuals to act rationally. Individuals rarely know their individual preferences, and they don't always know how to gather and analyse information in order to make rational decisions. For instance, many students will prefer ice cream that costs 50 cents over ice cream that costs $1 when asked to choose between the two. But when a third choice of ice cream that costs $2 is thrown into the mix, they tend to switch their preference to the $1. This is strange because adding irrelevant alternatives should not impact rational decision making. Additional examples might illustrate that people in general – and also those working for government – do not always act rationally and that they tend to make mistakes. If someone asks whether more or less than 20% of African nations are members of the United Nations, an individual might guess 40%. When that same person is asked whether more or less than 50% of African nations are UN members, he or she might increase their response to 70%.

These examples demonstrate that adding irrelevant alternatives to a choice is in no way irrelevant for individual decisions, that opinions are anchored by the parameters of the choice, and that people have a conservatism bias in that they prefer to retain an existing situation over altering it, no matter the consequences. Furthermore, psychological experiments point out that people are risk averse, have no idea about probability calculus, and give, for example, more to charity if told about a single victim of poverty than when confronted with graphs showing the seriousness and degree of poverty in general. Individuals tend to perceive nonsensical arguments as strong and valid simply because they concur with the conclusion, and they may see options as more dissimilar when they analyse them simultaneously instead of separately. Finally, people tend to interpret events differently depending on how they are framed. In a country with one million adolescents, stating that 5% of them regularly commit criminal acts is much less disturbing than stating that 50,000 adolescents in that same society regularly commit criminal acts, even though both sentences are identical. There are many other biases in how individuals tend to make decisions that diminish the probability of optimal decisions. All of these tendencies in decision making explain why people keep buying lottery tickets even though the probability of winning a prize and the prize itself are very small (cf. Kahneman, 2011).

These same tendencies apply to public decision makers. In the process of decision making, they are likely to be susceptible to bias and to make mistakes. They make mistakes in gathering, interpreting, analysing and using information, and they make mistakes in their implicit calculation of the expected utility of alternatives. However, these sub-optimal public decisions affect society at large, so they come under public scrutiny and are likely to be criticized. Public decision making is a serious business because these decisions are funded by taxes and they affect the citizens who pay those taxes. Given the substantial number of public decisions made each day, it is relatively easy to find examples of flawed decisions thus creating a negative image of the public sector. As a result, much research in Public Administration is focused on preventing decision bias and optimizing public decision making despite the human deficiencies at doing so.

Before addressing solutions suggested by the research, one must analyse the context of public decision making. In addition to human deficiencies, the specific context in which public decisions are made also affects the possibilities for optimizing them. This context is partly found in the institutionalization of decision-making processes and partly in the features of the broader societal context in which public decisions are made. The remainder of this section focuses on these two dimensions.

The institutional context

From a Public Administration perspective, one of the problems in the fully rational approach to decision making is the assumption that decisions are made in a vacuum without incorporating the institutional context – the whole of formal and informal rules and regulations as given in the organizational structure, cultural features and historical developments – and the situation as it exists and develops. Given this institutional structure, some scholars in Public Administration even doubt whether public decision makers should strive for optimal decisions by considering as many alternatives and solutions as possible. Based on the *logic of consequentiality* they question whether decision makers should always try to maximize the positive effects and minimize the negative effects of their decisions. They suggest that, in reality, because of institutional boundaries, this position is unattainable and therefore different behaviour is desirable.

This was first suggested in the late 1940s by the later Nobel laureate, Herbert Simon, who argued that inherent to decision making is the notion that it *cannot* be based on full information, that the rationality guiding it is by necessity bounded and that decision makers are more often 'satisficers' than 'optimizers'. Institutional boundaries limit the ability, time and resources available to decision makers and they are thus confined in their attempts to make completely rational decisions (Simon, 1957). Simon argued that instead of seeking to be fully informed, decision makers have to find a way out by comparing – not simultaneously but sequentially – only a limited number of alternatives, basing their judgments on a limited number of criteria and opting for the first alternative they judge to be *satisficing* in that it meets a certain threshold (Simon, 1947). They do not need to search for more optimal solutions once a satisficing solution has been found.

In the 1950s, Charles Lindblom continued this line of thinking by arguing that decisions are embedded within previous decisions, existing practices and cultural and political institutional settings. In his view, these boundary conditions result in decisions which mostly conform to the existing institutional setting and minimally deviate from previous decisions. Hence, decisions tend to reconfirm existing arrangements or result in incremental change. *Incrementalism* – changing the current situation step-by-step – dominates in the public sector and revolutionary decisions that result in significant changes in the organization or the policies of that organization are rare. According to Lindblom, incrementalism is a smart solution since it allows for: flexibility – the changes that result from the decisions are so small that they can be reversed; learning – if there is any change in outcomes, one knows that the incremental change caused it, since it was the only thing changed; and reduced risk and resistance – since the changes are so small, their impact will be small so there will be few objections to them.

In the 1970s, Cohen, March and Olsen (1972) argued that the institutional setting of decision making is more determinative for the kind of decision made than the rational balancing of the estimated effects of decisions. Their analysis is more radical than those of Simon and

Lindblom. In their perspective, expertise and information do not influence decision making at all; at least, much less than expected in classic theories on decision making. According to them, research and information gathering preceding decision making is mostly symbolic and is only conducted to signal to the external world that decision making is taking place as it is ought to, namely controlled by information. Decision-making processes are viewed as positive if this appears to be case, and decision makers are eager to suggest this vision. Since decision makers know that optimizing decisions are unattainable, the only alternative is to act as if decisions have been made rationally. According to Cohen, March and Olsen, people in the public sector make the decisions they make because they think it is proper to make those decisions and not because of a rational balancing of the effects of such decisions. In their view, the *logic of appropriateness* dominates public decision making.

In the late 1980s, March and Olsen specified this kind of decision making in their classic volume *Rediscovering institutions* (1989). They argued that decisions in organizations often emerge randomly as the consequences of anarchical processes best described using the metaphor of the *garbage can* – in which problems, solutions, opportunities and actors flow independently and randomly until they accidentally merge and result in completely unpredicted decisions. March and Olsen further suggest that most theories about decision making suffer from reductionism, utilitarianism, instrumentalism and functionalism that falsely explain decisions by the logic of consequentiality. In this view, decision making is all about well-calculated intentional choices based on personal preferences in which the estimates of the merits of alternatives and their expected consequences play a central role. From their point of view, the main question is whether there is an alternative model that is better able to explain decision-making processes and that poses a real alternative for reductionism, utilitarianism, instrumentalism and functionalism.

The alternative approach focuses on the institutional structure in which decisions are made. This institutional structure provides order and influences decisions. Between the context in which decisions are made and the motives of individual actors, there is the institutional setting. This is a collection of standard operating procedures and structures that define and defend values, norms, interests, identities, and beliefs and decision-making methods (March & Olsen, 1989, p. 17). Within such institutions, routines, procedures, conventions, roles, strategies, organizational forms and technologies are crucial. This institutional structure results in rule-bound decisions involving nothing more than matching a specific situation that needs to be handled to the demands of one's own position (March & Olsen, 1989, pp. 22–23). Decisions are based predominantly on obligations and responsibility, instead of being deliberate choices. This is what March and Olsen mean by *the logic of appropriateness* as distinguished from *the logic of consequentiality*.

They go even further, to state that not only decisions, but also perceptions, interpretations and preferences are shaped by institutions, resulting in the situation where individuals often only see what they are expected to see and like what they are expected to like. People prefer to see what they like, like what they see, like the people they trust, and see what others whom they trust see (March & Olsen, 1989, p. 44). All of these institutional constraints result in decisions devoid of any consideration to the consequences of those decisions. March and Olsen's perspective has been widely applied. Kingdon (1995) developed the most well-known application with the *multiple-streams model* – using the same idea of independent flows of problems, solutions and actors, which accidentally merge and create a window of opportunity for decision makers – as a theory on how public policies come about.

Critics of these theories have emerged (cf. Bendor et al., 2001). They argued that the assumption of the existence of four streams which flow independently, namely problems, solutions, actors and opportunities, is difficult to imagine because these four streams cannot exist independently. They are necessarily linked; sometimes by definition, sometimes by mere logical reasoning. March and Olsen's approach, which emphasized organizational anarchy in decision making, has been criticized for paying too little attention to the role of power, leadership, authority, control, delegation and incentive systems within organizations that try to achieve as much congruence and coherence as possible. A third criticism focuses on the ambiguity and lack of clarity of many of the phrases March and Olsen use. These critics state that it is unclear what March and Olsen meant when they defined their logic of appropriateness. They asked whether the logic of appropriateness is not just a selfish interpretation of the logic of consequentiality, in which a narrow range of effects is taken into account, namely only those effects that refer to consequences of the decision for the decision maker's own position.

Finally, the critics of the garbage can model would like to see more nuances. While they agree that decision makers are never able to take all information into account, differences among decision makers exist to the degree that they are rule followers or information followers. According to the critics, how decisions are made has to be investigated empirically and depends, in part, on the *aspiration levels of decision makers*. From the standpoint of the critics, they question whether we have analysed behaviour thoroughly when we conclude that decisions have been made without using the information at hand, and that they are based solely on customs, norms and the position the decision maker was in.

The extent to which decision makers are inclined to search for information, fully use the information available and strive for optimal decisions might also be dependent on *characteristics of the decision-making process*. What are the rules and regulations that prescribe the decision-making process? Is the decision made by a single individual, by a small group or are multiple actors involved? Who has access to the decision-making process and who does not? Is the decision-making process transparent? Are the decision makers accountable for their decisions? The prevailing idea in Public Administration is that when decision-making procedures are more strictly regulated and more transparent, when the decision makers are accountable for their decisions and when the number of stakeholders involved in the decision-making process increases, decision makers will be inclined to gather more information and to try to make sound analyses based on that information. In such cases, they will be more meticulous in their decisions, because they are obliged to do so by law, because they might be forced by the participants in the decision-making process to support their decision and because decision makers might fear the consequences of being publicly accused of having made a wrong decision. Furthermore, the participation of stakeholders might in itself be a source of information.

The extent to which decision makers are inclined to seek information, fully use the information available and strive for optimal decisions might, besides the aspiration level of decision makers and the features of the decision-making process, also be dependent on *the nature of the issue* the decision maker faces. In this regard one can distinguish issues on the basis of the number of available alternatives determining whether a compromise could be negotiated; whether they are mainly pragmatic and principled, which is determinative for the kind of argumentation needed to make the decision; and whether they concern the provision of collective goods or the reduction thereof, determining whether either a lose-lose, a win-lose, or a win-win solution is the likely outcome. Dependent on the nature of the issue, decision makers might be more or less inclined or forced to search for specific information and to make a sound analysis of that information before making a decision. Other aspects of the issue that might explain whether or not a decision maker is inclined to search for information are the urgency of the issue, which might pose time constraints, and the difficulty and costs involved in gathering and analysing additional information, which might pose capacity constraints.

The societal context

Many scholars suggest that the causes of suboptimal public decisions can be found in societal structures and governments' position in that society. Two extreme perspectives are the Marxist and the neo-liberal views. In the first theory, the class structure of societies with a wealthy upper class and a resource-poor working class results in an unequal distribution of power and conflicts of interests; and these, in turn, result in decisions that are only profitable for the former and are disadvantageous for the latter. Public decisions always involve conflicts of interests and those in power positions, especially economic power, make or encourage decisions that serve only their own interests. Such theories conclude that public decisions most often serve the interests of the business community.

A classic example of these theories is found in *Marxism*, where it is assumed that governmental decisions will always support the dominant class and serve the interests of the owners of capital instead of the working class. More generally, this socio-economic perspective suggests that societies are layered, and that decisions made by the elites – the upper class – will be biased because the elite's interests are different from the interests of the masses and the former's power is decisive in decision making. The generative mechanisms are that the elite, or upper class, has better access to the decision-making process, can, because of its position in society and its wealth, impose its will on the public decision makers, is better able to organize itself and can better express its preferences and promote its specific interests. The elite also has the resources to back its interests with supporting evidence, commissioned research and by gathering additional information, at least to a greater degree than the masses can. Therefore public decisions will be biased in favour of those who already are advantaged.

A rather different explanation for suboptimal decisions in public decision making is that they are public and, therefore, by definition, suboptimal. This point is raised by neo-liberalists, proponents of a limited government and of *laissez faire* policies. The less a government regulates, steers and dominates the economy, the better for a society's economic development. Whether just or not, these theorists base their view on the writings of the eighteenth-century Scottish moral philosopher *Adam Smith*. Smith pointed to the 'invisible hand' through which the pursuit of selfish, individual interests is not contrary to but, in an aggregated form, helpful in furthering the public interest. According to Smith, one should always be suspicious of any attempt by governments to propose new laws and regulations which limit people, industry and commerce in the pursuit of their self-interests, because this more often is detrimental than advantageous for society as a whole. Modern interpretations of this theory conclude that government should limit itself to protecting private property and maintaining security, but should not steer or regulate business or wages because this would distort the socio-economic development of the country and negatively impact the *wealth of nations*, referred to in the title of Adam Smith's classic book.

In addition to these explanations that emphasize societal structure and the position of government, the nature of decision making can also be explained by how the public sector is internally organized. First of all, the regime type might influence decision making because the number of actors (and their interests) involved in public decision making is likely to vary per regime type. In palace-type regimes, decisions need the consent of a single individual, the monarch. In club-type and temple-type regimes, public decisions are usually made by a small cohesive group of individuals who share some belief or have been trained in a similar way (military regimes) or have a common background and education (as in, for instance, colonial regimes). In democracies, the interests of different societal actors, or at least the majority thereof, are usually represented in decision-making processes through legislative/parliamentary and/or presidential elections. Nonetheless, some democracies are characterized by a winner-takes-all mentality, in which the party that lost the elections will rarely be involved in decision-making processes. In such cases, elections can result in an administration composed of members of the winning party with all important positions in the country concentrated in the hands of individuals with similar convictions and ideas.

This brings us to the issue of group decision making and its merits compared to individual decision making. On the one hand, concentrating decision-making power in the hands of a single actor makes the decision-making process easier and faster. Single actors do not have to negotiate, they can choose the optimal option in their view, and they do not have to consider and aggregate different opinions in a single outcome. They can hire experts to collect information or ask advice, but they can also ignore that advice and abstain from considering information.

This is the easy life of the dictator who is authorized to make whatever decision he or she wants.

Making decisions single-handedly also has its drawbacks. Individuals have limited knowledge of the needed combination of organizational theory, path dependencies, economics, law, management, politics and social sciences. They will also be limited in their specialized skills and will almost certainly not be experts in strategic thinking, coordinating, staffing, finance and budgeting, organization, management and planning. Last but not least, individuals can handle uncertainty, dynamics and complexity only to a limited degree. Hence, there are good reasons for group decision making especially when the issues at stake are far from simple.

Group decision making is also not without drawbacks. The composition of a group is extremely influential in determining the quality of the decision-making process. In 1971, Irving Janis elaborated on the theory of *groupthink*. According to Janis, especially when decision-making groups are very cohesive and insulated, when leadership within the group is directive and there is high stress in terms of deadlines or a manifest outside threat, a form of self-censorship and a trend towards conformity will emerge within the group (Janis, 1982). This results in a tendency to prohibit deviant opinions, to consider only one or a few, not necessarily the best, alternatives, to exclude criteria on which the alternative preferred by the majority in the group scores negatively, to stereotype outsiders with different preferences and to silence group members who disagree with the majority opinion. The outcome of such groupthink – the ultimate decision – can be a fiasco because of these variables.

Increasing the size of the group and making it more heterogeneous might help to prevent groupthink, but while reaching consensus in a large group (>15 persons) can be more democratic, it can also be exhausting and time consuming. Hence, procedures have to be established for decision making, including rules for aggregating individual opinions, the number of participants, the number of meetings, et cetera; this can unintentionally bureaucratize the decision-making process.

An additional contextual factor is the governmental level authorized to make the decision. The location of the decision-making power, i.e. the national, regional or local government level, plays a role in determining the possibilities of public participation, the need for standardization and formalization of the decision-making process, the possibility for tailor-made decisions, the availability of knowledge and expertise to analyse this information, the skills of individuals involved in the process, the extent to which one can learn from past experiences and from other layers in government, the complexity of the issue underlying the decision-making process and the awareness of the participant of such complexity. When decision making is centralized, the possibilities for public participation decrease as do the possibilities for tailor-made decisions. On the other hand, the capacity, knowledge and skills of the central apparatus is often greater than at the local level, especially in cases of high uncertainty and dynamics and when the origin of such dynamics is outside the local level.

A final contextual factor is that participants are often representatives of interest groups, societal organizations, NGOs, governmental agencies, et cetera. The opinions they offer in decision-making processes do not always reflect their personal preferences but should reflect the preferences of the organizations or societal groups they represent. They are expected to care for their organizations' interest, even though their personal opinions might be quite different. A representative from retail will prefer nearby, free parking in order to attract as many customers as possible, while representatives from an environmental interest group might oppose building a parking lot since they want to ban cars from the neighbourhood. The residents are likely to want to keep the current situation unchanged or may opt for an underground parking with parking lots free of charge for themselves and high parking costs for commuters in order to guarantee sufficient free space for their own cars and those of their family and visiting friends. An administrator might have a keen eye for his or her own departmental interests and personal position or might just want to earn a reputation as a problem solver who accomplished the construction and maintenance of the parking within a predetermined budget. And politicians may just want to please as many of their voters as possible. Such organizational interests can frustrate decision-making processes since they interfere with the flexibility needed to arrive at optimal decisions; instead, they can result in polarization. Institutional ties also frustrate the outcomes of decision-making processes, because instrumental rationality might tend to dominate the decision-making process and other types of rationality, as mentioned in the previous section, become subordinate to instrumental rationality.

The main conclusion of this section is that decision-making processes are often difficult processes in which individual biases and errors, institutional boundaries and groupthink, and complex societal contexts – especially in conflicting interests and structural power disparities – blend together and inhibit extensive collection and sound analysis of information, thus blocking the way towards optimal public decisions.

Towards improved decision making

Public Administration scholars have been researching what can be done to approximate the ideal of rational decision making – and even optimal decision making – in spite of the inhibiting factors mentioned in the previous section. Many solutions have relied on increasing deliberation – in both of its meanings: increasing the thoughtfulness of decision makers and making them consult with stakeholders to discuss the merits of alternatives. Increasing the thoughtfulness of decision makers can be achieved through individual training and capacity building and by creating institutions aimed at providing decision makers with the needed information and analyses. Consultations can be accomplished by broadening the decision-making process in order to induce decision makers to seek out the opinions of a multitude of stakeholders and debate alternatives through public participation in order to avoid the inherent bias in the societal context, and by changing the format of decision-making processes, for instance by making them more transparent. This section provides a brief overview of the rationale behind these proposals.

Capacity building to make decision makers more thoughtful

The first recommendation to improve public decision making is to better think decisions through beforehand. Ancient philosophers pointed to the need for wisdom and virtue among individual public officials and the need to train them well. At the individual level, one can empower decision makers by making them aware of potential biases in decision making and their own decision-making deficiencies. This can be achieved, for instance, with training in:

- *formal logic and statistics*, including all the biases and fallacies
- *attention management*, making decision makers focus on relevant aspects of the decision and to avoid them becoming distracted by insignificant facts
- *dialectic thinking*, presenting alternative scenarios and discussing each of the options
- *lateral thinking*, forcing them to look at the decision from a completely different perspective in order to move them outside their usual frame of reference
- *intuitive thinking*, making them committed and responsible for the outcomes and inducing them to search for elegant solutions

- *inquisitive thinking*, training them to ask the right questions
- *the argumentative turn*, teaching them how to make a sound sub-stantive argument to counter political–strategic argumentations, and to distinguish types of support for a claim in an argument, such as arguments which are based on authority, pragmatism, ethics, intuition, analogy, causality and analytics (cf. Fischer & Forester, 1993).

In addition, one can introduce public servants to the techniques developed in operational research intended to aid the decision-making process, including impact assessments, scenario methods, brainstorming, the Delphi technique and simulations, emphasize the potential for these techniques to improve the decision-making process, and train decision makers in using these instruments.

Institution building to make decision makers better informed

At an institutional level, information generating institutions can be established, such as think tanks and planning agencies, decision-management units within governmental agencies, political–professional advisory committees and university researchers. One could institution-alize regular evaluations to provide the necessary information that decision makers are unable to collect themselves, analyse that informa-tion and translate it into building blocks for decision making.

Just to elaborate on *think tanks*, these conduct contract research on behalf of decision makers which, unlike academic research, has a strong focus on applied knowledge in public decision making and policy making and provides advice and training to public decision makers. Some are university-based, others are linked to political parties or ideologies, while still others are created and sponsored by govern-ments or business. Some think tanks are completely independent and have received their funding from donations. The first formal think tank involved in domestic public decision making was believed to have been established in 1884 by the *Fabian Society* as the first ideologically (socialist) based think tank. It attracted many academicians wanting to influence public decision making.

Nowadays, many countries have think tanks. With regard to pub-lic decision making and public policies, the most famous American think tanks are the Brookings Institution and the RAND Corporation. Canada is home to the Institute for Research on Public Policy (IRPP). In Brazil, the *Fundação Getulio Vargas* (FGV) is well known, and in Peru, the *Grupo de Análisis para el Desarrollo* (GRADE) holds a prominent place. In Mexico, the CIDE (Center for Research and Teaching in Economics) specializes in public policy and public choice. In Asia, the major think tanks are the Development Research Center of the State Council (China), the Japanese National Institute for Research Advancement and the Nomura Research Institute (Japan), and the Centre for Civil Society (CCS) (India). In Germany, the Max Planck Institute for the Study of Societies is a major think tank on public decision making. And in Saudi Arabia, the Gulf Research Center (GRC) and in South Africa, the Centre for Education Policy Reform are influential in public policy making.

The phenomenon of think tanks has evolved rapidly since the 1950s and nowadays there are over 1,800 think tanks in the USA alone. There are over 400 in China, over 250 in the UK and India, and over 150 in France and Germany. In 2013, South Africa had 88 think tanks and even small countries like Iceland, Gabon, Laos and the Seychelles have multiple think tanks (McGann, 2013). These numbers are a good indicator for widespread attempts to rationalize public decision making.

Transparency to make decision makers accountable

A different approach to improve public decision making is opening up the process by making it more transparent. In a 2009 memo to his lead executives, President Barack Obama stated: 'We will work together to ensure the public trust and establish a system of transparency, public participation, and collaboration. Openness will strengthen our democracy and promote efficiency and effectiveness in Government.' Nowadays, transparency is seen as a major dimension of good governance. It is a classic concept in that governments should make information about its laws, regulations and public policies and decisions to change them publicly available, because only then can citizens abide by the law. Also, because governments use public money, it makes sense to have oversight and accountability in order to ensure that government spends this money well. As early as the 1800s, moral philosophers such as John Stuart Mill considered transparency to be the principal check against misrule and abuse of power and the primary means to ensure accountability to the public.

In the age of e-government, transparency involves more. For instance, governments are increasingly able to use information and communication technology (ICT) and as a result, they face an increased demand for open government. There is a growing consensus that governments need to provide timely, reliable and accessible information to all relevant stakeholders, about economic, social and political developments, about its decisions and actions and about the data it collects and stores, and that they make laws and regulations ensuring that stakeholders have access to that information in order to empower them. A World Bank report noted such open government improves risk management, economic performance and bureaucratic efficiency in governments (cf. Islam, 2003). It concludes that: 'Governments that do not produce, organize and share information will be hampered in policymaking. Good policymaking requires up-to-date information on the economic situation; good policymaking requires the sharing of information for better coordination, analysis and monitoring' (p. 36). This view is shared by many governments. As the Australian government stated, 'Once public sector information is liberated as a key national asset, possibilities are unlocked through the invention, creativity and hard work of citizens, business and community organizations'. The Spanish minister for tourism stated, 'Data are crucial for the knowledge economy. By publishing Public Sector Data, more (economic) value can be generated. The data are a source for the development of new products and services. In addition, data are important to exercise one's democratic rights. Citizens are better informed about and engaged in government' (cf. Huijboom & Van den Broek, 2012, p. 3).

Transparency can have a positive impact on the quality of decision-making processes by making decision makers more cautious and open to public scrutiny, and thus increasing efforts to achieve effectiveness and efficiency. Furthermore, transparency can prevent favouritism, nepotism, bias and deceptive and strategic behaviour based on information asymmetry. Of course, not all information can be made public; for instance, in the case of national security or public procurement, but, as has been argued, such 'first-order secrecy (in a process or about a policy) requires second-order publicity (about the decision to make the process or policy secret)' (cf. Thompson, 1999, p. 185).

Such transparency can be improved by laws on access to information, laws on the protection of information, laws on administrative procedures and regulations about rights to observe decision-making processes and to be heard. Countries and regions vary in their degree of openness, and this is summarized in the Open Data Barometer survey. It is based on Right to Information laws; Open Government Development initiatives in central, regional and local governments, demand for open government and whether such data can be reused. In 2013 (see Table 7.1), the Barometer recorded distribution among regions with regard to the degree of transparency, in which the scores are composite scale values based on factor analysis, after which they were recoded to a scale of 1–100:

Table 7.1   *Open Government Index around the world in 2013*

	Right to Information Act	*Open Government initiatives*	*Demand from civil society*	*Government support for Open Government innovations*	*Local and regional initiatives*
Europe	61.36	55.45	61.82	38.89	47.47
Americas	60.77	50.77	42.31	29.06	34.19
Asia Pacific	56.92	50.00	46.15	29.06	23.93
Middle East & Central Asia	22.50	38.75	21.25	8.33	8.33
Africa	35.71	28.57	28.10	14.81	5.29
Total	49.48	44.68	42.47	25.83	25.69

Note: Regional breakdown of Open Data Barometer survey responses. Higher scores are better
Source: Davies, 2013

Besides aggregate results, the report also presents huge variations within regions (cf. Davies, 2013). In Africa, for example, there is a huge difference in Open Government with Kenya having relatively high scores and Mali, Nigeria and Zambia having low scores. In the Middle East, Israel and Bahrain vary dramatically from Yemen. In the Americas, differences can be found between the USA and Canada on the high side and Venezuela, Ecuador, Peru and Jamaica on the low side. In Europe, differences exist in the scores for Open Government between the UK and Sweden on the one hand and Greece, Turkey and Hungary on the other.

Involving stakeholders to give decision makers a balanced perspective

A final suggestion for improving public decision making is including societal groups, interest groups, business, NGOs, experts and all other groups with an interest or specific knowledge about the issue at stake in the decision-making process. Groups who receive products from a public service agency, groups whose behaviour is to be steered by public decisions and any other group that has specific interests and knowledge can contribute to more effective and efficient public decisions. This could create support and legitimacy for those decisions, increase trust in government and create a more favourable image of government. At the very least, talking and consulting reduces the risk of violent confrontation since it serves to make societal groups aware of what options are being considered and why a certain alternative is chosen. Furthermore, broadening the decision-making process could increase the available information about the issue at stake, be a means for incorporating more information in the decision and improve the linkage between existing problems and the proposed solutions – since the problems that societal groups experience can be very different from the problems as defined and framed by decision makers, and because multiple actors usually know more than one individual actor. Finally, it forces decision makers to provide sound support since involving societal groups also functions as a form of checks and balances. Charles Lindblom called this the potential intelligence of democracy.

One may doubt whether such public participation is always possible and whether it will always produce the effects expected in theory, especially in the case of remote rural and poor areas where people have no experience in such participation and lack administrative, organizational and political skills. Recent research into community-managed schools in Honduras and Guatemala showed that governments can stimulate participation even in remote and poor rural areas and thereby produce changes in individuals' civic and political behaviours (Altschuler & Corrales, 2013, p. 8). Even in these least likely situations, inexperienced and non-educated participants did become more skilled through their involvement in such relatively simple activities as school council membership. It taught them how to visit government offices, submit proposals and petition government and other actors for assistance and gave them a keen eye for the essence of public goods. Participants in such small-scale organizations can and do learn the basic skills for participating in organizations and they did tend to use these skills by becoming active in other organizations and situations also. This is indicative for citizens' participation on a very small scale to have a spillover effect on their capacity to influence government in general. Such effects occur especially when the participation in small councils is supported by government, when there is leadership rotation in school councils and when such councils have ample autonomy. Nonetheless, the same study also pointed to remaining issues related to individual capabilities and experiences. Participation by inexperienced individuals only has a minor impact on the content of actual public policies. There remains a difficulty in participating in and influencing policies in more demanding areas and the impact on the establishment of local civil society is minor. An important issue is also that participation might result in a biased representation in the management of the organization in terms of gender and socio-economic position of the participants (Altschuler & Corrales, 2013, p. 176 ff).

Therefore, not all forms of public participation have the expected effects. The intensity and goals of participation can influence the outcome. One of the first to distinguish different levels of participation was Sherry Arnstein. She sees 'a critical difference between going through the empty ritual of participation and having the real power needed to affect the outcome of the process' (p. 216). As early as 1969, she distinguished eight steps on a ladder, with the lowest steps representing minimal or what she called 'non-participation', namely participation as disguised manipulation and therapy. The real objective in these cases is not to enable people to participate, but to educate or 'cure' the participants. The next three steps she denoted as 'tokenism', namely participation as information, consultation and placation. The decision makers still don't have to give up any part of their decision power. It is only further up the ladder that citizens are empowered, namely through partnership which enables citizens to negotiate and be delegated power, and citizen control in which citizens get the majority of decision-making seats (cf. p. 217).

Later, she further differentiated between citizens being inactives, spectators, advisors at the end, advisors from the start, co-deciders, partners and initiators of decisions. With regard to the use of social media, an increasingly important means to influence decision making, Forrester (2007) introduced a social-techno ladder in which he distinguishes inactives, spectators, joiners, critics, collectors, conversationalists and creators according to their impact and efforts in the process. The inactives are not at all seen or heard on the social media, the spectators only read blogs, listen to podcasts, watch videos, read online forums and read tweets. The joiners visit network sites and maintain a personal homepage. The collectors use RSS feeds, vote for websites and add tags to websites or photos. The critics post ratings, comment on someone else's blog, contribute to online forums, and contribute or edit articles in a wiki. Conversationalists update status on a social network site and post updates on Twitter. Creators publish blogs, publish their own web pages, upload videos and write articles and stories and post them (Li et al., 2011).

All of this implies that participation can and does vary over time and over situations and countries and that one has to be careful not to judge every participation process as similar in its contents and in its effects. In general, the trends can be distinguished by four criteria:

- *the right to know*, implying the disclosure of relevant information (transparency and open government) and the dissemination of information about opportunities for participation. In the communication between government and citizens (social) media play a crucial role
- *the right to be heard*, implying that societal groups can voice their grievances and problems, make proposals, add alternatives and criteria, and participate in hearings
- *the right to affect decisions*, obliging decision makers to take the opinions of participants into account and to provide good reasons and sound support when the ultimate decision deviates from the preferences of participants
- *the right to appeal*, if a decision maker does not sufficiently grant societal groups these rights.

Recent research in public decision making

Research in public decision making continues in all of the directions described in this chapter, including psychological experiments into individual deficiencies in decision making; the features of the context that can inhibit rational decision making; the merits of capacity building – especially in developing countries in which billions of dollars are involved; institution building to create Open Government and to enhance transparency; and within Public Administration the effectiveness of public participation and deliberative decision making.

Research into the contextual setting

One of the novel trends in research tries to understand collective decision-making or collective choice processes by investigating the extent to which the context, i.e. the institutions and the organizational setting, influences the decisions that are made. This approach, in which Nobel laureate Elinor Ostrom did extensive research, challenges common assumptions that individuals are bounded in their rationality and that they are unable to cooperate to achieve optimal outcomes. Ostrom argued that this depends on the formal and informal rules by which decision processes are governed, the awareness of the participants of these rules, the organizational setting and what is at stake. Individuals may not be fully informed, but this is not necessary for the following reasons: (1) scope and authority rules normally limit the number of allowable actions to choose from, (2) the set of participants in an action arena is usually limited by entry and exit rules and position rules, and (3) the process itself is normally regulated by a set of aggregation rules, information rules and pay-off rules (Ostrom, 1995). Within such rule-bound contexts, we can consider individuals to be fully informed. They don't need to take every possible option into account. Some choices will not be made and others will be more probable, and the necessary information for making decisions is therefore limited. Much information is redundant. Moreover, in addition to the operational rules that directly affect decision making are formal and informal collective-choice rules that affect the operational rules by prescribing, forbidding and invoking certain behaviour, and monitoring, applying and enforcing the operational rules. And in addition to these collective choice rules, there are constitutional rules which, at a more abstract level, provide internalized values and norms that prevent some actions or decisions from being considered; participants know that some options will have severe consequences. Supporting these constitutional rules are metaconstitutional rules that define certain decisions as self-evident and others as taboo because of ingrained habits, culture, history or religion. These operational, collective-choice, constitutional and metaconstitutional rules provide incentives to individual participants in collective-choice processes making them less vulnerable to fallacies and biases, and to mistakes, because it is self-evident that some options, for instance dishonesty or political manoeuvring, will be disadvantageous in the end.

Research into neuro-economics

A second approach for influencing individual decision making is the recent research in *neuro-economics*, though its relevance for public decision making is still unclear. It investigates what parts of the brain – parietal cortex, striatum, medial prefrontal cortex, frontal-parietal circuits or basal ganglia – are activated when people make decisions. What part of the brain is activated when an individual calculates a utility function? What part is activated when an individual falls victim to a fallacy or becomes biased? Currently such research points out that taking decisions involves an interaction between different parts of the brain, in which brain parts responsible for activating emotions are dominant or subordinate to brain parts responsible for activating cognitive utilitarian calculating behaviour. By activating or suppressing certain brain functions it has proven possible to change individual decision making, making it more moral or selfish and more or less sensitive to the biases inherent to decision making. The dominance of two systems within the brain makes individuals seek either social justice or egocentric results, makes them more or less sensitive to immediate need satisfaction, makes them impatient or patient, and makes them able to show a quick reflex to problems or able to conduct abstract and rational reasoning. An important finding is that when individuals are faced with a decision, the brain parts involved in activating emotions are activated prior to the brain part that activates cognitive behaviour.

The next chapter will show that, although this research is still in its exploratory phase, in some countries policy makers already use its results in their attempts to change the behaviour choices of target groups that opt for undesirable behaviour. In the future, medical solutions might be sought for influencing or improving individual decision making.

Research into the impact of ICT

In the search to optimize the deliberative aspects of public decision making, ICT and e-governance hold a prominent place in recent research. As we have already seen, ICT can be used for creating transparency and involving societal groups in the decision-making process. This research investigates, for instance, how social media can ease the participation of citizens and societal groups in decision-making processes, but can also mobilize individuals to demonstrate and even start an uprising.

To be mentioned is that the impact of the rapid introduction of ICT in government and the novel research in this area is not limited to its direct effects on deliberation and decision making. ICT has had a profound impact on the workings of the public administration in general, on the transparency of public decision making, on service delivery by governments, on intergovernmental relations, on the internal organization of governmental organizations, on working in government, on the relation between government and citizens and on the relations between citizens and, as such, it has also had indirect effects on decision making and policy making. ICT has changed the public administration enormously and created new dilemmas.

At first ICT was mainly focused on the standardization and automation of administrative and registration processes. Investigations explored to what extent ICT could improve the efficiency, effectiveness, legality and democracy of administrative activities. In that phase dilemmas existed between standardization of administrative systems with a minimum of flexibility and customer orientation, and between the need to formalize logistics in an environment characterized by political and social dynamics. A central topic of research also became how ICT could result in less hierarchical and more horizontal decision making, in which the Weberian hierarchical organization is replaced by a kind of network organization, and a shift to multi-level governance crossing local, regional and national boundaries is possible (Snellen, 2005, p. 6).

Afterwards ICT also became seen as an enabler of the spread of performance measurement and benchmarking. It became a tool to get more value for money and to improve the organization and management as well as public service delivery. As such it connected well with the reforms going on in many governments through NPM principles. ICT is said to have resulted in increased interdependences within government, resulting in new possibilities to change intergovernmental relations such as joined-up government at the central level, cooperation between municipalities through the creation of shared service centres and the emergence of multi-level government enabled by the increase of information through sharing data. The dilemmas that emerged simultaneously concern the issue that the meaning of information, the definition of concepts, had to be standardized; that ICT resulted in a transformation of service delivery, enabling one-stop shops and intragovernmental information sharing between departments thus changing the information available in decision making and policy making; and that the speed of information transfer could result in a conflict between the necessary meticulousness and the also necessary innovation and risk taking. Further dilemmas arose at this stage: public officials may perceive a loss of autonomy, it becomes ambiguous who owns a problem and new information sharing possibilities may result in a loss of discretion at the work floor.

According to David Brown, nowadays e-government relates to the entire range of government roles and activities, shaped by and making use of ICT (Brown, 2005, p. 242 ff.). This involves a number of issues: such technologies require new skills and human capacity development of public officials; e-democracy and e-governance impact on the legitimacy of government and its relations with citizens; it changes government operations and administrative processes; it even impacts on international relations between governments since governments can influence one another's citizens without having to use the previously formal channels; and it changes the relations between citizens as virtual communities are created unlimited by geographical or organizational distances and beyond previous obstructive institutional frameworks.

Governments are expected to become Open Governments, sharing information and cooperating internally and with their citizens, to increase the transparency and accountability of government functions vis-à-vis civil society and to improve and increase citizens' participation, now enabled by widespread access to information. However, this might create tensions between countries as there are huge differences between developed and developing countries in terms of their electricity and telecommunications infrastructure. Therefore, scholarly research into the impacts of ICT in the public sector has become a major topic, not just with regard to decision making.

Social-techno solutions seem to lead us away from the basic concept that public decision making is about the provision of public goods in order to improve the welfare of the people, i.e. to reduce poverty and to improve health care and education. The four solutions to suboptimal decision making – capacity building, building institutions for decision support, increasing transparency and broadening the decision making process –, as well as the major recent research, all attempt to approximate optimal decision making or at least try to understand how rational decision making is possible despite the limitations.

Conclusions

This chapter addressed the theme of decision making and especially the role of rationality in decision making. It began by presenting three inhibitors to rational decision making, namely individual deficiencies, institutional boundaries and the socio-economic structure of society at large. It continued with four ways for improving rationality in decision making. At the individual level, decision makers can be trained to become more knowledgeable and skilled in making rational decisions. Knowledge-building institutions, such as planning agencies and think tanks, can increase the knowledge and analysis needed to make rational decisions. At the level of the decision-making process, suggestions to increase transparency and allow public participation are key. This would also increase the amount of information in the decision-making process and could counter the bias that is likely to occur because of the conflicts of interests and power disparities in society.

There are many other proposals for improving the quality of decision making. Recent research focuses especially on making rational use of the irrationalities, on the important role of institutions in providing formal and informal rules that support collective choice and on ICT solutions for improving decision making. One of the key themes in Public Administration is whether we should strive to maximize rationality to achieve optimal decision-making processes, whether we should be more pragmatic and content with decisions that are feasible and satisfactory for the stakeholders – even though they might be second-tier choices – or whether we should just abandon the whole idea of rationality since it is unattainable anyway.

A substantial amount of research has been done on how to improve on rational decision making and many tools with the same aim have been developed in operational research. At the time of writing, the trend in research is towards rationalizing decision making. This may change in the future because the discussion will continue. Some scholars exert great effort trying to find innovative ways to improve on rational decision making while others persist in believing that using such tools are only symbolic – primarily to create an image of rationality for public consumption because the decisions have already been made and they are primarily determined by political factors and cannot be changed with additional information but only when power positions are altered. They argue that because giving subjective meaning to facts is more important than the facts themselves, achieving agreement among stakeholders is already a significant accomplishment, even if the resulting decision is ineffective and inefficient. They may, however, in light of the institutional analysis done by Ostrom, have to re-examine their assumption that we have to accept the political and irrational nature of decision making and the resulting suboptimal outcomes. Her research supports the idea that, with certain institutional conditions, it is possible to reach agreement and simultaneously achieve optimal outcomes of decision-making processes in spite of the deficiencies in individual decision making.

Further reading

Ariely, Dan (2008). *Predictably irrational: The hidden forces that shape our decisions*. London: HarperCollins.

Altschuler, Daniel & Corrales, Javier (2013). *The promise of participation: Experiments in participatory governance in Honduras and Guatemala*. London: Palgrave Macmillan.

Gaynor, Gerald H. (2015). *Decisions: An engineering and management perspective*. Hoboken, New Jersey: Wiley & Sons.

Kahneman, Daniel (2011). *Thinking, fast and slow*. London: Palgrave Macmillan.

Kleindorfer, Paul R., Kuhnreuther, Howard C. & Schoemaker, Paul J. H. (1993). *Decision sciences: An integrative perspective.* Cambridge: Cambridge University Press.

Poteete, Amy R., Janssen, Marco A. & Ostrom, Elinor (2010). *Working together: Collective action, the commons, and multiple methods in practice.* Princeton: Princeton University Press.

Simon, Herbert A. (1947). *Administrative behavior: A study of decision-making processes in administrative organization.* New York: Macmillan.

Chapter 8

How can public policies solve social problems?

This chapter addresses the last key issue of Public Administration, and provides an introduction to theories explaining the varying connection between public policies resulting in collective goods and the collective problems to which public policies are supposedly an answer. It also focuses on research which aims to strengthen the relation between public policies (as answers to problems) and the problems themselves.

Problems are nasty things and collective problems are nasty things for society as a whole. By definition, problems are something different from what you want or desire. If you want to be an Olympic champion and you just keep on losing games, you have a problem and this is also the case if you want to date that beautiful guy or girl, but he or she is not interested at all. This chapter is about problems and the way to solve them. It is not about your personal ones, but about those problems that affect many people simultaneously; in other words, collective problems. It is therefore not just about policies but about public policies.

That is easy to say, but what makes a problem a collective problem in need of the provision of collective goods? When you want to buy a car, but lack the money, it could be seen as an individual problem. Not so in Thailand and Singapore. In those countries, the government heavily subsidizes the purchase of a first car. The same goes for having children and lacking the time or resources to raise them well. One could say that is something to be taken care of within the family, but some governments, especially in Scandinavia, give huge amounts of child support and allow the father as well as the mother full-paid leave for a year. In other countries, the government tries everything to diminish the number of births, like in China during its one-child policy. In the latter case, it was a problem if you wanted more children, but society told you that having more than one is despicable.

These examples are, although very serious for those involved, still relatively simple. There are also structural problems varying in magnitude all over the world, but affecting all countries, such as climate change because of environmental pollution, the proliferation of nuclear weapons, the availability of clean water and energy, urbanization and growing public financial deficits. Especially in developing countries, problems prevail concerning child mortality, hunger and poverty, lack of primary education, lack of basic health care and the spread of infectious diseases like HIV/AIDS and malaria, shortage of drinking water and socio-economic and gender inequality. In developed countries the greying of society, the lack of spatial areas, unemployment and unsustainable economic growth pose serious challenges.

This chapter focuses on the main problems in the world and governments' answers to them through public policies. First, it focuses on the definition of problems and policies and gives the common features of problems and policies. Next, the variance in the interpretation of a problem is addressed and four approaches to problem definition are presented. Subsequently a section focuses on diagnosing problems; that is, framing problems in terms of causes and effects. Such framing is seen as the generative mechanism through which collective problems are related to public policies. The chapter continues with an overview of what is at stake when developing public policies and implementing them and ends with a concise outline of recent research into the understanding of public problems and public policies.

Terminology

Public policies

Just as with all other terms used in this book, public policy is also defined in varying ways by different scholars. Dye (1992) defined it simply as whatever governments choose to do or not to do. Easton (1965) described it broadly as the 'authoritative allocation of values' for society and Dewey described it as focusing on the public and its problems. Howlett and Ramesh (2003, p. 3) state that 'public policy is, at its most simple, a choice made by a government to undertake some course of action'. Still others have defined public policy as 'being the result of an interaction process between many actors of whom only a few are government bodies' (Klijn, Koppenjan and Termeer, 1995, p 439). As Paul Sabatier stated, policy making is all about the manner in which problems get conceptualized and brought to government for solution; governmental institutions formulate alternatives and select policy solutions, and those policies get implemented, evaluated and revised (Sabatier, 1999, p. 3).

Sabatier sees this process as extremely complex since it involves many actors – interest groups, governmental agencies, legislatures, researchers and journalists – because it often takes a long time, more than a decade, to go from problem definition to public policy, because it involves multiple programmes and public debate, and because disputes around policies often involve deeply held values and interests.

In order to make sense of such complex processes it makes sense to decompose this process into each of its elements, the policy stages. Until recently this was the dominant way to proceed to analyse public policy-making processes. Even critics of such stage models were nonetheless inclined to distinguish the policy-making process according to its stages, going from the occurrence of a problem, the transformation thereof to a policy problem through the agenda-setting process, the development of a policy proposal including the formulation of goals and means to achieve those goals, the formal decision about the policy by transforming the proposal into a law or regulation, and the implementation – the application of the means in practice (Lerner & Lasswell, 1951). Sometimes an evaluation stage, a policy reform and policy termination stage are also distinguished.

One point of dispute between scholars is whether they see these stages as elements in a linear process which reflects the sequence in the practice of policy making, as a cyclical model to be used to ease the analysis of the dynamics in policy processes, as a heuristic model to get an analytical grip on a specific policy process, or just as elements which together constitute the policy process but not necessarily in the suggested sequence, and in which it is not necessary that all elements occur. This points to symbolic policies which are not intended to be implemented, to policies which do not pose an answer to a problem, to policies which are implemented in practice but which were never decided upon, or to policies which start off from implementation feasibility and return to what this implies for possible decisions on which instruments to use, afterwards determining which goals could be achieved given these means, and only at the end determining what problems they could solve.

Problems

Scholars do agree on the desirability of a connection between public policies and public problems, because problems are annoying things one wants to resolve through policies. Problems are defined as the difference between what one wants or desires, one's standards, or yardstick and what one sees or foresees in reality. Hence, if you see poverty, defined as having to live on less than one dollar a day, and your normative idea or ethical standard is that there should be no such poverty, you see a problem. It can also be that you foresee a trend which you interpret as problematic, because you judge the trend to have negative effects.

In this regard it is interesting to see that people in economically developed countries have a different opinion about the world's severest problems than people in developing and developmental countries. Both see enduring poverty as the main global problem, but when asked what the next major problem is, people in the EU predominantly mention potential threats for their welfare and their concerns about what they foresee, such as climate change, the economic situation, international terrorism, the availability of energy, increasing global population, the spread of infectious disease, nuclear proliferation and armed conflict. For people living outside economically developed countries the main problems are related to what they experience, namely hunger, social and economic exclusion, pollution, war, a lack of health care, HIV/AIDS and other diseases, failing agriculture and a shortage of electrical supply and drinking water. It is the difference between fearing a possible deterioration of one's situation and experiencing huge problems and fearing that one's situation will not improve.

The subjectivity in problem definition

The definition implies there are two sides to problems, one's desires and what one experiences or foresees, and that there is always something subjective about problems, given one's wants and desires and what one experiences or foresees, and thus how one defines the problem. The main question is always, 'What is exactly the problem?' The answer to this question can vary and determines if and what kind of action is needed. One distinction is whether one perceives a problem as an individual or a collective problem, or as something in between. When the answer to this question is given, one can still differ on the nature of the problem.

If it is one's opinion that the use of the psychoactive drug 'cannabis' is a problem, it is still not clear what the problem exactly is. Is it a problem because the use thereof causes health problems, because the use is illegal or because the use is so expensive that addicts are likely to become criminals and tend to steal money to be able to buy the drugs? Governments all over the world differ in their definition of this problem. The Netherlands were long known for judging the use of drugs as a health problem, with street workers and government institutes constantly warning of the toxic effects and official quality checks of drugs at events where such drugs are frequently used. Thailand sees it mainly as a legal problem with heavy penalties if one is caught in possession of cannabis or when drugs-trafficking. Recently, Uruguay legalized the production, sales and use of cannabis, because its being illegal was judged to be the main problem. In that country it was judged to have grave economic consequences through which criminal organizations made huge profits and addicted users were forced into criminal behaviour because they could not afford it.

The ownership of problems

Another question is *whose problem* it is. When a multinational company decides on the closure of one of its divisions, the definition of the problem varies across stakeholders. From the point of view of the multinational the division could be seen as making too small a profit or even a loss. This problem is of a quite different nature than the problem for the workers who lose their jobs, for the unions who have to negotiate redundancy plans or for the municipality or regional government in which the factory was located. The latter is faced with increased unemployment and perhaps social benefit expenses.

The varying way in which one and the same event results in varying problems for different stakeholders results in the issue of ownership of problems.

The complexity of problems

Problems also vary in their complexity, which refers to their *dynamics*, the *dimensions* involved, their *interrelatedness* with other problems and the number of *stakeholders* involved, which results in a varying *uncertainty and disagreement* about the nature of problems.

Problems tend to be dynamic through time and space. First, problems are dynamic in the long term as they change in magnitude. This is the case for poverty, urbanization, climate change, economic growth, budget deficits et cetera, all being indicative of problems that change in magnitude and become more or less pressing through time. In the short term, dynamics are visible in the *definition of problems*. Imagine an explosion in a fireworks factory. This happens in many countries. Immediately after such incidents, the definition of the problem is in terms of death toll, houses destroyed, material damage and the search for survivors. After some days, the problem definition might change and begins to focus on the lack of controls, the running of the factory without proper licence, the absence of contingency plans, officials inside the factory or inside government who are to blame or laws not upheld.

Problems also have the tendency to move through space. This is seen when governments forbid prostitution in a specific area and take action. The prostitutes are likely to move elsewhere and thus move the 'problem' from one area to another. This is also the case when a local or regional government tries to attract industries by creating an industrial area in order to reduce its unemployment. Such an action might cause unemployment in the place the factories were located before. Another example is given in house owners taking action against burglars by establishing a neighbourhood watch, making the burglars move to other neighbourhoods.

Problems mostly have several dimensions. Unemployment can be perceived at the micro and macro level, or through its political, economic, social or psychological dimension. One can distinguish between voluntary and involuntary unemployment, frictional and structural unemployment, long-term and short-term unemployment and official and hidden unemployment. The dimensions enable one to distinguish between different aspects of unemployment and measure it in its varying manifestations. Deciding which dimensions to distinguish in a problem analysis is not just a matter of rationality and substantive argumentation. It also depends on the efforts of actors to get a specific dimension of unemployment to the front.

Another complicating factor is that many problems are mutually interrelated, making it difficult to decide where to start in resolving the problem – if it is even possible to define 'the' problem. For instance, poverty, lack of health care, hunger, lack of schooling, unemployment, infant mortality, bad infrastructure, lack of hygiene, shortage of drinking water, lack of electricity, lack of financial resources on the part of government, corruption and sometimes even civil war can accumulate into one big seemingly unsolvable mess, comparable to the Gordian knot, perhaps best, but too abstractly, defined as 'the suffering of a population' and more positively as 'low human development'.

A complicating factor is also that collective problems by definition involve many stakeholders, i.e. varying actors having their own vested interests, their own specific problem definition, their own particular analysis of the causes and effects of the problem and thus each promote different policies to solve the problem. One of the peculiarities of problems with many stakeholders each having their own interests, being mutually dependent but also with their own autonomy and decision powers, is that complex networks arise in which rationality is likely to give way to strategic behaviour.

The last complicating factor is that the knowledge about problems is sometimes extensive and at other times limited and that this can differ among actors involved. This knowledge concerns the facts as well as the normative valuation of those facts and uncertainties. That limited knowledge can make problems very complicated was seen in the Ebola outbreak in West Africa in 2014. Ebola is a deadly disease. At the time of the outbreak it was a disease without a cure, and believed to be contracted by the scratch or bite of a specific kind of bat, by eating undercooked bush meat or by physical contact with a person who already contracted Ebola through which sweat or saliva was transmitted.

Medical doctors and nurses structured the problem in terms of its contamination risk. By putting people in isolation in hospitals they tried to prevent further contagion and to control the outbreak. Part of the population in the West African countries was, however, not knowledgeable about the disease and many rumours spread synchronous with the disease. Some pointed out that the disease did not exist and that people were put in isolation in hospitals to harvest organs and steal blood. Hence, infected patients were fetched away from the hospitals by their families making the outbreak escalate. Other rumours told that the medical doctors had imported the disease, resulting in people wanting to burn the hospitals down, because they were angry with the health workers and didn't believe they were there to help. Still others were convinced Ebola was a government conspiracy to undermine certain tribal groups, steal organs or get money from international donors (cf. 'Ebola in Sierra Leone: Myths and misconceptions', 2014).

The example of poverty

As described above, opinion polls show that poverty is judged to be the most severe global problem for people in wealthy countries as well as for people in poor countries. Its eradication belongs to what the United Nations defined as Millennium Development Goals which all countries and international organizations should strive for.

Measuring the magnitude of problems

All the dimensions of problems as mentioned in the previous section are also seen in the definition and measurement of the magnitude of poverty. It is full of dubious assumptions and arbitrary thresholds which makes its measurement less of a technical matter and more a compromise. This is seen first of all in the attempts to measure poverty by defining an absolute poverty line. Quoting the UN 2014 report on the magnitude of poverty, 'About one in five persons in developing regions lives on less than $1.25 per day' (United Nations, 2014, p. 8). This threshold is important since it determines unequivocally who is seen as poor and who is not, and was suggested in 2008 by the World Bank after decades of having a poverty line of $1 a day. Officially the absolute poverty line is since then '$1.25 a day at 2005 purchasing-power parity'. Although generally accepted, this absolute threshold is arbitrary. Increasing the threshold slightly, half the people in the world would belong to the poor, since 3.5 billion people have to survive on less than two dollars a day. According to the official indicator they are near poor, but in reality as vulnerable as the extreme poor (EList10, n.d.).

There are more problems involved in the measurement of poverty through such an absolute threshold. Taking $1.25 as the dividing line implies that there would be no poverty in the affluent countries since there are hardly any people in those countries having to live on less than $1.25 a day. However, also in those parts of the world there are many people who face social exclusion and who have difficulty in finding food, clothing, housing et cetera each day and thus could be designated as poor. This issue was recognized and in 2008 the World Bank set the absolute poverty line for transitional economies at $4.30 per person a day. Affluent countries have their own thresholds. In the USA the poverty line is adapted yearly to the consumer price index. In 2013 it was set at $31.50 for a single person a day increased by $11 for every additional person in a household (Federal Register, 2013).

Adaptations were indicative of the complexities of absolute poverty lines and resulted in the development of relative poverty indices. According to this view people are not just poor because they lack money, but because they cannot participate in society and are excluded. Poverty is then seen in each society. As to its measurement, the OECD suggested taking 50% of the median income as a yardstick for poverty. The arbitrariness of that yardstick is again dubious, since Eurostat, the statistical bureau of the EU takes 60% of the median income as the poverty line. The question also arises: 50% or 60% of which median income? If in the EU the threshold is

60% of the median national income, the poverty in Luxembourg – despite this country being ranked second in the world's wealthiest countries, with a GDP per capita of nearly $80,000 a year – would be three times higher than the poverty in Portugal with a GDP per capita that is three times as low. If 60% of the median income in the European Union as a whole would be taken as the yardstick, the poverty in Portugal would be approximately 20 times as high as in Luxembourg. The relatively high income inequality and GDP per capita in Luxembourg compared to Portugal accounts for this. However, in the latter scenario, over 80% of the population in the EU member states in Central Europe would be labelled as poor, given the much lower GDP per capita in those states compared to the Western European EU member states.

Poverty can thus be measured by absolute and relative indicators both resulting in their own peculiarities and always involving arbitrary choices. This has made international organizations and scholars rethink the concept of poverty. Nowadays the dominant view is that poverty entails more than just a lack of money and that it is about vulnerability and lack of resilience in general. Poverty became defined as 'the failure of basic capabilities to reach certain minimally acceptable levels' (Sen, 1992, p. 109). By redefining the concept in this way, it was connected to other Millennium Development Goals, such as the fight against illiteracy, gender inequality and infant mortality, since improving on these factors would enable people to satisfy their basic needs even if their financial resources were small.

Not only at the individual level, but also at the national level the original indicator to distinguish between developed and developing countries and countries in transition changed. Before the 1990s GDP per capita was *the* indicator. Since then more elaborate indices such as the Human Development Index (HDI) as used by the UN have been developed. The HDI is a composite index of life expectancy, years of schooling and income. Table 8.1 provides an overview of the differences in the concentration of this human development in the world.

The third column of this table shows that in some countries the life expectancy at birth is below 60 years, while in others it is above 80 years. The fourth column shows that in some countries the average amount of schooling is less than five years, while in others it is over ten years. The last column tells us that in some countries people have to live on average on less than $3,000 a year, while the average income in other groups of countries is above $40,000 a year.

Table 8.1 *Human Development Index 2014**

	Human Development Index (HDI)	Life expectancy at birth	Mean years of schooling	Gross national income (GNI) per capita
Countries	2013	2013	2012	2013
Very high human development	0.890	80.2	11.7	40,046
High human development	0.735	74.5	8.1	13,231
Medium human development	0.614	67.9	5.5	5,960
Low human development	0.493	59.4	4.2	2,904

*Human Development Index (HDI): A composite index measuring average achievement in three basic dimensions of human development – a long and healthy life, knowledge and a decent standard of living.
Life expectancy at birth: Number of years a newborn infant could expect to live if prevailing patterns of age-specific mortality rates at the time of birth stay the same throughout the infant's life.
Mean years of schooling: Average number of years of education received by people ages 25 and older, converted from education attainment levels using official durations of each level.
Gross national income (GNI) per capita: Aggregate income of an economy generated by its production and its ownership of factors of production, less the incomes paid for the use of factors of production owned by the rest of the world, converted to international dollars using purchasing-power parity (PPP) rates, divided by midyear population.
Source: United Nations Development Programme, 2014, p. 163

People in countries in sub-Saharan Africa especially suffer, while those born in OECD countries tend to prosper. The highest values on the HDI are found in Norway, Australia, Switzerland, the Netherlands, United States, Germany, New Zealand, Canada, Singapore and Denmark, while at the bottom of the ranking countries like Niger, Congo, Central African Republic, Chad, Sierra Leone, Eritrea, Burkina Faso, Burundi, Guinea and Mozambique appear (United Nations, 2014, p. 163).

What makes matters even more problematic is that within those countries being worst off in terms of general human development, the inequality is also largest. Table 8.2 gives the data on inequality for different regions.

Table 8.2   *Inequality in regions*

	Coefficient of human inequality	Inequality in life expectancy at birth	Inequality in education	Inequality in income
Index group of countries	2013	2013	2012	2013
Very high human development	12.0	4.9	8.7	22.4
High human development	19.3	10.7	17.4	29.9
Medium human development	25.2	21.9	35.1	18.6
Low human development	32.4	35.0	38.2	23.9

Source: United Nations, 2014, p. 171

The figures in this table point out that the prospect of a life that is long, in which basic education is provided for and in which severe financial problems can be avoided are favourable in countries with a high score on the HDI, even if one is born in a not too wealthy family, while such a prospect is slim if one is born in a country with low human development and extremely low if one is born in such a country within a lower-class family. The latter can be indicative for a life-expectancy at birth of less than 40 years, that is, if one survives the first five years, of less than one-and-a-half-years of education, if any, and of incomes of less than the absolute poverty line of $1.25 a day.

Nonetheless the table should be interpreted with caution. One should be aware that the three indices of unequal opportunities for 'the good life' as given in such aggregated tables can present a somewhat skewed picture of reality. For instance, the highest income inequalities are found in countries in Latin America and the Caribbean, while the largest inequalities in education are found in countries in the Arab region, and inequality in life expectancy is highest in sub-Saharan African countries.

In countries with a low human development the proportion of deaths that occurs during the first month after birth is still increasing and as to infectious and mortal diseases, in Swaziland, Lesotho and Botswana more than a quarter of the population between 15 and 49 have contracted HIV/AIDS. This significantly reduces the life expectancy at birth. With regard to education, in such countries as Benin, Burkina Faso and Niger less than 30% of the adult population is literate. This might still be an overestimate since literacy is minimally defined as 'the ability to just read and write a simple sentence about their everyday life with understanding' as measured through surveys. Another indicator for the problem is that countries like Uganda, Ethiopia, Mozambique, Madagascar, Angola and Rwanda, but also Nicaragua, where the official literacy rate among adults is somewhat higher than in the three countries mentioned, score much higher on basic school drop-outs, as more than half of their children already drop out before finishing basic school.

Framing problems

The previous section showed that the measurement of a problem is always partly based on subjective notions about thresholds and yardsticks. One can push the issue further by pointing at the varying ways one can frame the problem. Framing a problem refers to isolating some of the basic frameworks of understanding events in order to make sense of the problem. Out of the many possible frameworks in which one can understand a problem one chooses and isolates a particular framework, thus steering the direction in which action is to be undertaken or inhibiting such action.

One of the original scholars on the theory of framing was the Canadian sociologist *Erving Goffman*. According to him framing involves two parts, namely constructing a primary framework and keying. Constructing the *primary framework* refers to looking at the facts and putting them in either a natural or a social framework. A *social framework* provides background understanding for events that incorporate will, aim and controlling effort (Goffman, 1974, p. 22). Someone or some human-made thing is to blame for the problem. A *natural framework* suggests that the problem is not intentionally guided and is something that occurs, or is for instance determined by biophysical, natural, historical or geographical factors.

The primary framework and keying can result in two main types of framing. The first type of frame emphasizes the magnitude of the problem, its causes and effects, possible policies as structural solutions and the instruments and resources needed, thus focusing on project management, being in control and being rational. The second type of frame focuses on the drama, the victims, heroes and villains, emphasizing the role of personal and relation managers and thus creates a more emotional frame for the problem.

As to poverty, an *emotional framework* could describe the poor in their awful situation, their desperate efforts to cope with everyday life, the constant search for food and shelter and the malnutrition of the children involved. An emotional framework with the opposite effect is to depict the poor as lazy, irresponsible in having children they cannot afford, making the wrong decisions and depicting their situation as their own fault. Similar framing, in that it is devoid of rational analysis and negates the necessity to take action, is by ennobling the problem: 'It is the will of the almighty'; by routinization: 'It's just a fact of life'; by denial: 'No, here in Japan, you cannot be poor, only people in developing countries are poor'; by lessening expectations: 'You cannot expect government to solve all of societies' problems'; and by externalization: 'It is not my problem' (cf. Dror, 1988).

Keying refers to modelling the problem. It implies adding a layer to which one anchors the problem and wants it to be interpreted and understood. One can key the problem of poverty as a problem of irresponsible individual behaviour of the poor themselves, but also as an economic problem of low wages, unfair international trade and global inequality. One can key the problem as a problem of social exclusion, as an educational problem focusing on illiteracy or as a survival issue focusing on health care. It can be keyed as a gender problem by pointing out that women are suffering more from poverty than men and that those women might be the ones who could provide the solution. Finally, one can key poverty as a public service delivery problem, involving the inadequacy of economic development, infrastructure, employment, schooling, health care and housing or the inadequate provision of clean water and electricity by local or regional government. It can also be keyed as a corruption problem since part of the aid to the poor ends up in the wrong hands or as a leadership issue pointing to the inefficient and wrong way political leaders in the countries in which poverty is prevalent spend their resources.

Problems such as poverty have many dimensions and keying refers to isolating one of those dimensions and making it dominant in order to guide, promote or inhibit specific actions to resolve the problem.

Societal interests

The framing of problems is not just a theoretical exercise, but is visible in many policy processes meant to resolve social problems. Especially when problems are 'wicked', in that there is no agreement about the values involved nor sufficient knowledge of the incidence of the problem and the causalities involved, conflicting frames are likely to emerge. Such unstructured problems are characterized by multiple actors, advocacy groups, non-governmental organizations, pressure groups, special interest groups and lobby groups, with varying power and interests. These actors not only want to have the problem as such high on the policy agenda or to prevent the problem getting high on the policy agenda but also strive to get their specific problem framing accepted by influencing public opinion, politicians and policy makers.

Their problem frames are determined, among others, by their knowledge of the problem, their perception of the severity of the problem, trigger events, sincere concerns, the proximity of the problem to them and their self-interest, and also by their position, the organization they belong to, their beliefs, the political ideology they adhere to and the (sub)culture in the peer group they belong to.

With regard to ideology, the left–right distinction is probably a classic one. Originally the terms can be traced back to the French Revolution, after the seating arrangement in the parliament of the time. Even though left and right are rather abstract concepts, they can be seen as guiding principles to understand political differences resulting in different policy preferences. Left and right are associated with other abstract terms like 'progressive' or 'conservative', or socialist, liberal, communist or fascist ideologies. 'Left' is associated with being in favour of social change and promoting equality, whereas 'right' is associated with maintaining the status quo, conservatism and being against social equality. A 'leftist' interest group has a favourable attitude towards an intervening government and a 'rightist' group will most probably be in favour of a withdrawing government. Typical issues of the left are about income redistribution, while the right is more concerned about maintaining 'law and order'. Leftist groups and parties stress democratic values, the need for governmental control over industries and the financial sector and social justice, while typical rightist issues are concerned with the efficiency of the public sector, promoting the free market system and scaling down government. A typical leftist frame of poverty would be that 'The 85 richest people in the world have the same wealth as the 3.5 billion poorest people', thus pointing to the need for social justice through income redistribution by, for instance, progressive taxes. A typical rightist frame would be that socio-economic inequality furthers economic growth by which the poor also profit, that governmental interference disrupts the workings of the free market, thus diminishing economic growth and that government by providing social benefits deprives the poor from incentives to seek work and become independent.

The way problems are framed is also culturally determined. As described in Chapter 5, in some countries people accept a high power distance and inequality, while people in other societies favour equality. In some societies collectivism dominates while in others individualism prevails. In masculine societies the interpersonal caring that is characteristic of feminine societies is absent, and in societies that lack a long-term orientation, people prefer quick results and a quick fix to address problems, while a long-term orientation is about having a grand purpose and commitment to a grand cause. Belonging to a specific culture influences the way one frames the poverty in it being morally wrong or not, whether it affects the quality of one's own life even if one does not belong to the poor or sees the problem as distant and whether one searches for relief and alleviation for those suffering momentarily or seeks the eradication of the fundamental causes of poverty in order to diminish poverty within decades.

Public administration interests

The inherent subjectivity in the definition of problems makes all the themes relevant to the internal workings of government, as addressed in the first part of this book, also relevant in understanding how problems are structured. As discussed in Chapter 2, one of the issues is whether the problem is to be seen as a collective problem in need of collective action or whether it is an individual problem outside the realm of the public sector. When a problem is judged to be a collective problem, the question arises of whether it should result in collective action at the national, regional or local level, as discussed under the label of centralization and decentralization in Chapter 3, and to what degree path dependences are at stake. The next question is how potential policies meant to resolve the problem are to be organized, as discussed in Chapter 4, and whether that impacts on the definition of the problem. Should it be taken care of within the existing organizational structures or should a new department or agency be established, and which department should get the responsibility and authority to deal with the problem and how does that influence the definition of the problem? What does this imply for the recruitment of new administrators, for managers and for leaders, the central topic of Chapter 5, and how are they involved in the framing of the problem? The framing of the problem is also likely to be determined by personal motivation of administrators who might see it either as a threat or as an opportunity to further their careers and their departmental interests. And policies might become less effective when decisions about them are suboptimal because of the inhibitors mentioned in Chapter 7.

All this makes it understandable that the definition of a social problem in practice is not only determined by its actual nature and magnitude, and public policies to address such problems are not only judged for their effectiveness and efficiency or their rationality and legitimacy. Factors inherent to the internal workings of the public sector cannot be neglected in analysing how problems are defined and solved.

It is most likely that the way problems are framed depends on the position of the person doing the framing, conforming the general adage known as Miles' law: 'Where you stand depends on where you sit.' This implies that organizational interests are often as important as collective interests in addressing collective problems. Someone working in a health department is likely to see poverty as a health-care problem, whereas someone working at the ministry of education will stress the importance of education and reducing illiteracy, and somebody working in the department of economics will see the same problem in terms of unemployment, absent economic development or downward international trade. Somebody at the ministry of justice might not see poverty as a problem at all, because resources allocated to alleviate poverty might come at the expense of his or her own budgets to fight crime. This individual may emphasize examples of abuse of social benefits by people who can hardly be called poor in order to discourage new policies to alleviate poverty.

All this implies that problems are not only framed and keyed, but also vulnerable to fabrication and *misframing*. Deception, make-believe and concealment of facts create vulnerabilities in the understanding of social problems.

From framing to public policies

The crucial question is when and how public problems result in public policies that are effective and efficient, rational and legitimate in resolving those problems. One way to analyse this is to decompose the policy process into each of its elements. The classic way of doing this is to distinguish different phases of the policy process, such as the agenda setting, in which the problem is recognized and deemed important enough to induce policies; the phase of policy development, in which the problem is analysed, goals are formulated and instruments are proposed to achieve those goals; and the phase of policy adoption, in which the policy is transformed in a law or regulation approved by the authority, after which the policy is implemented, the instruments are actually applied, and the policy is evaluated and judged for its effectiveness, efficiency, rationality and legitimacy.

These phases can be seen either as elements in a linear process, in which there is a one-way direction from problem formulation through agenda setting, policy development and policy adoption, to implementation and evaluation, or as a policy cycle in which the process is seen as a recurrent process because the magnitude of the problem might change due to the policy, but does not disappear, or new issues may arise, resulting in a repetition of the process through which the contents of the policy are changed in order to make it more effective and efficient, rational and legitimate, after which the process repeats itself again.

Much research has been done into each of these phases and has, among other things, shown that this phase model is far from a straightforward process.

Getting the problem on the agenda

With regard to *agenda setting* Public Administration scholars have pointed out that it is not easy to get problems addressed by policies. Policy makers have to be made aware of the magnitude and urgency of the problem, they have to be convinced that the development of a public policy is in order and that investing in such a policy will result in a policy that is politically, economically, culturally and administratively feasible, and they need to be not too busy addressing other urgent problems. Hence, it is not easy for problems to reach the policy agenda. This needs *policy champions* who continuously invest in placing the problem to the fore by distributing knowledge, making thorough analyses and/or building an interest group which has to become active and get attention in the media and thus influence policy makers by making them aware of the magnitude and effects of the problem. The role of interest groups can be, through manifestations, conferences and demonstrations, to increase awareness.

Scholars point to the crucial role of the media as intermediaries between societal groups and policy makers, and the importance of the role of investigative journalists. Also deemed important are trigger events, events that receive a lot of media attention, and that suddenly and unexpectedly may make policy makers aware of the urgency of the problem. Finally, the outcomes of evaluations that may point to the failure of existing policies or to the catastrophic effects of the neglect of the problem, and outcomes of research by experts or university scholars that point to the seriousness of the problem, might make policy makers take the problem seriously. In the agenda-setting process, in which meaning is given to problems by way of framing, the way the problem is presented is crucial for its recognition as a policy problem by policy makers.

Two examples of problems which have been proven difficult to get on the policy agenda are global warming and the Ebola outbreak in West Africa in 2014. Global warming, previously known as the greenhouse effect (a term apparently not so appealing), still has difficulty in being taken seriously by many policy makers, despite the presence of all the factors mentioned for decades. The Ebola outbreak took several months, the growth of the problem to 1,000 deaths in West Africa (apparently a symbolic figure) and the death of an American medical doctor in particular (the trigger event) before affluent countries started to take action to stop the outbreak. By the time money, medics and equipment became available, border controls were introduced for people coming from the three hardest hit countries – Liberia, Sierra Leone, Guinea-Bissau – and measures were taken in neighbouring countries to counter the spread of the disease by people entering from those countries, the number of people with the disease had exceeded 13,000, the death toll in West Africa had neared 5,000 people and the number of countries affected included Nigeria and Mali.

Developing the policy

The next step in the policy process, the development of a public policy, is also far from straightforward. It involves making an analysis of the problem, deciding where one wants to interfere, which policy instruments should be used and weighing the costs and benefits of the policy.

From a purely *rational approach to policy making*, a policy maker would first want to find out *the dimensions involved* in a problem and who suffers for it where, how and when, in order to get adequate insight as to where an intervention would be most effective and efficient. As to policies to reduce poverty, the first question asked would be what is poverty and what are its dimensions? Is it just about low income, or is it also about child mortality, nutrition, unemployment, health, education, social exclusion, fear of violence, access to loans and credits, and access to resources such as land and other property? Are there gender inequalities and how do children suffer? One would also ask whether there are statistics pointing out its magnitude, regional variations, and its concentration in rural and urban areas, in order to answer the question of where poverty is especially found. Secondly, one would ask what is known about the *causes and effects* of poverty, about its underlying causes and about the root causes, as well as about the direct and indirect effects of poverty. A simplified example of such an analysis is given in Figure 8.1.

Such causal analyses can be based on scholarly research, expert opinions and other in-depth investigations, but their content and application are also dependent on the way a problem is framed, the dimension of the problem that is emphasized, the position of a policy maker who has to deal with budget constraints, and the demands of the department, political authorities and other stakeholders involved. It might also be dependent on ideological, political, cultural, economic and organizational factors. Thirdly, the causal model underlying the policy to be developed might be imposed by funding agencies or authorities,

Figure 8.1 *The causal analysis of a policy problem*

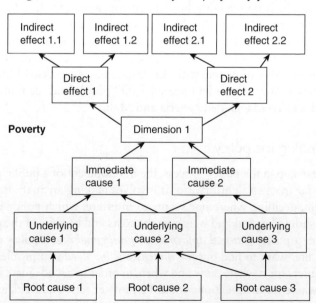

who only want to allocate money to make the implementation of a policy possible if a certain aspect of the problem is addressed in the policy – for instance the promotion of good governance, democracy or combating corruption – irrespective of whether there is a direct link between this aspect and poverty reduction or whether its effects on poverty reduction are remote. (For an overview of theories on policy processes, see Sabatier, 1999.)

Irrespective of the validity of the schema used, it is meaningful to reconstruct it in order to get insight into the rationality behind public policies and to understand what the assumptions of the policy makers were when they designed the policy. For policy makers the information such schemas contain could become the basis for an intervention through a policy aimed at the level of the root causes, underlying or immediate causes, to address the problem itself or to act in order to alleviate the direct or indirect effects of the problem. Acting with the aim of removing the root causes of poverty could imply trying to change global, national or local inequality. Acting with the aim of removing the underlying causes of poverty might involve improving on education, health care or national infrastructure, or trying to attract business and foreign investments in order to create employment, while acting on the immediate causes might make a policy maker decide to make it easier for the poor to get work, force them to work or give them access to loans in order to start their own business. Acting on the effects of poverty, the policy maker might decide to provide flour at a subsidized price, to provide cheap housing or provide access to electricity, drinking water and health care at reduced rates, and acting on indirect effects a policy maker might invest in order and security to prevent those affected by poverty from using illegal means to survive, protesting or even rising up. In this process the rational policy maker develops a policy in which one of the elements in the previous schema is removed or reduced and takes possible side effects of his or her policies into account. This is visualized in Figure 8.2.

Figure 8.2   *The contents of a policy*

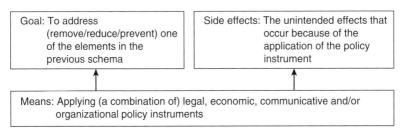

In order to achieve the policy goals a range of instruments is available: organizational, legal, economic and communicative. As to *organizational instruments*, one can try to improve a situation or resolve a problem by arranging things in a different way. If a traffic intersection crossing leads to a dangerous situation, one can change the current situation; for instance, by changing the intersection into a roundabout. If, within a public administration, the performance is below expectations, one can start a departmental reorganization or change the intergovernmental relations by decentralization and privatization, as we have frequently witnessed in previous decades. Although classic policy analysis does not acknowledge organizational instruments as a separate instrument and restricts itself to the next three types of policy instrument listed above, recent research gives such organizational instruments a more prominent place within policy making (see the end of this chapter under the section on 'nudging').

The *legal instruments* consist of laws, rules, instructions, resolutions, ordinances, jurisprudence and treaties. In the case of the traffic intersection one can change the rules of precedence or forbid car drivers to approach the crossing at a speed above 30 km per hour. *Economic instruments* consist of subsidies, premiums, levies but also financial sanctions. One can fine car drivers that do exceed the speed limit or who do not abide by the law. In *communicative instruments* the policy maker tries, through means like advice, counselling and information transfer, to change the opinions and behaviour of business and citizens. Warning messages or flashers could be placed along the roads to the crossing, to make traffic aware of the danger ahead of them.

In the case of poverty alleviation, applying organizational instruments could be done by improving the infrastructure of a country, by building roads, airports and railways, building industrial areas, ensuring the provision of clean water and electricity, enabling (fast) internet and building hospitals, schools, et cetera in order to provide the basic conditions for socio-economic development. Recently, it has also been repeatedly tried to reorganize development aid organizations in order to make the aid to the poor more effective.

Legal instruments can in the case of poverty alleviation be applied, for instance, to create and guarantee equal opportunities, to ensure social assistance and social benefits to the poor, to fix prices of commodities and to accomplish minimum wages, safe working conditions or fair trade. Poverty is partly created and maintained by law and laws can also be tools for redistribution.

As to economic instruments, international organizations can give aid to poor countries in order to alleviate the poverty. Governments can subsidize or facilitate the development of small and medium and micro enterprises. Some governments like the one in Egypt heavily subsidize the price of wheat in order to make the purchase of food affordable. Other governments use progressive tax to reduce income inequality. International banks have started micro-credits which are used to enable the poor to borrow money to start a business.

Communicative instruments can be used to get a better understanding of poverty, to inform the poor about opportunities to escape from poverty or to make the rich aware of the seriousness of the problem in order to induce them to give more to charity.

Policy instruments are part of the collective goods provided by the public sector and therefore are to be judged for their effectiveness, efficiency, rationality and legitimacy as described in Chapter 2. To classify them into four categories does not imply that there is a limited number of policy instruments. The imaginable variation in policy instruments is only limited by one's creativity, although the actual variance depends on their effectiveness, efficiency, rationality and legitimacy within the contextual boundaries. The actual preference for certain types of policy instruments does not only depend on their expected effectiveness and efficiency. Some regimes favour legal instruments, other regimes prefer economic instruments and still others use communicative instruments, irrespective of the problem at hand. The preference depends on the level of government, be it national, regional or local; on the nature of the organization that develops the policy, its culture, its type of management and organization; the preferences, capabilities and motivation of individual policy makers; and their capacity to analyse the problem at stake and to make sound decisions. Furthermore, the actual choice for certain policy instruments is partly determined by the rules as mentioned in the previous chapter – whether or not the process is transparent and stakeholders are involved and so forth and so on. The content of policies is embedded in the organizational and institutional structure in which such policies are developed.

In the practice of policy making such schemas are not often generated and remain implicit. First, because there might be uncertainty and a lack of knowledge about the causes and effects of social problems, and second, in the case of extensive knowledge, such schemas tend to become complex and even cluttered because of the multitude of factors involved and the many crossing lines. In the latter case such schemas result in confusion rather than in clarity.

It is more likely that policy makers asked to develop a public policy to address a certain problem will investigate first whether such policies have already been developed elsewhere, instead of analysing the problem themselves. If so, they will search for information about the effectiveness and efficiency of those policies and whether the policies could fruitfully be copied to their own situation. In case of national policies the question is often whether something can be learned from (best) practices in other countries and in case of local policies whether something can be learned from policies developed in other municipalities. There is a risk that copying policies from one context to another might result in disappointing outcomes, because differences in both contexts might affect the effectiveness and efficiency of the copied policies. It is the problem of so-called 'one-size-fits-all policies' implying that if contextual differences are not properly addressed, best practices in one place may turn into worst practices in another place because policies that work in China will not necessarily be effective in the USA and vice versa. Much research into the copying of public policies has been done under the label of *policy diffusion* (Rogers, 1962). Such research points out that policy diffusion is promoted by personal contacts between policy makers, by shared membership of organizations that promote certain policies, and by the participation of policy makers in conferences, symposia and other meetings in which public policies are discussed. Structural factors are also important; for instance, the physical proximity of organizations, the hiring of policy consultancy firms and the promotion, or even imposing, of policy diffusion by higher authorities, funding agencies and international organizations.

The formal decision on the policy

After a policy has been proposed, it needs formal approval, i.e. a law passed, and implementation will be based on this approval. As such, this is a major phase since proposals are turned into established policies. Two issues that can arise in this phase are *policy drift* and *symbolic policy making*.

Policy drift occurs when the relation between the policy and the problem it addresses becomes confused and unclear. This can happen when power, interests and strategic rationality enter the process, as is so often the case in political decision making.

In his classic 1964 book, Murray Edelman introduced the concept of *symbolic policies* by which politicians just want to appear as if they are actively solving a problem. They do this by using symbols, which 'by definition stand for something other than themselves and evoke an attitude, a set of impressions or a pattern of events associated through time, space, through logic or through imagination with the symbol'

(Edelman, 1964, p. 6). Their function is to gain support even if the polices are not effective in reducing the problem. The second function of symbolic policies is to reduce complexity and to appeal to the public by reducing a complex issue to appealing one-liners (Edelman, 1964).

Policy proposals tend to drift or become symbolic particularly when authorities are influenced by lobby groups or ground their opinions in political ideologies, motivated by their desire to maximize popular support for themselves or by their desire to maximize profit for themselves. Political decision makers can make minor or dramatic changes to the policy proposal; for instance, to mitigate the effects for groups that will suffer from the policies, by complicating policies and by altering responsibilities for the implementation of policies.

In the Netherlands, for instance, a proposal was put forward to scale up regional government by amalgamating the provinces in order to reduce costs and the complexity of domestic institutional arrangements. When political support was sought for the plans, politicians from the green parties demanded extra money to merge environmental policies handled by the provinces; and the social liberals wanted additional money for education policies in exchange for their support to amalgamate mid-level governmental institutions. The costs for accommodating the varying political demands that complicated the original policy proposal became so high that the proposal was withdrawn.

Similarly, in Indonesia in 2012 there was a push to reform junior high-school education. The original problem was based on the low ranking of Indonesian students on PISA scores, an international ranking produced by the OECD on the basis of reading, mathematical and problem-solving capacities of 15-year-old high school students. PISA is an acronym for OECD 'Programme for International Student Assessment'. The 2012 outcomes placed Indonesia second to last for all countries included in the research. Indonesia's ranking was particularly low in maths: 75.7% were deemed to be low achievers – the highest of all countries. Because of the negative publicity, education reform was in order. Two years later, this educational reform policy was ready to be implemented in the schools. The main changes were an increase in mandatory school hours for elementary and junior high school children, new textbooks, new teaching methods and more lessons per week on religious studies. Somewhere during the process, the reform policy must have drifted away from the original problem.

Brazilian politicians faced similar problems in education, measured in IDEB scores – the Brazilian Education Quality Index – a national equivalent to PISA scores. They opted for decentralizing authority and responsibility for education by merging state and municipal schools into municipal schools and by improving the education of teachers based on the slogan 'training the trainers'. Although both policy options seemed reasonable at first sight, a causal analysis revealed that the variance in the achievement scores was most dramatic between poor and affluent regions and between private and public schools. As a result, the merger of public schools at the local and state level was merely a symbolic policy; in order to have real effect, they should have called for additional funding to bring public schools, be they state or municipal, to the same level as private schools. As for the policy of training the trainers, empirical research suggests that while the level of education of teachers is related to students' achievements, it has very little influence on achievement scores when controlled for the poverty in the region. That finding suggests that the level of education of teachers and the region they work in is strongly related. It implies that well-educated teachers do not tend to seek employment in the poor regions. Policies aimed at improving teachers' education might therefore reinforce the differences between regions and could mainly benefit those regions that are already well off (cf. Andrews & de Vries, 2011). Such effects are characteristic of symbolic policies.

Implementing the policy

Policy drifting can become worse during implementation, the last phase in the policy process. The application of the policy instruments in practice and the actual provision of collective goods and services are often carried out by different actors than those who developed and decided on the policies. Educational policies have to be implemented by teachers, security policies by the police and health-care policies by medical professionals. And policies developed at the national level often have to be implemented at the local level.

Until the 1970s policy implementation was rarely considered as a problem. It was assumed that policies would simply be implemented exactly how they were intended and developed. Nowadays, implementation issues are the major obstacle in achieving the policy goals; implementation reduces the effectiveness and efficiency of policies. The causes of failed implementation can be found in all of the issues described in the previous chapters in this book, i.e. government structures, centralization, organizational structure, poor leadership and management, individual corruption, poor decision making and lack of clarity in policy making.

In 1973, Pressman and Wildavsky investigated a large welfare project developed by the US federal government to be implemented in Oakland and other US cities. The goals of the policy were ambitious, namely reducing racial differences, increasing employment opportunities for black citizens and improving the city's infrastructure. The policy required substantial investments in the deployment of human and financial resources. However, five years into the project, Pressman and Wildavsky found that very little had been accomplished and the outcomes were disappointing. This led to the famous subtitle of their book 'How great expectations in Washington are dashed in Oakland' (Pressman & Wildavsky, 1973).

They concluded that the implementation failed because the ambitious goals proved to be mutually conflicting in the implementation phase, that during the implementation phase the project experienced conflicting legal demands, bureaucratic obstruction and conflicts of interests between participants, and that uncertainty arose about the desirability and feasibility of local projects. They concluded that these issues related to this specific project could be generalized to implementation processes in general: implementation has a natural tendency to fail, all superficial solutions have as many drawbacks as advantages and that it is better to develop more modest goals and objectives.

A similar analysis could be conducted for the Millennium Development Goals formulated in 2000 and the eight more ambitious global goals added in 2015, namely poverty eradication, universal primary education, gender equality, reducing child mortality, improving maternal health, combating the most serious diseases, ensuring environmental sustainability and developing an open, rule-based, predictable, non-discriminatory trading and financial system. This is especially the case because international organizations such as the UN acknowledge that limitations at the local level, i.e. their capacity to implement policies, play a large role in meeting the Millennium Development Goals.

The research by Pressman and Wildavsky led to a vast amount of research on implementation issues. Initially, this research suggested the need for more control on implementation, hierarchical relations, authority and loyalty, the need to consider the availability of resources for policy implementation, the need for extensive communication between policy makers and implementers in order to achieve agreement about goals and means and the validity of the policy, and the need to remove organizational, institutional and individual barriers to implementation. It sought reasons for failed implementation in the inadequacies of the *top-down* relations between policy makers and those who have to implement them.

This view changed with the publication of Michael Lipsky's book in 1979. Lipsky studied the actual workings of what he called 'street-level bureaucrats'. He argued that the work of these individuals – responsible for implementing public policies developed by others – has a number of characteristics that contribute to implementation problems. Their performance is often impossible to measure, they often lack adequate resources and therefore have a high workload, they are confronted with ambiguous policy goals and they have substantial policy discretion in their interaction with clients. The combination of these characteristics can transform committed individuals at the start of their career into cynics later on when they start to simplify reality, externalize responsibility and are increasingly inclined to move to standard operating procedures, instead of being caring and motivated to serve the public. Lipsky sees the solution in a *bottom-up* approach in which policy makers listen to those who have to implement their policies, in which policies are developed by those who have to implement them and in which implementation issues are the input instead of the output of policy development.

Since these two early studies, much additional research has been done into implementation processes (cf. Hill & Hupe, 2002). The findings suggest that there are many factors and characteristics of the individual actors who carry out the implementation that influence it. Some have argued that before proposing any additional factors, we should abandon existing ones. The research into implementation focuses on how such processes should be organized and who should implement policies. It is about whether public or private actors (or some combination) should take the lead, and whether the public, NGOs and societal organizations (or some combination) should be involved. This brings us back to our first key theme in Public Administration from Chapter 2; namely, how to solve collective problems with the provision of collective goods.

Recent research on problem analysis and policy making

Evidence-based policy making

One of the novel treads in public policy analysis is evidence-based public policy. Since many policies fail to achieve their goals or prove ineffective and inefficient in solving problems, researchers are led to ask what works and why (World Bank, n.d.). This information could be obtained by systematic monitoring and evaluation of existing policies. With regard to education policies, for example, Gary Banks concludes that changing them into evidence-based policies might significantly alter their content. He argues this by pointing to existing research. 'The long-term policy goal of reducing class sizes has received very little empirical support. In contrast, the importance of individual teacher performance, and the link to differentiated pecuniary incentives, are backed by strong evidence, but have been much neglected.' (Banks, 2009)

This evidence-based approach to policy making uses policies as experiments in a manner similar to medical research where treatments and their effects are studied. The supposed connections between policy instruments and policy goals and between goals and problem solving are hypotheses that could be tested through scholarly research. Such research evidence and analysis that is robust and publicly available can serve as an important counterweight to the influence of sectional interests and political–strategic rationality (Banks, 2009).

In some ways, evidence-based public policy is reminiscent of Donald Campbell's classic work in 1966. He advocated for an experimental society and for conducting policy experiments with experimental and control groups with pre-testing and post-testing to determine what works and what does not. Such policy evaluations were widely conducted in the 1960s, but they were criticized for their failure to point to statistically significant effects of policies, even though policy makers were convinced that their policies had the intended effects.

Perhaps evidence-based policy is best reflected in the literal as well as the figurative meaning of the sentence 'there is nothing like evidence-based policy making'. Figuratively, the sentence suggests that this type of policy making is superior, that it would be ideal if policy makers would think their plans through beforehand, would make more use of scientific findings and could base their policies solely on such knowledge, experience and evaluations. The literal meaning suggests that genuine evidence-based policy making is impossible. This is evident from the factors that affect policy outcomes that are mentioned in this chapter as well as in the previous one. These pointed to a number of reasons that policies might fail in achieving their goals including deficiencies in the implementation process, in the decision-making process, in framing problems, in motivating public administrators, in management and leadership, in the structure of the organization, in the governmental structure and in the regime type. All of these factors could negatively affect policy effectiveness and efficiency, but failing policies can be explained by factors other than the absence of evidence supporting the relation between means and goals, causes and effects.

Nudging

One of the novel trends in policy research within the evidence-based policy making movement investigates the policy implications of individual deficiencies in decision making, and focuses on the possibility of changing individual behaviour. If individual choices are dependent on how the alternatives are presented (the choice architecture), if irrelevant alternatives *do* matter for decision making, and if there are numerous types of biases, perhaps this information can be used to come to more effective decisions by changing individual behaviour in a favourable way without forbidding or prescribing it. Thaler and Sunstein recently suggested the effectiveness of *nudging* (2008).

Nudging implies influencing the choice architecture in an attempt to alter people's behaviour in a predictable way without removing any options or significantly changing their economic incentives. For instance, if we want to combat obesity and induce people to avoid eating fast food, we can place healthy food at the front of stores and snacks at the back.

If we want to decrease gambling addiction we can add restrictions to betting licences in order to counter the temptations to gamble; for instance, by installing visible spending monitors in slot machines to counteract the seduction of the machines and by making gamblers aware of their losses. One can impose additional restrictions by ordering the separation of gambling from drinking through a partition between the slot machines and pubs and bars, cafeterias and coffee shops, or altering the environment in which gambling takes place in other ways.

In order to reduce excessive speeding, laws can be passed that increase the probability of being caught, provide more information, and increase fines; all of these can be costly and ineffective. Nudging would determine the motives of drivers who fail to comply with the rules, and investigate the context in which drivers make their choices and alter the characteristics of the context as a result of this new information. Speeding in residential areas is especially dangerous. Social–psychological research into the underlying motives of drivers has pointed out that the isolated environment inside automobiles made drivers unaware of the outer environment, and this results in more aggressive driving and risk taking. Nudging would adapt the outer environment in such a way that it forces drivers to become more aware of their surroundings. Policy makers can accomplish this by restructuring residential roads, placing blocks and planters, narrowing the entrance to residential roads and painting road surfaces, instead of constructing roads in the classic way by making them as wide as possible to increase the traffic flow. By using social research and investigating what determines human choice behaviour and subsequently changing the relevant aspects of the context, one can alter individual behaviour towards the desired direction without forbidding or prescribing behaviour (cf. Whitehead et al., 2011).

Nudging is based on a number of main assumptions: human rationality is bounded, without countermeasures individuals repeat irrational behaviours, market incentives do not correct – and sometimes encourage – irrational decision making, and characteristics of the physical and procedural context in which decisions are made impact the likelihood of irrational decisions. Governments that are reluctant to forbid or prescribe individual behaviour by law can induce people to make the desired choice by giving them a small push – nudge, the effectiveness of which is determined beforehand by the outcomes of social research (cf. Whitehead et al., 2011).

The same kind of nudging can be used to change the behaviour of individuals working in a bureaucracy. Some Public Administration scholars have associated bureaucracy with an iron cage in which officials become dehumanized and rigid as they need to conform to the hierarchical, rule-based instrumental rationality that is dominant in this type of organization. (Temporarily) changing this environment, for instance sending civil servants to the participants' locale for decision making as opposed to having the participants come to them, might make a difference in supporting innovative ideas and allowing substantive rationality in decision making.

It is an innovative way of thinking about policy making because it transforms the weaknesses, biases and fallacies in decision making into an opportunity for developing more effective public policies. Providing individuals with specific information presented in a well-considered way, changing the context in which they make decisions, giving them incentives for short-term rewards – which apparently most people favour – and pointing out the risks of unfavourable options – which people apparently give greater weight to than opportunities – will change their choice behaviour. *Framing* is closely related to nudging.

The use of nudging in public policies has its critics. Such policies are sometimes depicted as libertarian paternalism since the action doesn't forbid or compel behaviour but changes how options are presented in order to influence behaviour. They are also considered somewhat dangerous since they often reflect only part of social research and social research often provides only partial answers to the questions posed by policy makers. A final risk is that nudging can be considered ethically dubious since it poses the risk of technocratic policy making without considering the opinions of stakeholders.

Network analysis

This last risk is balanced by recent research into the social context in which public policies are developed. This widely researched field concerns the analysis of policy networks. It investigates how a multitude of actors work together to accomplish a common policy. The findings of this research suggest that in order to understand policy development, one has to understand the hierarchy of networks, the degree to which interests coincide or conflict and the degree to which the actors in the network are mutually dependent or relatively independent in being able on their own to achieve beneficial outcomes.

The first systematic studies, on networks, networking and building coalitions in and between organizations are from the late 1950s and early 1960s (Evan, 1965). This classic research described interactions among individuals across organizations. These individuals aimed to create networks for getting things done and for exchanging information by going beyond the formal structure of their own organization. Current research focuses on the importance of the following factors:

- Features of the network context, i.e. its complexity, uncertainty, ambiguity, dynamics and institutionalization. The network itself is a layer restricting or enabling participants in their choice behaviour. Complexities and adversities in the context of the network necessitate huge investments in the mutual relations of the participants. Scholars focus on the institutional environment typical of the society in which a network is formed. They investigate the political, legal and cultural issues that influence the possibilities for network formation. Another important factor is whether a network is created voluntarily or whether it is a mandated network, and how long it has been in existence.
- The developmental phase of the network. Some studies conclude that once network relations are established, experience within the network has evolved, mutual learning has taken place and network participants know one another, further networking relationships are reinforced and policy-making processes are eased.

- The type of governance of the network, i.e. its management, the centrality of certain actors and of the network as a whole, and their resource dependency. It has been argued that the most effective governance depends on the level of trust and goal consensus among the actors, the size of the network and the nature of the policy. Research suggests that shared (non-hierarchical) network governance will be most effective when trust is widely shared among network participants, when there are relatively few network participants and when network-level goal consensus is high. However, hierarchy within the network is needed when trust among network participants is low, when there are many network participants and when goal consensus is low.

- Structural features of the network, i.e. size, density, reciprocity, connectivity, cohesion, interconnections, goal consensus, trust, legitimacy, formalization and social embeddedness are deemed important to bringing about effective public policy for solving the underlying problem. Research concludes that the density of a network (the number of actual ties between participants given the potential number of ties in a network) and trust serve as conditions for information exchange, building know-how, searching for best practices, innovativeness and improving performance. If the connectivity of a network increases, this in itself could establish shared direction and purpose in the network as a whole. Trust can also substitute for formal governance.

Conclusions

The key theme addressed in this chapter concerns the relationship between public problems and public policies as an answer to public problems and ways to strengthen this relationship with the aim of making public policies effective and efficient in achieving their goals.

It began by addressing the structuring of problems in general and the poverty problem in particular and subsequently described the issues involved in different phases of the policy-making process. It argued that policies have a tendency to drift from the underlying problem, and that as a result it is difficult to optimize outcomes in terms of problem resolution. Policy drift can be caused by a lack of problem structuring, incomplete analysis of the relation between goals and means, symbolic policies and flawed implementation. As described in several chapters, recent research has taken two paths. Researchers in the first path rationalize the policy-making process by making it evidence based, but they run the risk of policy making becoming technocratic. Researchers in the second path analyse policy networks in order to better understand the social complexities in policy processes which concern numerous stakeholders as a way to balance technocratic solutions.

Evidence-based policy making directly addresses the relationship between power and knowledge and tries to counter political strategic rationality by pointing to the need of substantive rationality based on the outcomes of social and psychological research. It puts the relationship between policies and problem solving back to the fore of policy making. For policies whose aim is to change individual choice behaviour, this field of research recently began investigating the possibilities for changing contextual features – the psychological infrastructure – in which individual choice behaviour takes place, in order to push/nudge individual decisions in the desired direction.

The analysis of policy networks tries to explain what it is in the context of the policy-making process that influences the policy developed. It investigates the impact of structural and governance features of policy networks and the degree to which policy network participants agree on policies in order to solve problems.

Current research focuses on the key theme of making public policies more effective and efficient by investigating whether adapting the social context in which the policy-making process takes place, i.e. the policy network, might serve as an alternative to closed and 'technocratic' policy-making processes. When individual choice behaviour is viewed as the problem to be tackled by a public policy, policies increasingly seek to apply the findings of social and psychological research to change the behaviour of the target group in the desired way by using organizational policy instruments as an alternative to legal, financial and communicative policy instruments. The uncertainty about the usefulness of the trend to emphasize the role of policy networks and the trend to make more use of evidence out of scholarly research in actual policy making and their helpfulness in the understanding of the effectiveness of policy making make this chapter's issue a continuing key theme in Public Administration.

Further reading

Dunn, William N. (2007). *Public policy analysis: An introduction.* Cheltenham: Pearson.

Green-Pedersen, Christoffer & Walgrave, Stefaan (eds) (2014). *Agenda setting, policies, and political systems: A comparative approach.* Chicago: University of Chicago Press.

Parsons, Wayne (1995). *Public policy: An introduction to the theory and practice of policy analysis.* Cheltenham: Edward Elgar.

Rochefort, David A. & Cobb, Roger W. (1994). *The politics of problem definition.* Kansas: Kansas UP.

Sabatier, Paul A. & Weible, Christopher (eds) (2014). *Theories of the policy process.* Boulder, CO: Westview Press.

Thaler, Richard H. & Sunstein, Cass R. (2008). *Nudge: Improving decisions about health, wealth, and happiness.* New Haven: Yale UP.

Chapter 9

Conclusion: The need for appreciation of the public sector

The first sentence of this book made its intentions clear. It is intended to make you think, to reconsider and to reflect on the workings of the public sector by addressing eight key themes in Public Administration. I take the liberty of using this final chapter to formulate a personal key theme in Public Administration. By now it should be clear that Public Administration means two things: it is a scholarly discipline (Public Administration) and it is the subject of that discipline, i.e., public administration as part of the public sector.

In this regard, something odd is going on in Public Administration. As scholars and academicians, we love our students when they are students. We educate them, impart knowledge and skills, and an academic approach to thinking. But as soon as they graduate and enter the public sector as public servants, we begin to loathe them, view them with suspicion, distrust, and pity and criticize them for laziness and failing to be efficient and client oriented. We are inclined to magnify all of their failures, faults and misconducts to the next generation of students. We tell them to initiate administrative reforms; no matter how they are actually doing things, they should do it differently.

Instead of blaming the public sector for everything that goes wrong – even for the consequences of the global financial crisis – and punishing civil servants by freezing wages and downsizing, it is time to be proud of what the public sector has accomplished in terms of public order and safety, health care, education and equity and handling those problems which commercial business calls externalities. Public administration has pursued these accomplishments in spite of the dilemmas and conditions discussed in this book. It addressed a number of dilemmas from the macro to the micro level, not to criticize the public sector, but in order to demonstrate the complexities involved in trying to resolve collective problems through collective action. Public administration is under constant scrutiny as it undertakes collective action. Administrations make public policies and try to ground them in laws and regulations, involving restrictions but also opportunities for citizens. Some individuals might depict these laws, rules and regulations as administrative burdens, but they are, in fact, primarily established in order to remedy the problems that individuals or the private sector cannot remedy alone.

Of course, some criticism of the public sector is justified. There are many examples of things that have not gone well. In spite of these examples, framing the public sector as something to be loathed neglects the merits of public sector work and is based on a misunderstanding of what is at stake.

Unfortunately, the field of Public Administration has not been helpful in balancing this skewed view on the workings of public administration. This chapter provides a concise overview of developments in Public Administration theories and argues that Public Administration theorizing needs to become more balanced. This might well be the ultimate key issue in Public Administration.

From identifying the field of Public Administration...

Although in Europe theorizing about public administration has a long history, at present the dominant theories come from the USA. In the USA, Public Administration theory started with Woodrow Wilson, Frank Goodnow, L. D. White, Luther Gulick and William Franklin Willoughby, and in Europe with Max Weber, although Weber would never have called himself a Public Administration scholar.

The study started on a relatively positive note. Wilson wanted to develop a separate study of administration distinct from political science administrative issues and constitutional issues. In his view, 'Public administration is the detailed and systematic execution of public law.' He wrote:

> Every particular application of general law is an act of administration. The assessment and raising of taxes, for instance, the hanging of a criminal, the transportation and delivery of the mails, the equipment and recruiting of the army and navy, etc., are all obviously acts of administration; but the general laws which direct these things to be done are as obviously outside of and above administration. The broad plans of governmental action are not administrative; the detailed execution of such plans is administrative. (Wilson, 1887, p. 208)

According to Wilson our duty is:

> to supply the best possible life to a federal organization, to systems within systems; to make town, city, county, state, and federal governments live with a like strength and an equally assured healthfulness, keeping each unquestionably its own master and yet making all interdependent and co-operative combining independence with mutual helpfulness (Wilson, 1887, p. 215).

That was quite positive.

Wilson was important in setting the tone for the new discipline. He identified it as distinct from politics and law in its emphasis on 'application' and on improving that application. His distinction was elaborated upon by Frank Goodnow, who distinguished politics and administration in government as follows, "Politics has to do with policies or expressions of the state will. Administration has to do with the execution of these policies" (Goodnow, 1900, p. 18). Where Wilson set the agenda for the new discipline, Goodnow provided the theoretical foundations and demonstrated the intimate connection between public administration and the law that it executes. Like Wilson, he tried to separate the discipline of administration from the (ugly) world of politics. The early years of the discipline focused on making Public Administration distinct in nature. With the benefit of hindsight, one can now say that while Lasswell defined politics in the 1950s as, 'Who gets what, when, and how', Public Administration could be defined in its early years as, 'What works, when, and how'.

Further contributions towards making Public Administration a distinct discipline were made by Leonard White who emphasized management as a crucial aspect of the study of Public Administration, which in his words consists of 'all those operations having for their purpose the fulfilment or enforcement of public policy' (1926, p. 6) and by Gulick who emphasized organizational patterns, authority, division of labour, and the tasks of leadership in such organizations as found in his acronym 'POSDCORB' (Gulick & Urwick, 1937).

In these early years, ideas about the discipline and its subject were relatively positive. The discipline should (1) become managerial, seeking to improve on the internal workings of government by means of management studies, (2) focus on improving the efficiency of the internal workings of government, (3) emphasize the scientific nature of public administration practices which is vital for government to deal with the entangled problems at stake, and (4) distinguish itself from business administration, as research shows how managerial and organizational principles work differently in the public sector.

Max Weber (1965) tried to understand bureaucracy by making it an ideal type, not ideal as a normatively appreciated phenomenon, but an ideal type as the purest form in which it could exist. He never witnessed a bureaucracy in its purest form, but he theorized that trends were definitely going in the direction of such a bureaucracy in which efficiency is central.

Hence, during the first half century in the evolution of Public Administration as an academic discipline, the aim was to define the discipline vis-à-vis the academic disciplines it emerged from and to point to the essentials of public administration in practice.

...through understanding public administration...

Just after the Second World War, the previous development of the discipline was severely criticized by Dwight Waldo (1948). He argued that Public Administration was just a kind of political theory and its aim to improve on efficiency was just one of the many possible things to improve upon in government.

Following Waldo's criticism, many Public Administration scholars began looking beyond efficiency to better understand the Public Sector. Herbert Simon (1965) tried to understand organizational behaviour, and he built a still-used theory on bounded rationality, the limits of optimizing behaviour and the likelihood of satisficing behaviour. Pressman and Wildavsky (1973) explained why implementation will always be flawed. Niskanen (1974) used economic theory to understand what bureaucrats try to maximize, which, according to him, was the growth of their budget and department. Anthony Downs (1967) tried to get a grip on public administration organizations through developing coherent hypotheses. Coase (1937) tried to understand the essence of organizations through transaction cost theory, and Selznick (1957) tried to understand authority, leadership and the binding relations between the organization and its environment. The Ostroms (1999) tried to understand patterns of decision making in the public sector.

The positive aspect of this period, which lasted until the late 1970s, was that scholars invested real effort in making Public Administration a distinct discipline by developing theories that enabled a better understanding of how to explain what goes on inside government. They did so by explaining such processes through more general theories such as transaction cost theory, bounded rationality, budget maximization, rational choice theory and polycentricity in public administration.

This development was needed to move the discipline of Public Administration further in having not only its own object of study or locus – administrative processes in the different spheres of government – but also its own focus in a variety of typical Public Administration theories that explained why administrative processes in the public sector proceed as they tend to proceed. It provided the discipline with tools to explain why the previous era in the development of the discipline – that focused on the optimization of efficiency through scientific management and organization – was one-sided in its focus, unfeasible in its aims, naïve in its futile attempts to improve the public sector, and limited in its understanding of the essence of public administration.

The drawback of this period was that the theories mainly resulted in criticism about the workings of government. Whatever the original *raison d'être* of the public sector, Public Administration theories pointed out that by its nature, the public sector is inclined to act irrationally. The provision of collective goods has numerous drawbacks such as inefficiency, free riding, overproduction and overconsumption; it can be viewed as exploitation of the rich by the poor; its decisions rarely aim at reaching optimal outcomes; it has an inherent tendency towards excessive growth that is not warranted by the magnitude of societal problems; and its centralized decision making and planning are likely to become dashed in the localities.

...towards reforming the public sector

The Public Administration theories developed between 1945 and the 1970s were unable to defend the public sector against the attacks that arose in the late 1970s. The attacks pleaded for downsizing government and, if that was unfeasible, for more efficient performance. It started with deregulation and privatization under the Thatcher regime in England and the Reagan administration in the USA. The latter became famous, or as others have said, notorious, by saying that government was no longer to be seen as the solution for societal problems, but instead to be seen as the problem itself (Reagan, 1981).

The discipline responded to these conservative leaders in the UK and USA, and later the leaders of most other OECD countries, by providing answers for reducing government. It resulted in the development of New Public Management (NPM) theory, in theories calling for converting collective goods into semi-collective goods and privatized goods, and in theories about the desired transformation of government from a Weberian bureaucracy to a more entrepreneurial administration. The methods for achieving these objectives included creating competition inside the bureaucracy and introducing performance measurement, pay for performance and lean management. NPM focused primarily on the ratio between inputs and outputs, i.e. efficiency. Minimizing inputs and maximizing outputs and thus achieving more value for money became the ultimate aim. These developments also changed the language. Policies became products and citizens became clients and customers. Public administration should become more client oriented.

More recently, good governance theory focused on improving the processes – the throughput – within government. Processes should be transparent, thus allowing for democracy and giving people a voice. Administrative processes should abide by the rule of law. There should be regulatory quality, control of corruption, efficiency – which was, by the way, sometimes equated with effectiveness – and a focus on maximizing political stability and minimizing violence and terrorism. It is only recently that the limitations of these two models of public administration reform have been acknowledged, but the call for more public sector reforms remains.

The need to balance

As was repeatedly argued, unlike the private sector, the public sector is not just making profits or protecting the interests of shareholders; it has to weigh the different societal interests, put the general interest to the fore, and take care of the interests of all stakeholders.

One of the complexities involved in achieving these multiple goals is that public sector processes do not conform to a simple principal-agent model. Instead, they are often characterized by a multiple agent-multiple principal model, in which multi-level government has to consider the interests of the public, politicians, domestic and international actors, and related governments at the same or different levels. Not only are there multiple agents, multiple principals, multiple goals and multiple criteria for achieving those goals, but the public sector is often faced with serious dilemmas and constraints. Another complexity is that public sector financing is done mainly through taxes and levies, which are not particularly popular with citizens and companies. Taxation is a continual object of criticism. The third complexity is that the public sector has to conform to multiple criteria such as 'good governance' and 'New Public Management'.

If all this is not enough, the development of policies is restricted and delimited by contrasting ideas (ideology, gaps, fears, unrest), actors with opposing interests (entrepreneurs, policy advocates, interest groups), path dependencies, rapidly changing external circumstances (crises), internal circumstances (institutional resilience), political factors and coincidental factors, all often magnified by the media.

As a result, the basic element of economics, scarcity, also applies to the working of the public sector: the means available for developing adequate policies are always less than the means necessary for developing adequate policies. Because of this scarcity and the resulting dilemmas, it is impossible to comply to all demands simultaneously. One has to prioritize, and therefore some demands are neglected. It is easy to criticize the public sector for what is not done or neglected. Appreciation for what is accomplished by the public sector given its almost impossible circumstances would be more appropriate, and would balance the one-sided view on the public sector. Therefore, my first proposal is:

> Public Administration should start developing theories that cherish the original *raison d'être* and accomplishments of public administration.

Changing the public sector through administrative reforms and reorganizations does not work, and it may even be counterproductive. The formulated goals are often not achieved, and such reforms have negative side effects. In public organizations that have experienced multiple reforms and reorganizations, employees tend to be fed up with the idea of yet another transition. Because of repeated administrative reforms, public employees tend to lose morale, pride and their public service motivation, and they tend to become more critical towards their work, their colleagues and their organization. Furthermore, they are inclined to convert purposeful, effective and strategic rationality into traditional rationality and become conservative. Finally, but importantly, the number of interpersonal conflicts is likely to increase because of the dynamics in the organization. Administrative reforms are not a cure-all, and they are often no better than educated guesses or last resorts. Recent research concluded that these reforms are similar to flipping a coin: sometimes they are effective, sometimes not, and no one seems to know or to care why the probabilities of success and failure are equal.

The literature is full of studies promoting structural administrative reforms based on theoretical arguments. Notwithstanding the eloquence of such arguments and their grounding in theory and logic, they often simply do not work in practice. In fact, there is very little research that demonstrates that the administrative reforms that have taken place in the last few decades have indeed improved the functioning of government. Therefore, my second proposal is:

> Theories in Public Administration should do more than just recommend administrative reforms.

The public sector has to pursue a number of goals including efficiency, effectiveness, accuracy and precision in order to ensure predictability, the application of and fidelity to the rule of law, the promotion of equality before the law and public integrity in order to create trust and legitimacy, and to perform according to the criteria for good governance. This implies checks and balances. Although such mechanisms and institutions may appear inefficient and are often seen as red tape, they are necessary in this regard. They require maintaining institutions such as an audit office, an ombudsman, an independent national bank, independent courts of appeal, a depoliticized public administration and the basics of the *Trias Politica*. Checks and balances imply that the state must be divided into multiple segments that function as checks against each other's power and perform different functions. Preferably, there is an external system of checks and balances, divided among organizations, in order to prevent individual selfishness and the abuse of power, nepotism, fraud and corruption, and to prevent the tyranny of the majority, under which minorities suffer.

Scandals such as Enron, WorldCom and the banking crisis demonstrate what happens when checks and balances fail. Such fiascos happen if one only pursues deregulation, outsourcing, decentralization and deconcentration without proper controls, adequate public procurement, public responsibility and the separation between institutions that control and institutions that advise. While the type of institutions required to accomplish the necessary checks and balances varies among cultures and context, what was witnessed during the last two decades is that nearly all countries have diminished the institutions responsible for checks and balances in favour of creating more efficiency under the excessive impact of NPM. In the furore to introduce reforms, it was neglected to ensure that public administrations would perform their tasks with precision and accuracy and as a result trust in the public sector has eroded. Hence the third proposal:

> Public Administration theory should provide a balanced view of the worth of the institutions that are built to ensure checks and balances in order to assure that the public sector itself upholds the rule of law and nurtures those existing public institutions that have proven their worth.

If anything, one needs to recognize that the public sector was not created to be efficient, but that the true essence of the public sector is to make the public safe and secure, to avoid the conflict of everyone with everyone, to protect property rights and to lay the foundation on which the country's economy and welfare can flourish. The emphasis in the concept of public administration should be on the word 'public', not 'administration'. If the administrative reforms of the last few decades have proven anything, it is that they have made the public administration less oriented towards serving the public. Administrative reforms result in an internal orientation of public administrators who become worried about what the reorganization means for their position within the organization, instead of what the reforms mean for the citizens, except in terms of taxes and costs. Therefore, my last proposal is:

> Public Administration theories should prioritize the 'public' side of public administration, instead of 'administration', by viewing the public side as the *explanandum* and administrative arrangements the *explanans*.

Conclusions

Despite all the criticism, more appreciation for the public sector is in order. The last two decades have witnessed a tendency and inclination to look down upon the public sector as something that needs continual reform and reorganization in order to resemble the private sector. This last chapter argued otherwise. It argued that we should cherish the original *raison d'être* of the public sector; discard the inclination to continuously initiate structural administrative reforms as a panacea; nurture those existing institutions that have proven their worth; and prioritize the 'public' side of public administration instead of the 'administration' part. Let us put an end to promoting reforms we don't know how to handle. Instead, we should be proud of our students and make our students proud to serve the public.

To this end, the recent research described at the end of each chapter is promising and welcomed. Public Administration scholars are trying to find ways to optimize the provision of collective goods, public management and organization, motivation and integrity, public decision making and public policy making by turning the issues into applied science without suggesting that the public sector is good for nothing. Recent research is also involved in investigating the contextual features that affect how public administration operates. It is about theories that rethink how to provide collective goods, rethink the merits of centralization and decentralization, rethink the essentials of bureaucracy and rethink cultural dynamics. It is also about research returning to the classics in governance, and about theories on institutional analysis and policy networks that show that public administrations all over the world are embedded within varying political, economic, historical and organizational contexts and transcend the simplistic notion that such contexts matter by investigating which aspects of those contexts matter and which do not.

Recent developments have resulted in an enormous research agenda for Public Administration scholars, and now they must live up to these expectations because if they fail to do so, future scholars may well view present-day research trends as the umpteenth hoax.

As stated at the beginning, this book intended to make you think, reconsider and reflect, but hopefully you will also now be encouraged to participate in this research based on the idea that there might be a strong case for contributing to a better world, through a properly functioning government; government that needs solid research and education in Public Administration.

References

Aberbach, Joel D., Putnam, Robert D., & Rockman, Bert A. (1981). *Bureaucrats and politicians in western democracies.* Cambridge, MA: Harvard University Press.

Allison, Graham T. (1992). Public and private management: Are they fundamentally alike in all unimportant respects? In G. M. Shafritz & A. C. Hyde (eds), *Classics of Public Administration*, pp. 457–474. Belmont, CA: Wordsworth.

Altschuler, Daniel & Corrales, Javier (2013). *The promise of participation: Experiments in participatory governance in Honduras and Guatemala.* London: Palgrave Macmillan.

Andrews, Christina W. & Michiel S. de Vries (2011). Distinguishing symbolic and evidence-based policies: The Brazilian efforts to increase the quality of basic education. *International Review of Administrative Sciences* 77(3), 435–450.

Arnstein, Sherry R. (1969). A ladder of citizen participation. *Journal of the American Institute of planners* 35(4), 216–224.

Arrow, Kenneth J. (1951). *Social Choice and Individual Values.* Yale University Press.

Ayee, Joseph R. A. (2008). *Reforming the African public sector: Retrospect and prospects.* African Books Collective.

Banks, Gary (2009). Challenges of evidence-based policy-making. Retrieved from: http://www.apsc.gov.au/publications-and-media/archive/publications-archive/evidence-based-policy (last accessed 29 September 2015).

Barrett, Richard (2003). *Vocational business: Training, developing and motivating people.* Cheltenham: Nelson Thornes.

Bass, Bernard M. & Ralph Melvin Stogdill (1990). *Bass & Stogdill's handbook of leadership: Theory, research, and managerial applications.* New York: the Free Press.

Behn, Robert D. (1998). The new public management paradigm and the search for democratic accountability. *International Public Management Journal* 1(2), 131–164.

Bendor, Jonathan, Moe, Terry M. & Shotts, Kenneth W. (2001). Recycling the garbage can: An assessment of the research program. *American Political Science Review* (95), 169–190.

Blaug, Ricardo (2010). *How power corrupts: Cognition and democracy in organisations*. London: Palgrave Macmillan.

Bowles, Samuel, Robert Boyd. Ernst Fehr & Herbert Gintis (1997). Homo reciprocans: A research initiative on the origins, dimensions, and policy implications of reciprocal fairness. *Advances in Complex Systems 4*(2/3), 1–30.

Bozeman Barry (1987). *All organizations are public*. San Francisco: Jossey-Bass.

Bozeman, Barry & Steve Loveless (1987). Sector context and performance: A comparison of industrial and government research units. *Administration & Society 19*(2), 197–235.

Brown, David (2005). Electronic government and public administration. *International Review of Administrative Sciences 71*(2), 241–254.

Campbell, Donald Thomas, Julian C. Stanley, & Nathaniel Lees Gage (1966). *Experimental and quasi-experimental designs for research*. Chicago: Rand McNally.

Center for Creative Leadership (2014). Leader effectiveness and culture: The GLOBE study. Retrieved from: http://www.ccl.org/leadership/pdf/assessments/GlobeStudy.pdf (last accessed 29 September 2015).

Civil servants to be taught ethical behavior (2011, 11 July). *China Daily*, p. 3.

Clements, Benedict, Gupta, Sanjeev, Karpowicz, Izabela & Tareq, Shamsuddin (2010). *Evaluating government employment and compensation*. Washington DC: International Monetary Fund Fiscal Affairs Department.

Coase, Ronald H. (1937). The nature of the firm. *Economica 4*(16), 386–405.

Cohen, Michael D., March, James G. & Olsen, Johan P. (1972). A garbage can model of organizational choice. *Administrative Science Quarterly 17*(1), 1–25.

College of Policing (n.d.). Code of ethics. Retrieved from: http://www.college.police.uk/What-we-do/Ethics/Pages/Code-of-Ethics.aspx (last accessed 29 September 2015).

Constitution Society (n.d.). Code of Hammurabi. Retrieved from: www.constitution.org/ime/hammurabi.pdf (last accessed 29 September 2015).

Council of European Municipalities and Regions (2011). *EU subnational governments 2010 key figures*. Brussels

Cowley, Edd & Smith, Sarah (2013). *Motivation and mission in the public sector: Evidence from the World Values Survey*. Working Paper No. 13/299. Bristol: Centre for Market and Public Organisation, University of Bristol.

Cribbin, James J. (1981). *Leadership: Strategies for organizational effectiveness*. New York: AMACOM.

Crozier, Michel. *The bureaucratic phenomenon*. Transaction Publishers, 2009.

Davies, Tim (2013). *Open data barometer. 2013 global report*. Retrieved from: http://www.opendataresearch.org/dl/odb2013/Open-Data-Barometer-2013-Global-Report.pdf (last accessed 29 September 2015).

De Balzac, Honore (1898). *Bureaucracy*. Dent.

de Vries, Michiel S. (1999). Toward a historical–comparative perspective on bureaucracies. *International Review of Public Administration* 4(1), 55–123.

de Vries, Michiel S. (2000). The rise and fall of decentralization: A comparative analysis of arguments and practices in European countries. *European journal of political research*, 38(2), 193–224.

Demographia World Urban Areas (2013). Retrieved from: www .demographia.com/ (last accessed 29 September 2015).

Denhardt, Janet Vinzant & Denhardt, Robert B. (2003). *The new public service: Serving, not steering*. Armonk, NY: M. E. Sharpe.

Denhardt, Janet Vinzant & Denhardt, Robert B. (2008). *Public administration: An action orientation*. Belmont, USA: Wadsworth.

Denhardt, Robert B. (2001). The big question of public administration education. *Public Administration Review* 61(5), 526–534.

Denhardt, Robert B., Denhardt, Janet Vinzant & Aristigueta, Maria P. (2002). *Managing human behavior in public and nonprofit organizations*. Thousand Oaks CA: Sage.

Deutsch, Karl (1974). *Politics and government: How people decide their fate*. Boston: Houghton Mifflin Company.

Dorfman, Peter W, Mansour Javidan, Paul J. Hanges, Ali Datmalchian & Robert J House (2012). GLOBE: A twenty year journey into the intriguing world of culture and leadership. *Journal of World Business* 47(4), 504–518.

Downs, Anthony (1967). *Inside bureaucracy*. Boston: Little, Brown and Company.

Drechsler, Wolfgang (2005a) The re-emergence of 'Weberian' public administration after the fall of New Public Management: The Central and Eastern European perspective, *Halduskultuur* 6, 94–108.

Drechsler, Wolfgang (2005b). The rise and demise of the new public management. *Post-Autistic Economics Review* 33(14), 17–28.

Drechsler, Wolfgang (2013a). Three paradigms of governance and administration: Chinese, Western and Islamic. *Society and Economy* 35(3), 319–342.

Drechsler, Wolfgang (2013b). Wang Anshi and the origins of modern public management in Song Dynasty China. *Public Money & Management* 33(5), 353–360.

Drechsler, Wolfgang (2015). Debate: Islamic PA – does it exist, what is it, and why and how should we study it? *Public Money & Management 35*(1), 63–64.

Dror, Yehezkel (1988). *Policymaking under adversity*. New Brunswick, NJ: Transaction Publishing.

Drucker, Peter (1955). *The Principle of Management*. Allied Publisher Private Ltd.

Drucker, Peter (1999). *Management Challenges for the 21st Century*. New York: HarperCollins.

Dulaure, Jacques-Antoine (1834). *Histoire de Paris*. Vol. 6.

Dye, Thomas R. (1992). *Understanding public policy*. Englewood Cliffs, NJ: Prentice-Hall.

Easton, David (1965). *A framework for political analysis*. Englewood Cliffs, NJ: Prentice-Hall.

Ebola in Sierra Leone: Myths and misconceptions (2014, 9 August). *The Guardian*. Retrieved from: http://www.theguardian.com/ global-development/2014/aug/09/ebola-sierra-leone-myths-misconceptions (last accessed 29 September 2015).

Edelman, Murray (1964). *The symbolic uses of politics*. Urbana: University of Illinois Press.

EList10 (n.d.). Top 10 major problems in third world countries. Retrieved from: http://www.elist10.com/top-10-major-problems-third-world-countries/#ixzz3B8NKxS9q (last accessed 29 September 2015).

Etzioni, Amitai (1996). *The new golden rule: Community and morality in a democratic society*. New York: Basic Books.

Evan, William M. (1965). Toward a theory of inter-organizational relations. *Management Science 11*(10), 217–230.

Evans, Peter & Rauch, James E. (1999). Bureaucracy and growth: A cross-national analysis of the effects of 'Weberian' state structures on economic growth. *American Sociological Review 64*(5), 748–765.

Faiz, Bilquees (2006). *Civil Servants' Salary Structure*, PIDE Working Papers No. 4. Islamabad: Pakistan Institute of Development Economics.

Fayol, Henri (1917). *Administration industrielle et générale; prévoyance, organisation, commandement, coordination, controle*. Paris: H. Dunod et E. Pinat

Fayol, Henri (1949). *General and industrial management*. Trans. C. Storrs. London: Pitman.

Federal Register (2013). Annual update of the HHS poverty guidelines. Retrieved from: https://www.federalregister.gov/articles/2013/ 01/24/2013-01422/annual-update-of-the-hhs-poverty-guidelines (last accessed 29 September, 2015).

Feldman, Martha S., & Dutton, Jane E. (1991). Order without design: Information production and policy making. *Academy of Management Review 16*(4), 825–827.

Fiedler, Fred E. (1964). A contingency model of leadership effectiveness. *Advances in Experimental Social Psychology 1*(1), 149–190.

Finer, Samuel E. (1997). *The history of government.* Vols 1–3. Oxford: Oxford University Press.

Fischer, Frank & Forester, John (eds) (1993). *The argumentative turn in policy analysis and planning.* Durham & London: Duke University Press.

Forrester Research (2007). Blog, http://blogs.forrester.com/groundswell/2007/04/forresters_new_.html.

Fottler, Myron D. (1981). Is management really generic? *Academy of Management Review 6*(1), 1–12.

Fry, Brian C. & Raadschelders, Jos C. N. (2008). *Mastering public administration: From Max Weber to Dwight Waldo.* Washington, DC: CQ Press.

Gilman, Stuart C. (2005). *Ethics codes and codes of conduct as tools for promoting an ethical and professional public service: Comparative successes and lessons.* Washington DC: World Bank.

Goffman, Erwing (1974). *Frame analysis.* New York: Harper & Row.

Goodnow, Frank (1900) *Politics and Administration: A Study in Government*, New York, The Macmillan company; London, Macmillan & co., ltd.

Gormley Jr, William T. (2001). Moralists, pragmatists, and rogues: Bureaucrats in modern mysteries. *Public Administration Review 61*(2), 184–193.

Goslin, David A. (ed.) (1999). *Handbook of socialization theory and research.* Chicago: Rand McNally. Greenhouse.

Greiner, Larry E. (1972). Evolution and revolution as organizations grow. *Harvard Business Review 76*(3), 55–60.

Grindle, Merilee S. (2004). Good enough governance: Poverty reduction and reform in developing countries. *Governance 17*(4), 525–548.

Gulick, Luther & Urwick, L. (eds) (1937). *Papers on the Science of Administration.* New York: Institute of Public Administration, Columbia University.

Haque, M. Shamsul (1999). *Restructuring development theories and policies: A critical study.* New York: SUNY Press.

Heady, Ferrel (1996). Configurations of civil service systems. In H. Bekke, J. Perry & T. Toonen (eds), *Civil service systems in comparative perspective*, pp. 207–226. Bloomington and Indianapolis: Indiana University Press.

Hersey, Paul & Blanchard, Kenneth (1979). Life cycle theory of leadership. *Training and Development Journal 33*, 94.

Herzberg, Frederick I, Bernard Mausner, Barbara Bloch-Snyderman (1959). *The Motivation to Work.* New York: Wiley.

Hill, Michael J. & Hupe, Peter L. (2002). *Implementing public policy: Governance in theory and practice*. London: Sage.

Hillwatch (n.d.). Quotations on bureaucracy and public administration. Retrieved from: http://www.hillwatch.com/PPRC/Quotes/Bureaucracy.aspx (last accessed 29 September 2015).

Hin, Koh Tek (n.d.). Corruption Control in Singapore. Retrieved from: http://www.unafei.or.jp/english/pdf/RS_No83/No83_17VE_Koh1.pdf (last accessed 29 September 2015).

Hobbes, Thomas (1651/1968). *Leviathan*. Harmondsworth: Penguin Books.

Hofstede, Geert (1980). *Culture's consequences: International differences in work-related values*. London: Sage.

Hofstede, Geert & Bond, M. H. (1988). The Confucius connection. From cultural roots to economic growth. *Organizational Dynamics 16*, 4–21.

Hofstede, Geert (1997) *Cultures and organizations: software of the mind*. McGraw-Hill: New York.

Hondeghem, Annie & James L. Perry (2009). EGPA symposium on public service motivation and performance: Introduction. *The American Review of Public Administration 75*(1). 5–9.

Hood, Christopher (1991). A public management for all seasons? *Public Administration 69*(1), 3–19.

Hood, Christopher (1995). The "New Public Management" in the 1980s: Variations on a theme. *Accounting, Organizations and Society 20*(2), 93–109.

Hood, Christopher, Rothstein, Henry & Baldwin, Robert (2001). *The government of risk*. Oxford: Oxford University Press.

Hooghe, Liesbet, Gary Marks & Arjan H. Schakel (2008). Measuring regional authority. *Regional and Federal Studies 18*(2–3), 111–121.

House, R., Javidan, M., Hanges, P. & Dorfman, P. (2002). Understanding cultures and implicit leadership theories across the globe: an introduction to project GLOBE. *Journal of World Business 37*(1), 3–10.

Howlett, Michael & Ramesh, M. (2003). *Studying public policy*. Toronto: Oxford University Press.

Huijboom, Noor & Tijs van den Broek (2012). Open data: an international comparison of strategies. *European Journal of ePractice*. Retrieved from: http://www.epractice.eu/files/European.Journal.practice.Volume.2012_1.pdf (last accessed 29 September 2015).

International Monetary Fund Economic Outlook (2015, October). World Economic Outlook Database. Retrieved from: www.imf.org/external/pubs/ft/weo/2015/01/weodata/index.aspx (last accessed 29 September 2015).

Islam, Roumeen (2003). *Do more transparent governments govern better?* World Bank Policy Research Working Paper 3077. Washington DC: World Bank.

Jandt, Fred E. (2006). *An introduction to intercultural communication: Identities in a global community.* Thousand Oaks: Sage.

Janis, Irving L. (1982). *Groupthink: Psychological studies of policy decisions and fiascoes.* Boston: Houghton-Mifflin.

Kahneman, Daniel (2011). *Thinking, fast and slow.* London: Palgrave Macmillan.

Kant, Immanuel (1785/1993). Trans. by James W. Ellington. *Grounding for the metaphysics of morals.* 3rd ed. Indianapolis: Hackett.

Kaufman, Herbert (1960). *The forest ranger.* Baltimore: John Hopkins UP.

Kaufman, Roger (1981). Determining and diagnosing organizational needs. *Group & Organization Management* 6(3), 312–322.

Kaufmann, Daniel, Aart Kraay & Massimo Mastruzzi (2003). *Governance matters III: Governance indicators for 1996–2002.* World Bank Policy Research Working Paper No. 3106. Retrieved from: http://ssrn.com/abstract=405841 (last accessed October 10, 2012).

Kayode, Asaju, Adagba, Sunday O. & Anyio, Silas F. (2013). Corruption and service delivery: The case of Nigerian public service, *Wudpecker Journal of Public Administration* 1(1), 1–6.

Kettl, Donald F. (1993). *Sharing power: Public governance and private markets.* Brookings Institution Press.

Kettl, Donald F. (2002). *The transformation of governance: Public administration for twenty-first century America.* Baltimore, MD: Johns Hopkins University Press.

Kingdon, John W. (1995). *Agenda, alternatives, and public policies* (2nd ed.). New York: HarperCollins College Publishers.

Kleindorfer, Paul R., Kuhnreuther, Howard C. & Schoemaker, Paul J. H. (1993). *Decision sciences: An integrative perspective.* Cambridge: Cambridge University Press.

Klijn, Erik-Hans, Joop Koppenjan, and Katrien Termeer (1995). Managing networks in the public sector: a theoretical study of management strategies in policy networks. *Public administration* 73(3), 437–454.

Kroeber, Alfred L. & Clyde Kluckhohn (1952). *Culture. A critical review of concepts and definitions.* Papers. Peabody Museum of Archaeology & Ethnology, Harvard University.

Laski, Harold J. (1939). The obsolescence of federalism. *The New Republic* 98(3), 367–369.

Lasswell, Harold D. (1950). *Politics: Who gets what, when, how.* New York: P. Smith.

Lerner, Daniel & Lasswell, Harold D. (eds) (1951). *The policy sciences.* Stanford: Stanford UP.

Li, Charlene, Josh Bernoff & Marike Groot (2011). *Groundswell.* Boston MA: Harvard Business Press.

Lindblom, Charles E. (1959). The science of 'muddling through'. *Public Administration Review 19*, 79–88.

Lipsky, Michael (1979). *Street level bureaucracy.* New York: Russell Sage Foundation.

Local Development International (2013). *The role of decentralisation/ devolution in improving development outcomes at the local level: Review of the literature and selected cases.* Brooklyn, New York: Local Development International LLC.

March, James G. & Olsen, Johan P. (1989). *Rediscovering institutions. The organizational basis of politics.* New York: Free Press.

Marx, Karl (1858/1993). *Grundrisse.* London: Penguin.

Maslow, Abraham, H. (1943). A Theory of Human Motivation.*Psychological Review 50*(4), 370–396.

Matheson, Alex, Weber, Boris, Manning, Nick & Arnould, Emmanuelle (2007). Study on the political involvement in senior staffing and on the delineation of responsibilities between ministers and senior civil servants. *OECD Working Papers on Public Governance, 2007/6.* Paris: OECD Publishing.

McGann, James (2013). *2013 global go to think tank index report.* Philadelphia: University of Pennsylvania.

McGregor, Douglas M. (1966). *The human side of enterprise.* Cambridge: MIT Press.

Menzel, Donald (2007). *Ethics management for public administrators.* New York: M.E. Sharpe.

Merton, Robert K. (1957). *Social theory and social structure.* Glencoe, IL: Free Press.

Michels, Robert (1915). *Political parties: A sociological study of the oligarchical tendencies of modern democracy.* New York: Hearst's International Library Co. (Original, in German, published in 1911.)

Mill, John Stuart (1859). *On Liberty.* London: Longman, Roberts & Green Co.

Mintzberg, Henri (1973). *The Nature of Managerial Work.* New York: Harper & Row

Mintzberg, Henri (1980). Structure in 5's: A synthesis of the research on organization design. *Management Science 26*(3), 322–341.

Mintzberg, Henri (1993). *Structure in fives: Designing effective organizations.* Englewood Cliffs, NJ: Prentice-Hall, Inc.

Mosca, Gaetano (1939). *The Ruling Class.* Trans. by Hannah D. Kahn. New York: McGraw-Hill.

Mosher, Frederick C. (1975). *American public administration: Past, present, future.* University of Alabama Press.

Niskanen, William A. (1974). *Bureaucracy and representative government.* Chicago & New York: Aldine-Atherton, Inc.

North, Douglas. C. (1990). *Institutions, institutional change and economic performance.* Cambridge: Cambridge University Press.

Oates, Wallace, E. (1972). *Fiscal Federalism.* New York Harcourt, Brace, Jovanvich

Obama, Barack (n.d.). Transparency and Open Government: A memorandum for the Heads of Executive Departments and Agencies. Retrieved from: www.whitehouse.gov/the_press_office/TransparencyandOpenGovernment (last accessed 29 September, 2015).

Olson, Mancur (1965). *The logic of collective action: Public goods and the theory of groups.* Cambridge, MA: Harvard UP.

Organisation for Economic Co-operation and Development (2007). Towards better measurement of government. *OECD Working Papers on Public Governance.* Retrieved from: http://dx.doi.org/10.1787/301575636734 (last accessed 29 September 2015).

Organisation for Economic Co-operation and Development (2008). The State of the Public Service. OECD Publishing, p. 37. Retrieved from: www.keepeek.com/Digital-Asset-Management/oecd/governance/the-state-of-the-public-service_9789264047990-en#page37 (last accessed 29 September 2015).

Organisation for Economic Co-operation and Development (n.d.). Acquiring capacity. Retrieved from: www.oecd.org/gov/pem/acquiringcapacity.htm (last accessed 29 September 2015).

Osborne, David (1993). Reinventing government. *Public Productivity & Management Review*, 349–356.

Osborne, David & Gaebler, Ted (1992). *Reinventing government.* Reading, MA: Addison Wesley.

Ostrom, Elinor (1990). *Governing the commons: The evolution of institutions for collective action.* Cambridge: Cambridge University Press.

Ostrom, Elinor (1995). *Understanding institutional diversity.* Princeton, New Jersey: Princeton University Press.

Ostrom, Vincent & Ostrom, Elinor (1999). Public goods and public choices. In Michael McGinnis (ed.), *Polycentricity and local public economies. Readings from the workshop in political theory and policy analysis*, pp. 75–105. Ann Arbor: University of Michigan Press.

Ouchi, William (1981). Theory Z: How American business can meet the Japanese challenge. *Business Horizons* 24(6), 82–83.

Overell, Stephen, Thomas Mills, Sam Roberts, Rohit Lekhi & Ricardo Blaug (2010). *The employment relationship and the quality of work.* London: Good Work Commission.

Page, Edward (1985). *Political authority and bureaucratic power: A comparative analysis.* Knoxville: University of Tennessee Press.

Painter, Martin & Peters, B. Guy (eds) (2010). *Tradition and public administration.* Basingstoke: Palgrave Macmillan.

Pfeffer, Jeffrey & Salancik, Gerald R. (1978). *The external control of organizations: A resource dependence perspective.* New York, NY: Harper & Row.

Pierson, Paul (2000). The limits of design: Explaining institutional origins and change. *Governance 13*(4), 475–499.

Pollitt, Christopher (2013). *Context in public policy and management: The missing link?* Cheltenham, UK and Northampton, MA: Edward Elgar.

Pollitt, Christopher & Bouckaert, Geert (2004). *Public management reform. A comparative analysis* (2nd edn.). Oxford: Oxford University Press.

Pressman, Jeffrey L. & Wildavsky Aaron B. (1973). *Implementation: How great expectations in Washington are dashed in Oakland.* Berkeley: University of California Press.

Pugh, Derek Salman & Hickson, David J. (1976). *Organizational structure in its context.* Westmead, Farnborough: Saxon House.

Public Service Commission South Africa (n.d.). Code of conduct for public servants. Retrieved from: http://www.psc.gov.za/documents/code.asp (last accessed 29 September 2015).

Ramos, Guerreiro (1965). *A Redução Sociológica – introdução ao estudo da razão sociológica.* 2ª Edição. Rio de Janeiro: Edições Tempo Brasileiro.

Rawls, John (1971). *A theory of justice.* Harvard: Harvard UP.

Reagan, Ronald (1981, 20 January). Inaugural address. Retrieved from: http://www.reagan.utexas.edu/archives/speeches/1981/12081a.htm (last accessed 29 September 2015).

Rogers, Everett M. (1962). *Diffusion of innovations.* New York: Free Press.

Rousseau, Denise M. (1995). *Promises in action: Psychological contracts in organizations.* Newbury Park, CA: Sage.

Sabatier, Paul A. (1999). *Theories of the policy process.* Boulder, CO: Westview Press.

Safran, William (1998). *The French Polity.* New York: Longman.

Saks, Alan M. (2006). Antecedents and consequences of employee engagement. *Journal of Managerial Psychology 21*(7) 600–619.

Schein, Edgar H. (1965/1980). *Organizational psychology.* Englewood Cliffs, NJ: Prentice-Hall.

Schein, Edgar H. (1978). *Career dynamics: Matching individuals and organizational needs.* New York: Addison-Wesley.

Schein, Edgar H. (1984). Coming to a new awareness of organizational culture. *Sloan Management Review* 25(2), 3–16.

Schumpeter, Joseph A. (1950). The march into socialism. *The American Economic Review*, 446–456.

Selgin, George (n.d.). Gresham's Law. Retrieved from https://eh.net/encyclopedia/greshams-law/ (last accessed 29 September 2015).

Selznick, Philip (1957). *Leadership in administration: A sociological interpretation*. Evanston, IL: Row Peterson.

Sen, Amartya (1992). *Inequality Re-examined*. Cambridge, MA: Harvard University Press.

Shah, Anwar (ed.) (2006). *Local governance in developing countries*. World Bank Publications.

Shi, Xiumei, and Jinying Wang (2011). Interpreting Hofstede Model and GLOBE Model: Which Way to Go for Cross-Cultural Research? *International Journal of Business and Management* 6(5), 93–99.

Simon, Herbert A. (1947). *Administrative behavior: a study of decision-making processes in administrative organization*. New York: Macmillan.

Simon, Herbert A. (1957). *Models of man, social and rational: Mathematical essays on rational human behavior in a social setting*. New York: Wiley.

Simon, Herbert A. (1965). *Administrative behavior*. Vol. 4. New York: Free Press.

Smith, Adam (1776). *An inquiry into the nature and causes of the wealth of nations*. London: Methuen & Co., Ltd.

Snellen, Ignatius (2005). Technology and public administration: Conditions for successful e-government development. In G. Petroni & F. Cloete (eds), *New technologies in public administration*, pp. 5–19. Amsterdam: IOS Press.

Sobis, Iwona & de Vries, Michiel S. (2011). The social psychology perspective on values and virtues. In Pan Suk Kim & Michiel S de Vries (eds), *Value and virtue in public administration*. Basingstoke: Palgrave.

Sobis, Iwona, van den Berg, Frits & de Vries, Michiel S. (2011). *The limits of leadership*. Paper presented at the 19th Nispa Conference, Varna, Bulgaria.

State Services Commission (2007). Code of conduct for the state services. Retrieved from: http://www.ssc.govt.nz/code (last accessed 29 September 2015).

Stigler, George (1957). The Tenable Range of Functions of Local Government. In Joint Economic Committee, Subcommittee on Fiscal Policy (ed). U.S. Congress. *Federal Expenditure Policy for Economic Growth and Stability*, page, 213–19. Washington, D.C: U.S. Government Printing Office.

Stiglitz, Joseph (2002). *Transparency in government. The right to tell.* Washington, DC: World Bank.

Takada, Yuji (2012). System of ethics of public servants in Japan. Retrieved from: http://www.unafei.or.jp/english/pdf/PDF_GG5_Seminar/GG5_Adviser6.pdf (last accessed 29 September 2015).

Thaler, Richard H. & Sunstein, Cass R. (2008). *Nudge: Improving decisions about health, wealth, and happiness.* New Haven: Yale UP.

Thelen, Kathleen (2004). *How institutions evolve: The political economy of skills in Germany, Britain, the United States, and Japan.* Cambridge: Cambridge University Press.

Thompson, Dennis (1999). 'Democratic Secrecy'. *Political Science Quarterly 114*(2), 181–93.

Transparency International (2011). What is public sector corruption? Retrieved from: http://blog.transparency.org/2011/12/02/what-is-public-sector-corruption/ (last accessed 29 September 2015).

Treisman, Daniel (2007). *The architecture of government: Rethinking political decentralization.* Cambridge, Cambridge University Press.

United Nations (2014) *The Millennium Development Goals report 2014.* New York: United Nations.

United Nations (n.d.). Universal Declaration of Human Rights. Retrieved from: http://www.un.org/en/documents/udhr/ (last accessed 29 September 2015).

United Nations Development Programme (2014). *Human Development Report 2014. Sustaining human progress: Reducing vulnerabilities and building resilience.* New York: UNDP.

United Nations Economic and Social Council (2006). Committee of Experts on Public Administration. Definition of basic concepts and terminologies in governance and public administration. http://unpan1.un.org/intradoc/groups/public/documents/un/unpan022332.pdf (last accessed 29 September 2015).

Van Dooren, Wouter & Van der Walle, Steven (eds) (2008). *Performance information in the public sector, how it is used.* Basingstoke: Palgrave Macmillan.

Waldo, Dwight (1948). The administrative state: A study of the political theory of American public administration. New York: Ronald Press.

Walker, David (1980). *The Oxford companion to law.* Oxford: Oxford University Press.

Walker, Richard M., Boyne, George A. & Brewer, Gene A. (eds) (2010). *Public management and performance: Research directions.* Cambridge: Cambridge University Press.

Weber, Max (1946/2009). *From Max Weber: Essays in sociology.* Abingdon: Routledge.

Weber, Max (1965). *Politics as a vocation.* Philadelphia: Fortress Press.

Weber, Max (1978). *Economy and society: An outline of interpretive sociology*. Univ of California Press. First published in German in 1921 as '*Wirtschaft und Gesellschaft*': *Grundriss der verstehenden Soziologie Vol. III*'

Weber, Max. (1994) *The profession and vocation of politics*. In: Weber, Max, Peter Lassman, and Ronald Speirs. Weber: *political writings*. Cambridge University Press, 1994. pp. 309–69. First published in German in 1926 as '*Politik als beruf*'.

White, Leonard D. (1926). *Introduction to the study of Public Administration*. New York: Macmillan.

Whitehead, Mark, Jones, Rhys & Pykett, Jessica (2011). Governing irrationality, or a more than rational government? Reflections on the rescientisation of decision making in British public policy. *Environment and Planning 43*, 2819–2837.

Wilson, James Q. (1989). *Bureaucracy: What government agencies do and why they do it*. New York: Basic Books.

Wilson, Woodrow (1887). The study of administration. *Political Science Quarterly 2*(2), 197–222.

World Bank (n.d.) Evidence-based public policy: Overview. Retrieved from: www.worldbank.org/en/topic/evidencebasedpublicpolicy/ overview#1 (last accessed 29 September 2015).

Name Index

Subject Index